Theorizing Childhood

WITHDRAWN

Theorizing Childhood

Allison James
Chris Jenks
Alan Prout

Teachers College
Columbia University
New York

CARL A. RUDISILL LIBRARY
LENOIR-RHYNE COLLEGE

HQ
767.9
.J364
1998
apr.1999

Published in the United States of America by Teachers College Press
1234 Amsterdam Avenue, New York, NY 10027

Published in Great Britain by Polity Press in association with Blackwell Publishers
Ltd. 1998

Copyright © Allison James, Chris Jenks and Alan Prout 1998

All rights reserved. No part of this publication may be reproduced or transmitted in
any form or by any means, electronic or mechanical, including photocopy, or any
information storage or retrieval system, without permission from the publisher.

Library of Congress Catalog Card Number: 97-62058

ISBN: 0-8077-3730-5

Manufactured in Great Britain

02 01 00 99 98   5 4 3 2 1

Contents

Part I
Imagining Childhood

1 The Presociological Child

Introduction

All writing occurs in time. That this book has been written in an era marked by both a sustained assault on childhood and a concern for children is no coincidence. Once childhood was a feature of parental (or maybe just maternal) discourse, the currency of educators and the sole theoretical property of developmental psychology. Now, with an intensity perhaps unprecedented, childhood has become popularized, politicized, scrutinized and analysed in a series of interlocking spaces in which the traditional confidence and certainty about childhood and children's social status are being radically undermined. This, we argue, offers new possibilities in the face of dogmatic reassertions of old certitudes and in this book we explore some of these spaces, mapping their emergence and their interconnections from within the recently established arena of the new social studies of childhood.

Our aim, in brief, is to theorize the field of childhood study by embracing the variety of approaches that will open up and also critique both extant and emergent debates about children. In epistemological terms, although we aim to set out a paradigm, it is necessarily hermeneutic, inviting engagement and simultaneously forbidding closure. In this opening section, then, we begin from a broad review of explanatory and theoretical models of childhood and consider those that are *presociological* in character. These, we argue, have become part of the conventional wisdom surrounding the child, informing both contemporary analytic as well as more everyday understandings of childhood. The second chapter, continuing this exploration, describes what can be called *transitional* models of childhood, which demonstrate the awakening of social theory's concerns with childhood, a concern fully realized in four *sociological* approaches. It is this exploratory typology which informs the main body of our text, offering both original formulations and, we anticipate, insights for future study in childhood research. These approaches are the *socially constructed* child; the *tribal* child; the *minority group* child; and the *social structural* child. And in each can be located particular interests, traditions and ideologies that together articulate different contemporary approaches to the study of the child.

However, these four models of the child also prefigure four dichotomous theoretical themes which create a narrative strand throughout the book and to which we constantly return: *agency–structure*; *universalism–particularism*; *local–global*; and *continuity–change*. Through the dynamic conceptual tensions that they provide, these dichotomies serve to demonstrate both the potential compatibilities and the possible grounds for divergence between the different sociological models of childhood which we have identified. Thus each of the four approaches and all of the four binary themes illuminate the empirical focus and substantive interests of the chapters that follow and demonstrate the ways in which the new social studies of childhood can contribute to social theory.

We must, however, be cautious at the outset. Childhood is not a new phenomenon. It was, of course, the historian Philippe Ariès (1962) who began the archaeology of childhood images with his breathtaking assertion that childhood has not always been the same thing. This established what Sennett (1993) referred to as 'the study of the family as a historical form, rather than as a fixed biological form in history' (1993: 92). Ariès, of whom we shall speak again, records the launching of childhood in Europe in the mid-eighteenth century. Adults in particular social classes, he told us, were steadily beginning to think of themselves as of not quite the same order of being as their children. An age-based hierarchy and eventual dichotomy was becoming institutionalized in the relationship between adults and children and the defining characteristics of these differences were, by and large, oppositional.

The obvious strengths of Ariès's approach lay in the relativizing of the concept of childhood. It provided the grounds for its analysis in terms of its social context, rather than abandoning childhood to a naturalistic reduction. On the other hand, the poverty of such historicism, Archard notes, lies in its 'presentism', that is, in the way that it appears to lock childhood into the realm of modernity.

Ariès understands by the concept of 'childhood' a peculiarly modern awareness of what distinguishes children from adults. This is manifested in morally appropriate forms of treatment, chiefly a certain separation of the worlds of child and adult. Previous societies, on Ariès's account, lacked this concept of childhood and whilst it does not follow that they treated children badly it is natural to think that they were disposed to do so. In reply it can be argued that the evidence fails to show that previous societies lacked a concept of childhood. At most it shows that they lacked our concept. (1993: 20)

We are not arguing in this book, then, that childhood is something new, an invention of modernity or the product of a capitalist, industrialized division of labour. Neither is it our concern to challenge the historian's evidence for the 'big bang' theory of the initiation of childhood. We do, however, remain preoccupied by the social and historical context that surrounds childhoods, beginning from the pertinent observation that childhood is very much an issue of our time.

Another historian, Raphael Samuel, reflects somewhat caustically on one manifestation of the current obsession with the child:

> Another genealogy which would repay attention would be the middle-class cult of childhood, with its celebration of the time-warped and its sentimentalisation of the nursery. It is brilliantly represented in theatre by the annual revivals of *Treasure Island* and *Peter Pan*; in ethnography by the Opies' *Lore and Language of Schoolchildren* . . . and in the auction rooms by the extraordinary prices paid for such vintage juvenilia as dolls' houses and toy theatres. (1994: 93)

But this sentimentalization is only a particular mannerism, perhaps a trivialization. Indisputably, over the last two, or at most three, decades childhood has moved to the forefront of personal, political and academic agendas and not solely in the West. The moving spirit of this process is extremely complex and can be seen in an entanglement of factors: a structural readjustment to time and mortality in the face of quickening social change; a re-evaluation and a repositioning of personhood given the disassembly of traditional categories of identity and difference; a search for a moral centre or at least an anchor for trust in response to popular routine cynicism; and an age-old desire to invest in futures now rendered increasingly urgent. In parallel with these ideational currents we might also note the more concrete aspects of contemporary social life which sharpen our focus on children and childhood: the demographic shift to an ageing population providing the idea of the child with an increased scarcity value and thus more 'precious' attention (Zelitzer 1985); and the well-documented change in family structure, instancing a fragmentation from an identity as a unit to the experience of a coalescence of individuals.

What these factors all presage is the rise of childhood agency, the transition from 'the child' as an instance of a category to the recognition of children as particular persons. Thus, although we cannot, with any certainty, offer a safe route through this complex milieu, we can begin by acknowledging the importance of the discovery of children as agents. In sociology this has been codified in the 'new paradigm' (James and Prout 1990b), as a call for children to be understood as social actors shaping as well as shaped by their circumstances. This represents a definitive move away from the more or less inescapable implication of the concept of socialization: that children are to be seen as a defective form of adult, social only in their future potential but not in their present being. And yet this rallying point of children's agency is embedded in and related to a much wider process through which the individual voices and presence of children is now being recognised and accounted for. Nasman calls this the 'individualization' of children, a path which she envisages in terms of an uneven working through of the individualist logic of the modern state:

> Children are identified, registered, evaluated and treated as individuals in some contexts as adult citizens but in others not. One could say that children are historically at the beginning of a process towards individualisation where men have long had an established position and women have achieved one during the end of the last century and increasingly so this. (1994: 167)

Whether matters are as teleological as this statement implies can be debated. None the less, it is undeniable that modern children are increasingly confronted with the opportunity (and, significantly, the requirement) that they are heard. Children globally now have civil rights encoded in the UN Convention on the Rights of the Child which, formally at least, have been ratified by large numbers of national states. These rights are constituted, it is true, within a confusing and not altogether coherent matrix of ideas concerning survival, protection, development and participation, and there are sometimes giant gulfs between the rhetoric and the reality. However, what is clear is that a discursive space has been established within which children are now seen as individuals, whose autonomy should be safeguarded and fostered and whose being can no longer be simply nested into the family or the institution. In English law, for example, the Children Act 1989 means that welfare agencies are now required to take into account not only, as was the previous formulation, children's 'best interests' but also the wishes and desires of individual children. Moreover, this right to be heard is now conditioned, not by chronological age, but by judgements about a child's developmental capacity to understand their situation and to form a meaningful opinion.

However, at the same time as there is a dynamic towards autonomous children, other contemporary social practices point in the opposite direction, emphasizing children's separateness and difference. Children are arguably now more hemmed in by surveillance and social regulation than ever before. In the risk society (Beck 1992) parents increasingly identify the world outside the home as one from which their children must be shielded and in relation to which they must devise strategies of risk reduction. This can be seen, for example, in the restriction of children's mobility because of their perceived vulnerability to physical harm, say in traffic accidents, or in the ubiquitous belief that 'stranger danger' constitutes a significant source of attack or abduction (Valentine, forthcoming). On the other hand, both public and private spaces are increasingly monitored by closed circuit television to contain the threat that unsupervised groups of children and young people are thought potentially to pose. Even the boundaries of the family are held to be at risk of penetration by insidious technologies like video and the Internet which could purvey serious moral threats to our children's childhoods. Rose notes this dramatic increase in agencies and ideologies that claim estate over the child:

> Childhood is the most intensively governed sector of personal existence. In different ways, at different times, and by many different routes varying from one section of society to another, the health, welfare, and rearing of children have been linked in thought and practice to the destiny of the nation and the responsibilities of the state. The modern child has become the focus of innumerable projects that purport to safeguard it from physical, sexual and moral danger, to ensure its 'normal' development, to actively promote certain capacities of attributes such as intelligence, educability and emotional stability. (1989: 121)

This is an illuminating thesis. It suggests that the parallel trends towards increased autonomy *and* increased regulation are not so contradictory as they might first appear. Furthermore, it highlights the extent to which children are now at the centre of political strategies in late modernity, but strategies designed to govern the individual through the capture of the inside, rather than constraint of the outside. So doing, it illuminates the subtleties of new forms of power-knowledge (Foucault 1977) in which children are enjoined to speak, make themselves visible and to regulate their own behaviour, as well as to be controlled by others. Rose's thesis therefore accounts for the emergence of a whole series of contesting voices, interests and discourses concerning the child which are detailed through this volume.

However, this is only part of the picture. Modern childhood has not come into being solely through a journey to the interior provided by the post-Freudian legacy. There is still an Enlightenment child who occupies a real concrete presence in our lives and in our thinking, as much a focus for popular celebration as for the academic futures markets of economics, politics, law, medicine, social work, history, education, psychology, communications, criminology, cultural studies, women's studies and, of course, anthropology and sociology.

Given the complexities through which modern childhood is embraced it would be easy to suppose, then, that the conventional wisdom about childhood rests somewhere within the spectrum of what Francis Galton in 1865 originally described as 'the convenient jingle of words', nature and nurture. However, our imaginings about the child have not always set out from the same starting point, and neither have they always had the same purpose in mind. The position espoused by Berger and Luckmann is seemingly straightforward:

> From the moment of birth, man's organismic development, and indeed a large part of his biological being as such, are subject to continuing socially determined interference.
>
> Despite the obvious physiological limits to the range of possible and different ways of becoming a man ... the human organism manifests an immense plasticity in its response to the environmental forces at work ... the ways of becoming and being human are as numerous as man's cultures. (1966: 66–7).

But childhood remains, we argue, a highly contentious topic. It is conceived from a number of different social, political and moral positions which we map out here and in the following chapter.

However, before doing so let us reflect once more on the apparent urgency that establishes 'the child' as a vivid presence both now and through history.

We might, for example, suggest that childhood presents a repository of the great unexplained in a manner that exceeds most phenomena. There is a wilfulness, even an anarchy, that the agency of childhood emits which resists containment and control through intelligibility. 'Knowing' about children or having ways of explaining their conduct neither holds them constant nor precludes the randomness of their interventions into adult life. And yet it is precisely this sustained otherness which is the necessary condition for understanding children, arising out of the difference comprising the adult–child relation. Thus, we would argue, children pose a potential threat or challenge to social order and its reproduction. But such a vision of the child is not the province solely of modernity or yet of learned debate. Instead, our adaptive everyday strategies towards handling this potential disruption crystallize around a series of discourses that are both of modernity *and* informed by earlier traditions of thought. In this chapter, then, the presociological discourses of childhood which we describe comprise a fund of increasingly entrenched and thus increasingly conventional wisdom which shapes our perceptions of childhood, *even within theory.* Our intention in the following chapter is to go on to reveal a movement away from such discourses through exploring the theoretical approaches that sociology provides[1] by recommending a particular turn to reflexivity. While everyday discourses of childhood seek to explain the 'truth' of childhood, the theoretical approaches which we offer in this book will allow us to explain and deconstruct those very discourses that have established taken-for-granted 'truths' about childhood.

In the light of the above, let us now begin an inventory of the presociological discourses of childhood. These, we anticipate, will provide an analytic taxonomy from which the reader can begin to engage more critically with the growing body of research into childhood.

The Presociological Child

This spacious category contains the dustbin of history. It is the realm of common sense, classical philosophy, the highly influential discipline of developmental psychology and the equally important and pervasive field of psychoanalysis. The gathering principle for the set of models assembled here is that they begin from a view of childhood outside of or uninformed by the social context within which the child resides. More specifically, these models are unimpressed by any concept of social structure.

The evil child

Though stemming from an earlier historical period, the first presociological discourse within which we can locate 'the child' finds echoes in contemporary criminology, public moralizing and current debates over pedagogic practice. It assumes that evil, corruption and baseness are primary elements in the constitution of 'the child'. Childhood, the context within which the otherness of the child is rendered safe, is therefore to be shaped by the exercise of restraint on these dispositions. More intrusively, they are to be exorcised by programmes of discipline and punishment. In the manner analysed and extrapolated by Michel Foucault into a metaphor for the form of solidarity and social control, the correct training of children is held to give rise to docile adult bodies. Docile bodies are good citizens, pliant members of the social order and, within this classical model (which however contains no theory of the interior or inner life), the child's body becomes the primary site of childhood. As Foucault put it: 'The classical age discovered the body as an object and target of power. It is easy enough to find signs of the attention then paid to the body – to the body that is manipulated, shaped, trained, which obeys, responds, becomes skilful and increases its forces' (1977: 136).

This image of the evil child finds its lasting mythological foundation in the doctrine of Adamic original sin. Children, it is supposed, enter the world as a wilful material energy; but in that their wilfulness is held to be both universal and essential it is not seen as intentional. Rather, children are demonic, harbourers of potentially dark forces which risk being mobilized if, by dereliction or inattention, the adult world allows them to veer away from the 'straight and narrow' path that civilization has bequeathed to them.

That the liberation of these forces threatens the well-being of the child itself is self-evident; perhaps more significantly, it also threatens the stability of the adult collectivity, that social order to which children in time will aspire. Such a mythology of primal forces remains a powerful theme in contemporary literature and cinema –

as in *Lord of the Flies* (Golding 1958), *The Children of Dynmouth* (Trevor 1976) and the film *The Exorcist* – and, we would argue, in more everyday contemporary public understandings of the child's capacity to murder or bully (James and Jenks 1996). Collectively these point to a Dionysian mythology:

> The child is Dionysian in as much as it loves pleasure, it celebrates self-gratification, and it is wholly demanding in relation to any object, or indeed subject, that prevents its satiation. The intrusive noise that is childhood is expressive of a single-minded solipsistic array of demands in relation to which all other interests become peripheral and all other presences become satellites to enable this goal. (Jenks 1995a: 182)

Threaded through this discourse is a concern, therefore, that these evil children should avoid dangerous places lest they fall into bad company, establish bad habits, develop idle hands; and be heard rather than just seen. 'Dangerous places' – from the shopping mall to the 'dysfunctional' family – are thus those which conspire in the potential liberation of the demonic forces already present within the body (and mind) of the child. And it is these which point to the need for restraint.

The philosophical antecedent for this evil child is to be found in the work of Thomas Hobbes. Though not dedicating his time to accounting for the condition of childhood, he produces an implicit specification of its content through his highly publicized conception of the human actor. Hobbes's initial scholarly education was within a Puritan tradition and he shared its commitment to the view that what is of most importance is good conduct. In his *Leviathan* of 1651 this produces a powerful advocacy of absolutism in relation to the continuity of the social order. The power of the monarch, and thus by analogy the power of parents, is absolute and stands over and above the populace or children, who have no rights or power. The source of this parental power is knowledge, which children can only attain by eventually becoming parents themselves. The powerful ogre of the state or the parent is omnipotent and the individual is 'saved' from the worst excesses of himself or herself by contracting into the society or the family. Without parental constraint, the life of the child is anarchistic.

Though stemming from the seventeenth century, such arguments remain pertinent to current public concerns about ' the child'. Breakdown in 'the family' and the loss of 'family values' are held to account for the unruly behaviour of children or for contemporary child lives that are 'solitary, poor, nasty, brutish and short' and without control. Old Testament Christianity echoes these sentiments and provides another significant contribution to the image of the evil child. Parental, God-parental and loco-parental guidance is a forceful introduction of the young to the humourless ways of the Almighty and has proved to be a lasting tradition in childrearing. This is despite, as Shipman (1972) has pointed out, the dramatic fall in infant mortality and the inexorable process of secularization through modernity which has reduced collective anxiety concerning the infant's state of grace. Described by Ariès (1962) in its sixteenth-century manifestation as a sign of weakness, the child was held to be susceptible to evil. It had little resolve and was easily diverted and corrupted. Such belief gave rise to the widespread practice of 'coddling' which, through the binding and constraining of children's bodies, yielded a material control over their supposed propensity to wilfulness.

However, the practice of coddling can also be treated instructively as a metaphor for a parenting style which confines children's urges and desires. It is at once a distant, strict and physical directing of the young. With the formalization of the model of the evil child in the sixteenth century, such socialization practices took the form of a contest, with the combatorial relation between adult and child closely paralleling the way that people 'broke' or tamed domestic animals in order to integrate their naturalness into the adult human world of culturalness (Stone 1979). Such harshness and indeed brutality in childrearing gained a powerful ideological bedrock from the zeal for greater reformation that accompanied the religious Puritanism of the sixteenth and seventeenth centuries and, as with the most oppressive social movements, the control and constraint exercised on the subject (in this case the child) was seen to be for its own good. Puritanism was determined that rods should not be spared in order to save children, and it was equally certain that the child should be grateful for the treatment it received. Though Puritanism was exhausted as a formal church, elements of the Puritan morality extended with an evangelical zeal into the nineteenth century, creating the Poor Laws and the campaigns against drunkenness, while still regarding children as being in need of correction. Thus much of the literature of this period employs the evil child as a symbol of an outmoded and hypocritical morality that continued to buttress an anti-democratic state. In Dickens's novels, for example, this institutionalized violence towards the young is depicted as a moral constraint, and in the late twentieth century we find a similar politics of restraint echoed in calls for 'boot camps' and 'short, sharp shocks' as desirable lessons for the child, lessons for the good of its and our own futures.

The innocent child

The innocent child represents the second of our presociological models of childhood and, in Coveney's (1957) critical work, it is set against the model of the evil child, encapsulating far more of what we have come to imagine as modern, Western childhood. In the romantic images of Blake and Wordsworth can be found the source of public standards for our demeanour towards children and for our expectations of policy and provision in relation to them. Essentially pure in heart, these infants are angelic and uncorrupted by the world they have entered. Although it would be cheering to believe that we had reached this view spontaneously, as part of the civilizing march of modernity, like all significant steps forward in human civilization the idea has an earlier architect in the person of Jean-Jacques Rousseau. An apostle of individual liberty, he began his *Social Contract* of 1762 with the assertion that: 'Man is born free; and everywhere he is in chains. One thinks he is the master of others, and still remains the greater slave than they.' He opened *Émile* with a similar view, namely that: 'God makes all things good; man meddles with them and they become evil.'

Children, then, have a natural goodness and a clarity of vision. Redolent with the reason that will form the society of tomorrow, their natural characteristics are those we can all learn from; they represent a condition lost or forgotten and thus one worthy of defence (and susceptible to sentimentalization). Indeed, Rousseau sought to banish all consideration of original sin and argued that, rather than treating children to a punitive journey into grace, we might more profitably idolize or worship the intrinsic values they bring to bear on the world.

Thus, rather than just instilling a sense of childhood innocence, Rousseau, more significantly, opened up the question of the child's particularity, a question that, as we shall see, remains central in contemporary theorizing. Through *Émile*, the child was promoted to the status of person, a specific class of being with needs and desires and even rights. And it is this personification which has paved the way for our contemporary concern about children as individuals. As Robertson put it:

If the philosophy of the Enlightenment brought to eighteenth century Europe a new confidence in the possibility of human happiness, special credit must go to Rousseau for calling attention to the needs of children. For the first time in history, he made a large group of people believe that childhood was worth the attention of intelligent adults, encouraging an interest in the process of growing up rather than just the product. Education of children was part of the interest in progress which was so predominant in the intellectual trends of the time. (1976: 407)

Our twentieth-century legacy is the serious recognition that children are not bundles of negative attributes, or incompletely formed persons waiting to become adults; they are who they are. As parents and educators we are contracted to bring up our children in such a manner that their state of pristine innocence remains unspoilt by the violence and ugliness that surrounds them. However, what we also note being instilled in the adult–child relationship here is the notion of responsibility, a responsibility which has to be reconciled with Rousseau's advocacy of freedom for the child. If childhood innocence is to be nurtured at all costs, then we must attain publicly recognizable standards in the treatment of children; all adults must assume responsibility for children in the same moment as they recognize their intentionality and competence. Children can no longer be routinely mistreated, but neither can they be left to their own devices. Within this discourse, then, children have become subject.

Our contemporary concern for children's education begins, therefore, with Rousseau and with a childhood that is recognizable through encouragement, assistance, support and facilitation. Jenks has likened this model to Apollonian mythology:

What now of the Apollonian child, the heir to the sunshine and light, the espouser of poetry and beauty? . . . Such children play and chuckle, smile and laugh, both spontaneously but also with our sustained encouragement. We cannot abide their tears and tantrums, we want only the illumination from their halo. This is humankind before either Eve or the apple. It is within this model that we honour and celebrate the child and dedicate ourselves to reveal its newness and uniqueness. Gone are the strictures of uniformity, here, with romantic vision, we explore the particularity of the person. Such thinking has been instructive of all child-centred learning and special-needs education from Montessori, the Plowden Report, A. S. Neill and the Warnock Report, and indeed much of primary teaching in the last three decades. This Apollonian image lies at the heart of attempts to

protect the unborn through legislation concerning voluntary termi-
nation of pregnancies and endeavours in the USA to criminalize
certain 'unfit' states of motherhood such as drug-addiction or HIV
infection. (Jenks 1996a: 73)

In the presociological discourse of the innocent child in the eighteenth and nineteenth centuries are the foundations of contemporary
child-centred education, of special needs provision, of nurseries and
kindergartens, of feeding on demand and of a whole host of adaptive childrearing strategies that are tailored to the needs of the
individual. We also see the seeds of the belief that children are
everybody's concern and that they constitute an investment in the
future in terms of the reproduction of social order.

The immanent child

Rousseau's child, touched by the *Geist*, is an idealist's creation. It
exemplifies the precedence of mind before matter and it is this
combination of intentionality and pure reason that renders this
child such a forceful creature, with a high priority in our scale of
human significance. Growing out of Rousseau's innocent child is,
then, a child imbued with a vitality and an immanence. However,
the blueprint for this model of the child was established over half a
century earlier by a philosopher from a radically different tradition.
John Locke concerned himself with the proper education of young
citizens in a 1693 tract called *Some Thoughts on Education*, but had
previously established his major thesis on cognition and the acquisition of knowledge in *An Essay on Human Understanding* of 1689.

That we cannot place Locke's thought within the model of the
innocent child is certain for he was quite clear that no such idealized
state of primitive kindness existed. Far from envisaging the free and
noble savage of Rousseau's dreams, Locke is much more hard-
headed in his unsentimentalized views on the cruel, spiteful and
incompatible dispositions of children. He does not view childhood
as an Elysian paradise of goodness and reciprocity – which is not to
say that he therefore regards it as intrinsically brutish either. For
him, children are intrinsically no-thing, but this is an epistemological statement rather than a disregard. Though from a Puritan family, Locke appeared to share none of their fierce attitudes towards
the young. On the contrary, famous for his epistemological contribution to the tradition of empiricism, Locke argued in the *Essay on*

Human Understanding that children do not possess inbuilt or a priori categories of understanding, or a general facility to reason:[2]

> Let us then suppose the mind to be, as we say, white paper, void of all characters, without any ideas; how comes it to be furnished? Whence comes that vast store, which the busy and boundless fancy of man has painted on it with an almost endless variety? Whence has it all the materials of reason and knowledge? To this I answer in one word, from experience: in that all our knowledge is founded, and from that it ultimately derives itself. (Book 2, ch. 1, sec. 2)

On the face of it this would appear to be the most radical of assertions. The tabula rasa appears in direct contrast to Rousseau's formulation of the child. However, Locke's theory of mind is tempered by his anachronistic liberalism: children are charged with a potential, as citizens of the future and as imperfect but latent reasoners. Thus, although in Locke's view there are no innate capacities, no knowledge lodged in a universal human condition, the drives and dispositions that children possess are on a gradient of becoming, moving towards reason. Like Rousseau, then, Locke believed that whatever children are, they are not inadequate or partially formed adults. They have a set of interests and needs that are special and should be recognized as such. Children should always be reasoned with, and parents, like pedagogues, have knowledge and experience and are in a position to exercise responsible control over them. Through education children will become rational, virtuous, contracting members of society, and exercisers of self-control. They will not threaten social order.

Although Locke's empiricism begins from a firm commitment to the view that knowledge is acquired through 'experience', there are inconsistencies in this belief. For example, he distinguishes between primary and secondary qualities of mind, suggesting that certain ideas are not simply reflections of objects but are created by the mind itself. In some circumstances, then, knowledge is the outcome of mental activity and perception. The gateway to 'experience' is predisposed by our own mental processes.

Rousseau's child is thus immanent in as much as it is innately charged with reason, reason which will develop given the appropriate environment. Locke's child is immanent in that it has mental processes and perception and, if we provide the appropriate environment, we can elicit the reason from it. According to Archard, Locke is offering us 'the earliest manifesto for "child-centred" education' through a delicate cocktail of idealist assumptions and empiricist stimuli (1993: 1). These are, of course, the very reinforcements which comprise much early learning in contemporary schools and homes. In recalling a much earlier model of the child as being at least motivated, if not anxious, to learn, the presociological model of the immanent child underlines our suggestion of the continuities, as well as discontinuities, in understandings of childhood.

The naturally developing child

It is within this model that we encounter the unholy alliance between the human sciences and human nature. Psychology, unlike sociology, never made the mistake of questioning its own status as a science and, in the guise of developmental psychology, firmly colonized childhood in a pact with medicine, education and government agencies. This has led in turn to enhanced prestige, authority and the power of persuasion, and a continued high level of public trust and funding. Developmental psychology capitalizes, perhaps not artfully but certainly effectively, on two everyday assumptions: first, that children are natural rather than social phenomena; and secondly, that part of this naturalness extends to the inevitable process of their maturation. The belief in children's naturalness derives from the universal experience of being a child and the persistent and commonplace experience of having and relating to children; the belief in the inevitability and even 'good' of their maturation emanates from a combination of post-Darwinian developmental cultural aspirations and, conflated with these, the post-Enlightenment confusion of growth and progress (Jenks 1982a; 1989).

The single most influential figure in the construction of the model of the naturally developing child is Jean Piaget. His work on genetic epistemology extended biology, quite successfully, into the vocabulary of the taken-for-granted and produced the most absolute, if materially reductive, image of childhood that we are likely to encounter. Ironically perhaps, he sets out from an idealism more deeply founded than Rousseau's, but one tempered by a voracious empiricism. Piaget seeks to reconcile reason with fact.

Piaget's child, poor biological creature that it is, is imbued therefore with a grand potential to become not anything, but quite specifically something. It is predicted, and in his work on the development of thought and bodily skills – the path to intelligence – Piaget lays out for us some inevitable and clearly defined stages of growth which are well signposted. Beginning immediately after birth with sensory-motor intelligence, children progress through preconceptual and intuitive thought to the final achievement of the 'normal' person in formal operations. Within the model, these stages are ordered temporally and arranged hierarchically along a continuum from infantile, 'figurative' thought, which has relatively low status, up to adult, 'operative' intelligence, which has high status. Figurative thought is realized in the form of very particularistic behaviour, an incapacity to transfer training and a concrete replication of objective states. Such behaviour is summoned by emotional responses in specific situations and the child is understood as being organized and orientated in relation to objective structures. Clearly, what is being demonstrated here is a lack of competence. By contrast, operative intelligence – that of the adult – displays action, informed, cognitive manipulation of objects and the transformation of those objects by a reflecting subject. Such action exemplifies logical process and the thinking individual's freedom from the constraint of immediate experience. What operative intelligence shows, then, is a competence achieved and deserved. What it provides, analytically and culturally, are some grounds to establish differences between adults and children. The control provided by adult competence justifies the supremacy of adulthood and further ensures that childhood must, of necessity, be viewed as an inadequate precursor to the real state of human being, namely being 'grown up'.

This prioritizing of the adult, complete state is revealed in Piaget's own definition of his purpose:

> Developmental psychology can be described as the study of the development of mental functions, in as much as this development can provide an explanation, or at least a complete description, of their mechanisms in the finished state. In other words, developmental psychology consists of making use of child psychology in order to find the solution to general psychological problems. (1972: 26)

Recently , however, there has been a growing dissatisfaction with this well-established orthodoxy in understanding human maturation. Fundamental objections have arisen concerning the view that there is a universal, standardized and inevitable programme of developmental stages (Richards and Light 1986; Morss 1990; Burman 1994). As Archard has put it:

First, his ideal of adult cognitive competence is a peculiarly Western philosophical one. The goal of cognitive development is an ability to think about the world with the concepts and principles of Western logic. In particular Piaget was concerned to understand how the adult human comes to acquire the Kantian categories of space, time and causality. If adult cognitive competence is conceived in this way then there is no reason to think it conforms to the everyday abilities of even Western adults. Second, children arguably possess some crucial competencies long before Piaget says they do. (1993: 65-6)

Other criticism has arisen. Reconnecting with the earlier ideas of Vygotsky, who believed that, far from passively growing into it, human beings actively take on or appropriate society, questions are now being asked as to whether biology provides an adequate model for the understanding of human cognition. Morss argues, for example, that developmental psychology is irrevocably embedded in a set of pre-Darwinian ideas that have long since been abandoned in the context of their own discipline. This, for Morss, means an inevitable compulsion to reduce all human maturation to an issue of development: 'What modern developmentalists measure, investigate, even perceive in their subject-matter is, therefore, still confined by these outdated biological concepts. What developmentalists discover in their empirical work may be determined in advance: by non-Darwinian . . . biology' (1990: xiii).

None the less, Piaget's genetic epistemology has, through its measuring, grading, ranking and assessing of children, instilled a deep-seated positivism and rigid empiricism into our contemporary understandings of the child. Under the hegemony of developmental stage monitoring it is not just iniquitous comparison with their peers which children suffer through testing and league tables, but also a constant evaluation against a 'gold standard' of the normal child. For those who fail to meet that standard, whether in education, bodily development or welfare, the repercussions and sanctions are strong.

The unconscious child

At the turn of the twentieth century the sudden impact of Freudian ideas and the new growth of interest in the human psyche produced something of a volte-face in our thinking about the child. After a long series of concerns with the idea of development and a continuous but unconcerted attention to futures, through our final presociological model of the child, childhood became the province of retrospectives. Whereas children had become firmly established in both theory and everyday consciousness as indicators of tomorrow, Freud opened up a concern with childhood as adult pasts. However, in one sense Freudian theory *is* dedicated to an account of human maturation: through his account of elements of personality, stages of development and complexes are revealed the childhood building blocks which sustain the architecture of an adult psychopathology.

Freudian development is a familiar process of the compatible bonding of three elements: id, ego and super-ego. The id comprises an elementary and primal broth of essentially libidinal drives which is both expressive and utterly inexhaustible. Visualized as a reservoir of the instinctive energies, the id is uncontrolled, dominated by the pleasure principle and impulsive wishing. Though a potential source of creativity, the id is wholly incompatible with a collective life and thus needs to be curbed. Successful development is, for Freud, the proper management of this 'curbing' or repression. Thus, in the id are awakened all the resonances of the model of the evil child, but at a later historical moment; once more childhood is predicated on constraint, management and the fear of an evil that resides within. But this time it takes the form of the unconscious. Recalled too in the ego is the model of the immanent child. This assumes the role of interaction in childhood, enabling the self to experience others through the senses. So begins an adjustment in behaviour through which the id is monitored. Consciousness and rationality are finally wrought through the supremacy of the super-ego, the experience of the collective other which regulates the presentations of self and integrates the child into the world of adult conduct.

In the growth of Freudian psychoanalytic influence in contemporary thinking can be seen, then, a new source of causality: the explanation, and in many cases the blame, for aberrant adult behaviour lies in childhood. As a resource for accounts of the deviant, the criminal and the abnormal throughout late modernity this has developed into an equation of parent–child relationships, transforming the child into the unconscious itself. All adults, it is argued, transport their childhood from action to action like a previous incarnation. However, although this model has opened up a vast potential for adult self-exploration, in line with the many journeys towards belief that modern society has spurred (Giddens 1991), it has done little to broaden our understanding of children. Freudian theory positions the child as no more than a state of unfinished business or becoming. Within this model, childhood is once again dispossessed of intentionality and agency. Instead, these are absorbed into a vocabulary of drives and instincts, with sexuality becoming the major dimension in the development of self and amnesia emerging, ironically, as the key to successful socialization.

Conclusion

Our review of presociological models of the child is instructive. It reveals how these understandings of children comprise, in different, sometimes contradictory ways, a complex array of motifs through which childhood has been and is still imagined. However, these are not the stuff of fantasy. Instead, as we shall see through this volume, they are models which continue to inform everyday actions and practices alongside more sophisticated sociological theorizing about childhood. As models, the import of their application should be carefully attended to.

2 The Sociological Child

Introduction

While concern with childhood is far from new, as we have seen, in the last decade it has attracted a rapid growth in sociological interest and attention. What is novel about this movement is a determination to make childhood itself the locus of concern, rather than seeing it as subsumed under some other topic, such as the family or schooling. As we show below, by keeping the focus on childhood itself, existing sociological approaches can be critiqued and a range of new ones advanced. A critical exploration of the various ways in which the sociological tradition has conceptualized childhood is our main purpose throughout this book, and in this chapter we set out the arguments against traditional conceptualizations and outline the alternatives.

We start by examining what until recently was the unchallenged dominance of socialization as the main interpretive device through which sociological understanding of childhood was pursued. This we characterize as 'transitional theorizing' because, from our perspective, it both draws on the presociological models that we have already described and provides the groundwork for the newer ideas which have emerged about how best to understand 'the child'.

Transitional Theorizing: the Socially Developing Child

The interest in understanding children's cognitive maturation that is found in developmental psychology finds close parallels in sociology in the model of the socially developing child. However, through its focus on the social context, this model of childhood represents an epistemological break between what we have termed presociological accounts of the child and the sociological approaches which follow. As a transitional theorizing of childhood, the model of the socially developing child thus bridges a conceptual divide in our understanding.

In some respects, however, sociology's project has always been concerned with the development of the child. Theories of social order, social stability and social integration depend on a uniform and predictable standard of action from participating members. In this sense, sociological theorizing begins with a formally established concept of society and works back to the necessary inculcation of its rules into the consciousnesses of its potential participants. These are always children and, within what here we call transitional theorizing about the child, the process of this inculcation is referred to as socialization. The direction of influence is apparent: the society shapes the individual.

This is not to imply that sociologists are ignorant of the biological character of the human organism. Indeed, the model of the socially developing child shares certain chronological and incremental characteristics with the naturally developing model outlined above. However, to demonstrate a singular commitment to an explication of its development within the social context, explanations in terms of natural propensities or dispositions are resisted in the sociological account. The socially developing model is not therefore attached to what the child naturally is, so much as to what society naturally demands of the child.[1]

Socialization is a concept that has been much employed by sociologists to delineate the process through which children, and in some cases adults, learn to conform to social norms (see Elkin and Handel 1972; Denzin 1977; Goslin 1969; Danziger 1971; Morrison and McIntyre 1971; G. White 1977). In this respect sociology's understanding of social order and its reproduction has depended largely on the efficacy of socialization to ensure that societies sustain themselves through time. This involves, in essence, the successful transmission of culture from one generation to another. Let us look at two definitions of the process. The first, written solidly within the tradition of socialization theory, is from Ritchie and Kollar:

> The central concept in the sociological approach to childhood is socialization. A synonym for this process may well be acculturation

because this term implies that children acquire the culture of the human groupings in which they find themselves. Children are not to be viewed as individuals fully equipped to participate in a complex adult world, but as beings who have the potentials for being slowly brought into contact with human beings. (1964: 117)

Speier, from a more critical, phenomenological stance, has stated:

Sociology considers the social life of the child as a basic area of study in so-called institutional analyses of family and school, for example. What is classically problematic about studying children is the fact of cultural induction, as I might refer to it. That is, sociologists (and this probably goes for anthropologists and psychologists) commonly treat childhood as a stage of life that builds preparatory mechanisms into the child's behaviour so that he is gradually equipped with the competence to participate in the everyday activities of his cultural partners, and eventually as a bona fide adult member himself. This classical sociological problem has been subsumed under the major heading of socialisation. (1970: 208)

The process has been conceived of in two ways. First, in what we might term the 'hard' way or what Wrong (1961) referred to as the 'oversocialized conception of man in modern sociology', socialization is seen as the internalization of social constraints, a process occurring through external regulation. The individual child's personality thus becomes continuous with the goals and means of the society itself; the individual is seen as a microcosm. Deriving largely from structural sociology and systems theory, the 'hard way' finds its most persuasive and influential exponent in Talcott Parsons, who defines the process as follows:

The term socialisation in its current usage in the literature refers primarily to the process of child development . . . However, there is another reason for singling out the socialisation of the child. There is reason to believe that, among the learned elements of personality, in certain respects the stablest and most enduring are the major value-orientation patterns and there is much evidence that these are 'laid down' in childhood and are not on a large scale subject to drastic alteration during adult life. (1951: 101)

What Parsons achieves in his theory of the social system is a stable, uniform and exact correspondence between individual actors and their particular personalities and the society itself. They are both cut to a common pattern. What he also achieves is a universality in the practice and experience of childhood, because the content of socialization is secondary to the *form* of socialization in each and every case. The potential for the expression of the child's intentionality is thereby constrained through the limited number of choices that are made available in social interaction. These Parsons refers to as pattern variables. In this way the model achieves a very generalized sense of the child at a level of abstraction and one which is determined by structure rather than pronounced through the exercise of agency. And, as this model is also based on a developmental scheme, the child is necessarily considered to be incompetent or to have only incomplete, unformed or proto-competencies. Therefore any research following from such a model cannot attend to the everyday world of children, or their skills in interaction and world-view, except in terms of generating a diagnosis for remedial action.

The second, and somewhat 'softer', way in which the socialization process has been conceived by sociologists is as an essential element in interaction, that is as a transactional negotiation that occurs when individuals strive to become group members. This is the version of socialization that stems from the symbolic interactionism of G. H. Mead and the Chicago School and involves a social psychology of group dynamics. This is really, however, a perspective on adult socialization. The Meadian analysis of child development is much more of a thesis in materialism. The basic theory of the acquisition of language and interactional skills is based very much on an unexplicated behaviourism, and the final resolution of the matured relationship between the individual and the collective other (that is, the 'self' and 'other') is a thinly disguised reworking of Freud's triumph of the super-ego over the id. Thus, though generating a wealth of sensitive ethnographic studies of small groups and communities, symbolic interactionism begins from the baseline of adult interactional competence. At this level, it shares much with the socialization theory espoused by Parsons and structural sociology.

To a large extent this accounts for sociology's long neglect of the topic of childhood and also demonstrates why children were only ever considered under the broadest of umbrellas, namely the sociology of the family. In all the manifestations of the model of the socially developing child (that is, socialization theory) as they have appeared in many forms of sociology, little or no time is given to children. That is why we relegate it here to a form of transitional theorizing about the child.

The Sociological Child

Here we introduce the series of approaches to child study that grounds our writing and our concern throughout this book to explore both the agency of children and their present social, political and economic status as contemporary subjects. However, in identifying four ways in which the child is constituted sociologically, we would add the caveat that these are not all part of a total mosaic. Nor are they necessarily compatible. Although sharing certain basic premises concerning the fundamentally 'social' and even 'social structural' character of their object of attention, the sociological perspectives on childhood considered in the following substantive chapters are divided, from the level of metatheory to that of methodology. It is also certainly the case, as we shall see, that many theorists do not see these approaches as standing in splendid isolation: they may routinely combine elements across the boundaries in their work. In introducing them here, then, we intend simply to sketch in some of the commonality between these approaches as well as their differences, while at the same time acknowledging that these approaches to childhood do not occur in an intellectual vacuum. Thus we note, en route, the felt traces of the many presociological models of 'the child' already encountered, which play a part in the shaping of current thinking about children and children's place within the social order.

The socially constructed child

What is now called social constructionism is a relatively new departure in the understanding of childhood. The approach has three major landmarks in the works of Jenks (1982b), Stainton-Rogers et al. (1989) and James and Prout (1990b). The perspective derives in large part from the 1970s reaction to the stranglehold that varieties of positivism were exercising on British sociology. A wave of critical, deconstructing phenomenology came into competition with the absolutist pronouncements of the structural sociologies and Marxisms that appeared to hold sway. Such theorizing also complemented the growing liberalism and relativism that were seeping into the academy in the wake of the 1960s when the dominating philosophical paradigm shifted from a dogmatic materialism to an idealism inspired by the works of Husserl and Heidegger. [2]

To describe childhood, or indeed any phenomenon, as socially constructed is to suspend a belief in or a willing reception of its taken-for-granted meanings. Thus, though quite obviously we all know what children are and what childhood is like, for social constructionists this is not a knowledge that can reliably be drawn on. Such knowledge of the child and its lifeworld depends on the predispositions of a consciousness constituted in relation to our social, political, historical and moral context. In their explorations, then, social constructionists have to suspend assumptions about the existence and causal powers of a social structure that makes things, like childhood, as they are. Their purpose is to go back to the phenomenon in consciousness and show how it is built up. So within a socially constructed, idealist world there are no essential forms or constraints. Childhood does not exist in a finite and identifiable form. Ariès (1962) had already shown us this historically and Margaret Mead and Martha Wolfenstein (1954) had made early demonstrations of this cross-culturally through their work on culture and personality, perspectives which move us to a multiple conception of childhoods, or what Alfred Schutz would have referred to as multiple realities. Social constructionism therefore stresses the issue of plurality and, far from this model recommending a unitary form, it foregrounds diverse constructions.

This approach to childhood is therefore dedicatedly hermeneutic. It also erodes the conventional standards of judgement and truth. Therefore if, for example, as many commentators have suggested, child 'abuse' was rife in earlier times and a fully anticipated feature of adult–child relations, then how are we to say that it was bad, exploitative and harmful? Our standards of judgement are relative to our world-view and therefore we cannot make universal statements of value. What of infanticide in contemporary non-Western societies? Is it an immoral and criminal act or an economic necessity? Is it an extension of the Western belief in 'a woman's right to choose'? Such questioning demonstrates social constructionism's intense relationship with cultural relativism and how, as an approach, it lends itself to a cultural studies style of analysis, or the now fashionable analysis of modes of discourse whereby children are brought into being.

Children within this approach are therefore clearly unspecifiable as an ideal type. Childhoods are variable and intentional. In direct refutation of the presociological models of childhood, there is no universal 'child' with which to engage. The following chapters bear testimony to such a view but, in passing, we note that such a perspective demands a high level of reflexivity from its exponents. It is also the case that social constructionists, through their objections to positivist methods and assumptions, are more likely to be of the view that children are not formed by natural and social forces but rather that they inhabit a world of meaning created by themselves and through their interaction with adults. In this model the child is to be located semantically rather than causally:

> There are no hard and fast principles for defining when disagreements about how things are seen become significant enough to talk about them as different social realities . . . When social constructionists look at childhood, it is to these different social realities that they turn. The interest is not just in learning about the constructions of childhood in history or in different cultures – it is also a technique that throws light on why we construct childhood as we do in our own time and society. (Stainton-Rogers 1989: 24)

The significance of social constructionism lies in its political role in the study of childhood. It is well situated to prise the child free of biological determinism and thus to claim the phenomenon, epistemologically, in the realm of the social. However, it is important to emphasize that this approach is more than a theory of the ideational. It is also about the practical application of formed mental constructs and the impact that this has on the generation of reality and real consequence. None the less, as we shall explore and guard against in the following chapters, social constructionism does run the risk of abandoning the embodied material child.

The tribal child

Our second approach – the tribal child – embraces a quite significant alteration in thinking, and not simply in terms of the particular theoretical perspective that it applies to the topic. Here we witness a moral reappraisal of the stratification system and power relation that conventionally exists between adults and children. It sets out from a commitment to childhood's social worlds as real places and provinces of meaning in their own right and not as fantasies, games, poor imitations or inadequate precursors of the adult state of being. However, it would be claiming too much to say that this approach takes children seriously, as this would suggest that those considered elsewhere have not. But it can be argued that there is a seriousness here which attaches to the child's own view. We have a sense of what Mayall (1994b) has referred to as children's childhoods: children's difference is honoured and their relative autonomy celebrated. In the manner of the enlightened anthropologist, those working within this approach desist from imposing their own constructs and transformations on children's actions and attempt to treat their accounts and explanations at face value in good neo-Tylorian fashion. Children are not understood as 'cultural dopes'; theorists do not begin from the premise that they have only a misguided, mythological, superficial or irrational understanding of the rules of social life. Their worlds are real locations, as are those of adults, and the demand is that they be understood in those terms.

An early and well-publicized excursion into the possibilities provided by this model is to be found in the copious ethnographic studies of Iona and Peter Opie in the 1950s and 1960s. The Opies, and other researchers following their lead, have argued for the long-overdue recognition of an autonomous community of children. The children's world is to be seen as not unaffected by, but nevertheless artfully insulated from the world of adults; it is to be understood as an independent place with its own folklore, rituals, rules and normative constraints. This is the world of the schoolyard, the playground, the club and the gang (Opie and Opie 1977).

What this approach encourages is an emphasis on children's social action as structured, but within a system that is unfamiliar to us and therefore to be revealed through research. In this approach childhood intentionality welcomes the anthropological strangeness that has been recommended by ethnographic and interpretive methodologies for, if the tribes of childhood are to be provided with the status of social worlds, then it is to be anticipated that their particularity will systematically confound our taken-for-granted knowledge of how other (adult) social worlds function. No doubt there will be homologies, but the purpose of this approach is to ensure that these do not legislate for or stand in a dictatorial relationship to the child's world.

The rich seam which such an approach mines anticipates that ethnographies of childhood will, and should, proliferate and although work within this approach does have a negative potential for generating whimsical tales – quaint fables of the tribes of children and anecdotal accounting – this should not be its purpose. Instead, although the child's ontology is spoken about in the literature as more aspiration than viable construct, this approach has the potential to ensure that such a form of childlife can begin to receive detailed annotation. This mapping of childhood practices, self-presentations, motives and assumptions provides the very basis for an attention to the intrinsic being of childhood time which, in turn, can make possible both more effective communication and latterly more apposite policy measures in children's everyday lives. A caution must however be sounded: on the child's side of the equation a successful and ultimately knowing intrusion into their tribal folkways inevitably brings the threat of increased strategies of control. The ever-looming panopticon vision, noted in our account of presociological models of the child, may explode into fruition once the interior and the ontological become readily available.

Double-edged though it is, there is one obvious benefit of the 'tribal child' approach. As the following substantive chapters amply illustrate, it has facilitated a sustained, and long-awaited, concentration on children's language, language acquisition, language games, and thus burgeoning competence. This can help us not only in our relations with children and in their education, but it can also advise us about the constitution of mind.

The minority group child

Our next approach can attend to children epistemologically in any number of ways for its binding feature is its politicization of childhood in line with previously established agendas concerning an unequal and structurally discriminatory society. Oakley (and see also Alanen 1992), in a paper that explicitly attempts to demonstrate parallels between the politics of women's studies and childhood studies, states the following:

> This chapter considers the emerging field of childhood studies from the viewpoint of the established discipline of women's studies. Women and children are, of course, linked socially, but the development of these specialist academic studies also poses interesting methodological and political questions about the relationship between the status of women and children as social minority groups and their constitution as objects of the academic gaze. (1994: 13)

Through ascribing to children the status of a minority group this approach seeks, therefore, to challenge rather than confirm an existing set of power relations between adults and children. Indeed, the

very title 'minority' is a moral rather than demographic classification that conveys notions of relative powerlessness or victim-
ization. Such an approach to the study of children begins, not from
an intrinsic interest in childhood, though this may certainly accompany the larger purpose, but instead from an indictment of a social
structure and an accompanying dominant ideology which, to quote
Oakley's conclusion, 'deprive[s] some people of freedom in order to
give it to others' (1994: 32).

It is certainly the case that sociology over the last thirty years has
striven to convert the natural into the cultural. This has not simply
been a completion of the Durkheimian endeavour to understand all
phenomena as if they were primarily social. What has been occurring, and what has finally given rise to this view of the child, is a
systematic move to redemocratize modern society and to disassem-
ble all remaining covert forms of stratification. Whereas classical
sociology attended primarily to the stratification wrought through
social class, modern sociology has begun to address all those areas
that have been treated as 'natural' or 'only human nature'. Thus
race, sex, sexuality, age and physical and mental ability have all
come under scrutiny and have all been shown to derive their meaning and routine practices from their social context. Childhood is
rather late in gaining both fashion and attention but it has finally
arrived. Standpoint epistemologies are being forged on behalf of the
child, never more powerfully, as we shall see, than when linked to
empirical findings derived from the other approaches to childhood
research.

The strengths of this approach derive, then, from its seeming
dedication to children's interests and purposes: a sociology for
rather than of children! In many ways children here are regarded
as essentially indistinguishable from adults, or indeed all people:
they are seen as active subjects. The weaknesses of this approach,
on the other hand, derive from the necessary categorical transformation of any social group into the status of a group for-itself
instead of just in-itself, through the imposition of a politicized
uniformity that defies the differences within. Thus the universal
child becomes a minority group with demands that have to be
heard; that that group is fractured and faceted in internal diversity
is less often remarked. This is analogous to the problems found,
for example, in applying the consciousness-raising of the white
middle-class woman to the everyday experience of black working-
class women. Approaches which stress children as a minority
group echo these problematics.

The social structural child

The social structural approach contains a good deal of sound sense, if not pragmatism, beginning from a recognition of the obvious – that children are a constant feature of all social worlds. As a component of all societies children are typical, tangible, persistent and normal. Indeed, they demonstrate all the characteristics of social facts: their manifestations may vary from society to society but within each particular society they are uniform. To this degree they constitute a formative component of all social structures. This approach begins from such an assumption: children are not pathological or incomplete; they form a group, a body of social actors, and as citizens they have needs and rights. In the model of the socially developing child we saw a social structure and a society made up of rational adults with children waiting to be processed through the particular rite of passage that socialization within that society demanded. Within the social structural approach, the constancy of the child is acknowledged, as is also its essentiality. From this beginning, theorizing proceeds to examine both the necessary and the sufficient conditions that apply to childhood within a particular society or indeed to children in general. Children are again very much a universal category and they are seen to emerge from the constraint that their particular social structure proffers.

Children, then, are a body of subjects but their subjectivity is neither wilful nor capricious. It is determined by their society and thus childhood is instanced as a social phenomenon:

> There is . . . a more positive, and more important reason for preferring to speak about *the* childhood, namely the suggestion that children who live within a defined area – whether in terms of time, space, economics or other relevant criteria – have a number of characteristics in common. This preference in other words enables us to characterize not only childhood, but also the society in which this childhood is situated as mutually both independent and indispensable constructions; moreover it allows us to compare childhood thus characterized with other groups from the same country, perhaps most notably other age groups like youth, adulthood and old age, because they in principle are influenced by the same characterizing and formative societal parameters, although in different ways; it also permits us to ask to what extent childhood within a given area has changed historically, because – typically – continuity reigns within one country more than within any other unit of that order; and finally, it

becomes possible, when the concept of childhood is used, to compare childhoods internationally and interculturally, because we are availing ourselves of the same types of parameters – e.g. economic, political, social, environmental parameters. (Qvortrup 1994: 5–6)

What such work demonstrates is the dual and non-contradictory view that children bear the same status as research subjects as do adults, but that they may also have a different set of competencies, all of which are recognizable features of the social structure. Although Frones has shown that there are multiple dimensions to the 'social structural' child, and that it always remains possible to investigate these dimensions separately, ultimately in his formulation 'the child' is to be understood in relation to the integrative, interrelated and functional constraints of the institutional arrangements within the overall social structure:

Childhood may be defined as *the life period during which a human being is regarded as a child, and the cultural, social and economic characteristics of that period* . . . most of the studies on childhood concentrate on aspects that fall into one of four main categories: relations among generations, relations among children, children as an age group, and the institutional arrangements relating to children, their upbringing, and their education. Factors from one category may, of course, be important in another, as when the institutional apparatus concerned with children is significant in an analysis of child culture or child–parent relations. (1994: 148, emphasis in the original)

The 'social structural' child, then, has certain universal characteristics which are specifically related to the institutional structure of societies in general and are not simply subject to the changing nature of discourses about children or the radical contingencies of the historical process.

Conclusion: a Way Forward

These four sociological approaches which we have identified as characteristic of the new social studies of childhood constitute the platform from which we begin to explore different sites of contemporary childhood through the following substantive chapters. Forming the central part of our text, part II on 'Situating Childhood' interrogates new loci of the childhood phenomenon and, through empirical examples, demonstrates the ways in which the new social studies of childhood are centrally placed to engage with the core dichotomies of contemporary social theory: *agency–structure; universalism–particularism; local–global;* and *continuity–change.* We set out from the contemporary metatheoretical dimensions of *space* and *time,* seeing these as critical in the shaping of human cognition and the establishment of social identity. In this sense they are inescapable contexts from which to begin to investigate reflexively both the contemporary condition of childhood and also our very understandings of children.

Next the everyday world of children, or what we might describe as the practice of childhood, which is often apprehended through a radical separation between the categories of work and play imposed by adult vision, is considered under two headings. *Childhood culture* explores play as that which signifies a difference and a differencing, rather than an aspect of leisure or a trivialization of time, and it is counterpoised by a consideration of *working children,* a designation which deliberately ironizes the economic metaphor. Thus in these two chapters we seek to explain children 'doing the business' of childhood, despite adult projections to the contrary. A final pair of 'sites' of childhood that we visit explores its potential multiplicity. *Childhood diversity* considers the infinite variety of the social contexts in which children live, leading to a deconstruction of childhood's conventional, singular and reductive form. Thus our focus becomes childhood(s), a perspective deliberately confronted and called into question through the following consideration of the material universality of *the body* in childhood.

A final substantive task is to explore the attendant *methodological* issues that accompany the new and yielding cartography of the social study of childhood. Our book is completed with an exposition of *theorizing childhood,* where the four explanatory approaches and our four generative binary themes are brought together in ideal-typical forms. This serves, in retrospect, to show how we have achieved our analyses. However, it also reveals how others might now proceed to engage theoretically with childhood. Thus the goal of our book is a synthesis of approaches to childhood, a demonstration of new paradigmatic possibilities and a recognition and celebration of our membership in the traditions of sociology and anthropology.

Part II
Situating Childhood

3 Childhood in Social Space

There is a trite segment of horticultural folklore which defines a weed as being 'any plant that is growing in the wrong place'. This is instructive of our understanding of the location of children in the suggestion that children are peculiarly noticeable in relation to their setting. To put this more vigorously we might suggest that children either occupy designated spaces, that is they are placed, as in nurseries or schools, or they are conspicuous by their inappropriate or precocious invasion of adult territory: the parental bedroom, Daddy's chair, the public house, or even crossing the busy road. Childhood, we might venture, is that status of personhood which is by definition often in the wrong place. Though all people in any society are subject to geographical and spatial prohibitions, whether delineated by discretion, private possession or political embargo, the child's experience of such parameters is, we suggest, particularly paradoxical, often unprincipled, and certainly erratic. In terms of social space children are sited, insulated and distanced, and their very gradual emergence into wider, adult space is only by accident, by degrees, as an award or privilege or as part of a gradualist rite of passage.

As Archard stated when discussing the cultural 'separateness' of modern Western childhood:

> Ariès is at least right to observe that the most important feature of the way in which the modern age conceives of children is as meriting separation from the world of adults. The particular nature of children is separate; it clearly and distinctly sets them apart from adults. Children neither work nor play alongside adults; they do not participate in the adult world of law and politics. (1993: 29)

Qvortrup concurs. For him one of the paradoxes of modern childhood is that while 'adults argue that it is good for children and parents to be together ... more and more they live their everyday lives apart' (1995a: 191). None the less, as this chapter will reveal, children are relentlessly subjected to the law and especially the politics of adult life, which works to position them firmly in their particularity.

It is indeed a peculiar state of being that has its ontology predicated upon trespass and its elementary learning understood through the sanction that accompanies it. But this is the understanding of childhood achieved through exploring children's engagement with social space, a monstrous behaviourist vision created through a power positivism of spatial relations. Drawing on the presociological models of childhood identified in part I, we can, for example, see how in the Freudian regression fables personality is said to be distorted through trauma, the shock often engendered through children's exposure to unlicensed frontiers. Hysteria, we are informed, is potentially induced and sedimented by the very sighting of a parent in a sacred adult place and thus prohibitions against access are needed to protect the child.

Such an emphasis on prohibition would seem quite contrary to that offered in another presociological view of the child: in the Enlightenment vision children are born free, and imbued with the a priori initiative of the explorer. If, as Rousseau advised and our late twentieth-century liberalism encourages, children are immanent in their capacities, then they must be allowed free rein to go where their journeying takes them and they must be encouraged in their pioneering spirit. And yet here, too, prohibition lurks. Physical, conceptual and moral boundaries circumscribe the extent of children's wanderings. From the closed arenas of domestic space to the infinite horizons of cyberspace, boundaries forestall and contain the child's movement. Erected by a gerontocratic hegemony and policed by discipline, the boundaries are legitimized through ideologies of care, protection and privacy.

The central issue to be explored in relation to childhood space is, therefore, that of control. Focusing on three spatial contexts – the school, the city and the home – we explore here how each is dedicated to the control and regulation of the child's body and mind through regimes of discipline, learning, development, maturation and skill. Often regarded as traditional, structured sites for socialization by teachers, parents and the peer group, we offer critical analysis of how it is that children might become aware of the close relation between the nature of their placement and the particular modes of control that are its necessary accompaniment. It is clear, for example, that schools, the dinner table, the playground, the street and children's own bedrooms all share control components, but of recognizably different natures. It is also clear that these can vary through time: the dinner table transforms into the site of drawing or painting and the bedroom becomes the spatial symbol of punishment. However, the licence for the switch in affective placement is largely the prerogative of adults, while the child's experience is more often that of continuous regulation. Thus the spaces and times of childhood (see also chapter 4) are intimately interwoven, and in this chapter we explore the ways in which space comes to fashion experience for children and, like time, to structure the social space of childhood itself. By way of conclusion, and prefiguring our later discussion of the body (chapter 8), we ask whether even the psychic space of childhood is now in subjection and children's agency thereby curbed.

An inkling of this double intent can be seen already in Prendergast's analysis of the control of childhood through the spaces of the psyche, the soma and the social. Drawing on empirical data she argues that adolescent girls' adjustment to and awareness of menstruation is not only a contextual issue in relation to the spatialization of their experience – which at school, for example, makes the onset of menstruation a potentially stigmatizing and embarrassing event with regard to the practical problems of obtaining sanitary protection or being excused from swimming. More crucially, it is a formal causality. That is, the space, in this instance the school, actually shapes this bodily experience and identity in relation to sex and gender (see chapter 8). In her research therefore Prendergast

> has laid out one very specific example of how the spaces of the school, pedagogical, social and material, may critically shape bodily experience and wider sense of self for young women at this time. Learning takes place at many levels, most particularly in the unconscious taking up of an authentic, seemingly natural, gendered embodiment which lies at the heart of what is considered properly feminine. At the same time this notion of the 'natural properly feminine' body, and the processes which contribute to shaping it in school reflect a crucial paradox in Western societies about the value given to the reality of adult womanhood. (1995: 360)

Thus, as we discuss in relation to childhood, social space is never a mere issue of neutral location; there is no garden from which we emerge and to which we return in our adult reveries as might seem possible within presociological discourses of 'the child'. Such a Romantic Wordsworthian image of 'a lost realm, somewhere in the past of our lives, and the past of our culture ' (Pattison 1978: 58) has no place in new sociological approaches to childhood. Instead, we must account for childhood as a social space tied into a modern, complex and global division of labour where, as Massey (1984) has argued, the very processes of capitalist production become manifest in that experience of spatiality. The placing of childhood within such a complex is loaded with intent. Consequently, children's spatial experience of that intent is formative of tomorrow's citizens. As Urry has suggested:

> Spatiality . . . has various aspects besides that of region including distance, movement, proximity, specificity, perception, symbolism and meaning: and space makes a clear difference to the degree to which, to use realist terminology, the causal powers of social entities (such as class, the state, capitalist relations, patriarchy) are realised. (1995: 13)

Clearly children, the group least in possession of power within modern Western societies, let alone on the global stage, are potentially most subject to the exercise of this realization, but as yet we have scant knowledge of their experiences. A consideration of childhood space, such as that beginning to emerge from the social geographies of childhood, is timely (Matthews 1992; Valentine 1996; forthcoming; Lowe et al. 1993; Sibley 1995). Smith and Katz have argued that

> With the reassertion of space in social and cultural theory, an entire spatial language has emerged for comprehending the contours of social reality. A response in part to the widespread historicism that has dominated 'Western' social thought over the last century and a half, this resurgence of interest in the space and spatial concepts is broadly based. It was the explicit goal of critical geographic and political economic theory from the late 1960s onwards, a central component of structural and post-structural social analyses, and a core concern of information theory. Most recently, space has provided an attractive lexicon for many feminist, postmodernist, and postcolonial enquiries, the focus for public art and geo art, and a grammar in cultural discourse more broadly. (1993: 67)

This chapter argues that such a language and politics of spatiality must now emerge in social theory for childhood too.

The Schooled Child

When infants graduate to 'toddler' status, a shift enabled in part by changes in the material body which permit a new body style of independent movement (see chapter 8), they instantly accelerate the likelihood of their collision with electric fires, or later, Internet pornography, or just adult conversation and intimacy. In this sense, as will become clear, the social space of childhood is also a temporal phenomenon. Chapter 4 will describe, for individual children, how age increases access to space, and, following Kovarik (1994), we can therefore conceptualize the structuring of childhood experience in terms of the 'stages and scripts' in which space and time are closely interwoven. These stages and scripts – primarily the family, the school and the peer group – generate not just the 'where' and 'when', but also the 'what' and 'how' questions that relate to children's environments. In this section we take the spatial/temporal scripts of the school as our main focus, exploring the ways in which these work to structure the institution of childhood for children.

In most Western societies children are obliged to spend a considerable period of their time in schools, a spatial positioning which provides a singular possibility for the focused and highly considered management and control of an extensive group within the population. Schools provide an ordered temporal passage from child to adult status; at the same time, on a daily basis, they restrict the ways in which children can spend their time (see chapter 4). Within this formulation, the unit of analysis becomes not so much the school regarded as a building or an institution, but the 'curriculum' as the social process that animates and gives meaning to 'the school' as a formal organization. The curriculum is strategic in mapping out the whole in-school experience of the child through a combination of space, time, location, content, proximity, isolation, insulation, integration and hierarchy. Though a commonsense view of the curriculum might lead us to view it as a collection of learning activities that occupies the day in educational institutions – curricula, in this sense, being not dissimilar to the production or work that goes on in a factory or office – to define an activity simply in terms of its being 'what people do' in particular contexts is to ignore the purposes of such activities. It is also to ignore the principles by which such activities are structured into recognizable forms.

Curricula, we would argue therefore, are more than the description of content. They are spatial theories of cognitive and bodily development and, as such, they contain world-views (Young 1971) which are never accidental and certainly not arbitrary. They involve selections, choices, rules and conventions, all of which relate to questions of power, issues of personal identity and philosophies of human nature and potential, and all of which are specifically focused on the child. In this sense, curricula are both social and political structures, containing assumptions about how people (that is, largely children) ought best to be. Understood within a historical context, they are from different points of view cumulative and stable, facilitating and resisting change. The knowledge that comprises the curriculum instances humankind's selection from and control of its world; its replication and repetition in paradigmatic style instances the control of others through the constitution of the child's body and consciousness into the form of an educational identity. Thus analysis of the school curriculum allows us to initiate our exploration of issues of control within the social space of childhood.

A central organizing principle of any curriculum is the timetable, which is itself a highly encoded spatialization of the politics of experience. Bernstein's classic essay (1971) on the political economy of educational knowledge, for example, treats the curriculum as a formal punctuation of time, crystallized for children into the 'lesson', the 'class' or the 'period'. Classes are in this sense spatial units of activity that, through time, are insulated from one another. Bernstein informs us that a content signifies what occurs within each distinct unit and the overall curriculum can thus be defined as the principle that brings units and contents together into a formal relationship. This leads to an analysis of units in terms of contents and also in terms of their time/space allocations. Introducing a further variable concerning either the compulsory or elective character of each bounded content, indices of the status of particular contents and their relative significance within a child's educational career begin to emerge.

A child's educational identity – as ' success' or 'failure' – is thus in part a function of the temporal and spatial controls exerted over time through the curriculum, which according to Foucault turns out to be not much about time at all:

> The time-table is an old inheritance. The strict model was no doubt suggested by the monastic communities. It soon spread. Its three great methods – establish rhythms, impose particular occupations, regulate the cycles of repetition – were soon to be found in schools,

workshops and hospitals. The new disciplines had no difficulty in taking up their place in the old forms; the schools and poorhouses extended the life and the regularity of the monastic communities to which they were often attached. The rigours of the industrial period long retained a religious air; in the seventeenth century, the regulations of the great manufactories laid down the exercises that would divide up the working day ... but even in the nineteenth century, when the rural populations were needed in industry, they were sometimes formed into 'congregations', in an attempt to inure them to work in the workshops; the framework of the 'factory-monastery' was imposed upon the workers. (1977: 149–50)

It is clear, then, that Foucault's work, which is highly spatial in its orientation and concerned with the social grounds of control in everyday life, may have much to offer to our understanding of the spatiality of childhood and, indeed, of children's experiences of that space. In his work *Discipline and Punish*, for example, Foucault provides us with an analysis of what he refers to as the 'anatomy of power' in Western culture. A caesura occurs, he suggests, in the eighteenth century, when the symbolic space occupied by discipline shifts from the public to the private arena. We are provided with two images of discipline which reflect two modes of control; these are, in turn, aspects of two forms of social integration. There is an old, medieval order, which in France gave way after the Revolution to a new order resonant with the modern industrial society. Penal theory was transformed and the new prison was born. All this is metaphoric of our concerns with childhood and space, for this new order provided a model of discipline and control which was not restricted simply to the jailhouse. Synchronic homologies emerged throughout the culture, including the hospital, the factory, the army barracks and, most significantly for our interests, the school.

Foucault's monograph begins with an account of the appalling violence and degradation inflicted on the individual found guilty of attempting to assassinate Louis XV. The awe-full excess of this exemplar is instructive of the spectacular, wholly public and demonstrable punishment that was characteristic of the old order, but by the twentieth century a transition had occurred. Notably there was a shift from an emphasis on the execution of punishment to the articulation of trial and sentence. It was as if a discrete rational process had overtaken excessive symbolism.

This is a clear index of modernity: relations between persons, or between state and persons, becomes marked by a greater humanitarianism. But this change in appearance is to do with far more than a change of attitude. What occurred, as Émile Durkheim predicted in *The Division of Labour in Society*, was that the juridical code of restitution replaced that of retribution. With modernity the disciplinary convention of physical violence against the body became subtly transformed into a far more intrusive correction and training of the psyche. In relation to childhood this transition from exterior space to interior space is evident in changing regimes of childrearing, pedagogy and educational psychology. Described by Rose (1989) as a governing of the soul, some of these we have already noted as instructive in both past and present imaginings of childhood (see part I). This , then, is the movement of the child through social space which we chart here and is a trajectory to which we shall return in our conclusion.

The central lesson to be drawn from Foucault for the social construction of childhood is that the exercise of discipline both requires and has developed historically a range of spatial conditions that make possible its successful implementation. To begin with, as Sheridan (1980) has put it, discipline is cellular. It localizes and places individuals, separates, isolates or combines them, thereby regulating individuals precisely according to space. People and units of space become synonymous:

> In organising 'cells', 'places' and 'ranks', the disciplines create complex spaces that are at once architectural, functional and hierarchical. It is spaces that provide fixed positions and permit circulation; they carve out individual segments and establish operational links; they mark places and indicate values; they guarantee the obedience of individuals, but also better economy of time and gesture. They are mixed spaces: real because they govern the disposition of buildings, rooms, furniture, but also ideal, because they are projected over this arrangement of characterisations, assessments, hierarchies. (Foucault 1977: 148)

The primary model for this cellularization is the monastery: each monk alone in his cell relating single-mindedly to the aims of the institution through a strict pattern of obligation and commitment. But this model opens up a variety of modern possibilities: the factory with the distribution of workers on the shop-floor according to the logistics of the particular division of labour and the ergonomics of specific task; the hospital with wings and wards, organized in relation to isolation, segregation and commonality, all according to the nature and the pacing of the patient's condition; and central to our concerns, the classroom, one of the most fundamental stages and scripts for childhood.

The placing of children in classrooms to enable the general communication of one teacher to reach all is a move towards the development of an educational machine, further facilitated by the emerging technologies of the blackboard, whiteboard, overhead projector, VDU and so on. But it is also a disciplined system of control. Children can be placed in rows, classes can be broken down into tables or groups and specialized into activities; individuals can be put in the 'reading corner', required to stand by teacher's table or come out to the front. Everyone can be evacuated, that is, sent out to exercise in the playground.

None of this speaks of the child's experience as being the experience of a 'neutral' space and, as Pollard and Filer (1996) have noted, this is indeed far from the case. In their discussion of the spatial and temporal contexts of British schools, they offer a complex and detailed account of the intimate conceptual relationship which is established for any individual child between the moral/knowledge space of the school and that of the home. In their view the national curriculum, supposedly designed to meet the needs of all children, is misguided in its failure to acknowledge the shifting spatial contexts of children's learning and in its 'lack of attention to learners and to social influences on the teaching and learning contexts which they experience'. According to Pollard and Filer, to grasp how education actually takes place it is necessary to understand the specificities of its temporal and spatial location by adopting a 'focus on pupil learners as *children* with identities and learning dispositions which are developed, fostered or constrained by experiences within the social contexts of home, classroom and playground' (1996: 314). These are the loci for the implicit regimes of control which work to shape particular educational identities for children.

Such disciplines of control, largely facilitated through the timetable, extend to shape much of children's activity. Play, for example, occurs in designated spaces within the curriculum so that four-year-old children quickly learn that 'styles of play appropriate to the playground [are] not permissible within the structured "educational play" of the classroom' (James 1993: 173). But in addition, as James notes, particular spaces and times within the school permit the learning of moral and conceptual values and prove formative for the new entrant:

Children new to Hilltop school ... soon learnt that adult rules defined when they were allowed to play on the grass, rather than the
tarmac. Adult rules designated which parts of the building they
could enter freely and which areas of the playground belonged to
older or younger children. The symbolic use made by adults of walls
and lines in the playground to identify publicly child miscreants
were visibly apparent. 'Naughty' children would be made to stand
still, against the wall or on a painted line. Like statues amid the
swirling hubbub of other children's games, they became temporary
symbolic reminders of the social order of the school. (1993: 173)

New children will also soon learn that school space is gendered.
They will note that the playground literally sidelines girls' play, as
the boys colonize its centre through their games of football. They get
to know that the Wendy House in the reception class is where

'Mummies' [girls] feed their babies, cook the dinner, go shopping,
control their husbands, speak on the telephone and smack their children. 'Daddies' [boys] go off to work. For much of the time they are
forced to stay outside the house, only gaining entry by permission
from the 'mummies' or, when refused, by violence and force. (1993:
187)

Thus, the institution of schooling, through the spatial discipline of
its curricula, creates the space of and for childhood, attributing the
status of 'child' to those who fall subject to its regimes of control.

In contexts outside those of Europe and North America, as schooling is extolled as a virtue, so its darker, disciplining aspect may
become more apparent. The particular spaces which schooling occupies in and creates for childhood may not be beneficial for all
children. Boyden (1994) points out, for example, that in many developing contexts an insistence on the intrinsic value of education and
compulsory school attendance may significantly increase, rather
than decrease child labour through the necessity to earn money to
pay for schooling (see chapter 6). Similarly, Field notes with alarm
that in contemporary Japan the concentrated disciplining of children at school – through long hours of study, excessive testing, the
beating of pupils and monitoring of conduct – has led to an increase
in children's suicides, alongside the appearance of so-called adult
stress-related conditions such as baldness and ulcers. Passage out of
childhood and into the space of successful adulthood is facilitated
by high examination achievement and so Japanese mothers eagerly
collude with teachers to enforce pedagogic discipline and control.

The irony is, as Field observes, that ' Japanese children are suffering and risking the loss of childhood itself by performing the socially defined tasks of childhood' (1995: 53).

Urban Children

Our second focus on childhood and social space is on a broader stage or space of modernity, the city, a space inhabited by an increasing number of children.[1] However, rather than examining the urban child, as if the space in question were merely substantive, we need to ask analytic questions of that city space. The city itself is anything but neutral with regard to social experience and creates a new set of parameters in relation to the child. It appears as the great public place, yet it is mapped fleetingly by private spaces and unpredicted geographies of power (Jenks 1995b). Conceptions of the urban have been slow in coming in social theory and they are rarely conceived within an active and critical theory of spatiality. Weber's account of the city, for example, was a historical tract in terms of the differentiation that urban life created in the experience of the citizen with the decline of feudalism; Simmel, as a theorist of modernity, analysed the ways of being and relating in the metropolis; and the Chicago School developed an ecological scheme to account for spatial zonality and a subsequent set of ethnographies to provide their classificatory scheme with a texture and content. Urry (1995) cites Castells (1977; 1978) as the first major breakthrough in disrupting the commonsense notions of urban, rural, local, community, city, etc. Just what is it that generates the city as an analytic category? For Castells it is 'collective consumption', a concept to which Pickvance (1985) has added 'localised political processes' and 'spatial density and proximity'.

The child in the city is therefore confronted by and contained within spatial structures that exaggerate the economic, the political and the social. The city generates an intensity of experience for children, as Connolly and Ennew point out, offering them 'the opposite of curricularization [by] providing arenas for doing nothing' (1996: 135). Increasingly, however, it also generates an intensity of risk:

> Unless participation in greeting, directing, watching, and helping others in the street is assumed, along with one's own right of way, the

path is soon fraught with danger. Here, then, we have a further exercise in the covenant of care that is vital to our children. For the look and feel of our city streets is an icon of our social and political life. It is also a source of personal harmony and aesthetic satisfaction to children as well as adults. For the city is in ruins when it looks ugly and feels dangerous, yet the city cannot be saved from ruin merely by design. (O'Neill 1994: 84)

However, the child's life in the city has not been and is still not a constant experience (see Ward 1977). For street children in South America the city is a complex moral, political and economic space which children appropriate, defining themselves variously as children in or of the street (Glauser 1990; see also chapter 6). Its streets are a place of work, of entertainment and, for some, their home. In harmony with the analytic trajectory considered above, however, for children in Western societies and especially those of the middle class, the city has developed from a public space to a private, adult place, one which they, as children, have little access to.

Taking Britain as an example, the available social histories of childhood and accounts of the rise of mass education attest to a wholesale relocation of the child throughout the nineteenth century. Mayhew's peripatetic ethnographies of 1861 of London's highways and byways have established a series of typifications of children now only credible in the collective imagination through the sustained popularity of Dickensian imagery. But these seasonally revived tableaux have a hard factual and material core that Mayhew was precisely striving to save from the status of fiction (see Mayhew 1985). The fierce competition and commercial predation that was bred through laissez-faire capitalism had converted the whole population into both consumers and producers and the market space provided by the city was permeated, quite promiscuously, by all generations of traders, as it continues to be, these days, in many cities in the world's South.[2] Children, like adults, possessed and roamed the streets. They were never out of place.

Mayhew's taxonomy introduces endless types: traders, mudlarks, apprentice costermongers, thieves of all varieties, beggars, street entertainers, prostitutes. All are of an age in the life course that we would now describe as childhood, but they are only amenable to today's sensibilities in the form of Dickens's 'Artful Dodger' or Arthur Morrison's 'Child of the Jago'. It is hard to conceive of them as real and utterly mundane features of the everyday urban scene (see chapter 6). As the eighteenth- and nineteenth-century image of the child shifted towards innocence, and the child's needs became increasingly articulated in terms of protection, refracted through the complex of presociological discourses of the Enlightenment (see chapter 1), so we witness the growth of movements and specific agencies to claim children back from the streets. As in contexts of the developing world today (Boyden 1990), the political motivation for this policy initiative was not always simply humanitarian. In her analysis of the impetus to institutionalize infant education in Britain in the early 1800s, Clarke points out that

> the interest in infant education has to be seen in the context of a more general interest in working-class education among liberal Whigs and Radicals who saw it as a necessary condition for social harmony. Education was seen as the solution to the social and political threat to the ruling class posed by the concentration of large numbers of working-class people in the rapidly expanding cities of the early nineteenth century and their political autonomy. The Sunday School movement and the establishment of monitorial schools in the late eighteenth and early nineteenth centuries may both be seen as attempts to control and contain the political energies of the working class. (1985: 75)

Though their welfare is of contemporary concern for the state, street children in many parts of the world may, none the less, also be most likely to experience statutory bodies as repressive:

> In countries as widely dispersed as Colombia, India, and Ethiopia, street children are constantly harassed by the police. In Puerto Plat, in the Dominican Republic, they are rounded up periodically to keep them from pestering the tourists. . . . They are usually held for some hours in penal establishments without food or drink. When the tourists have gone they are transported to distant beaches and left to make their own way back to town on foot. (Boyden 1990: 205)

This demonstrates that in these contexts, as in nineteenth-century Britain, children do not constitute a general category of persons but, instead, one that is divided by social class and/or ethnicity.

Thus the history of the city is marked by a developing segregation of space in terms of class, gender and, most importantly for our purposes, age. In Britain a hierarchy of mobility in relation to public space appears to have emerged towards late modernity. As both Buck-Morss (1986) and Wolff (1985) have demonstrated, women relinquished what little control and access to the public street they may have previously established. Markets were no longer for them and their sole access to symbolic exchange took place in the context of the newly developed, more private and enclosed department stores. This accompanies the change that Hall (1985) has documented as a ghettoizing of the female role within the realm of the domestic, that is, the private space of cities. And as women, both by degrees and by social class, withdrew into the private space of home, so also did the child. Although the street urchin did not disappear in a day and, as we have seen, its eventual disappearance was not wholly directed by care and attention, nevertheless, as the reserve army of domestic labour retreated behind the doorstep, new ideologies of motherhood and nurture ensured that the child withdrew alongside.

In a paper concerning Britain from the mid-nineteenth century up to the beginning of the First World War, Cockburn investigates the spacing and eventual placing of working-class children in Manchester, the zone of Engels rather than Mayhew. Concurring with the argument stated here, Cockburn shows the emergence of a new cartography of childhood through a relentless purging of streets and workplaces, which led to a systematic privatization of the child in the controlled spaces of homes, schools, playgrounds and clubs. This clearance, he suggests, was driven by school authorities, religious organizations and child protection agencies, and it created new and highly formalized childhood spaces. Cockburn concludes:

> The spaces available to children and young people were dramatically different between 1850 and 1914. This period witnessed the removal of children from the 'public spaces' of the streets and workplace to their homes, schools and organised entertainments. By 1914 if children were seen unaccompanied on the streets of Manchester at about 8 at night they were liable to be stopped by a policeman and questioned. This movement towards control must not be separated from the mood that was concerned with the training of young citizens into future participation in the electorate and defenders of the Empire . . . Children's role in social life had changed and their movements in public spaces been restricted. (1995: 14)

Thus in Britain the placing, or 'housing', of street children was not achieved through a concerted social policy and practice but rather through what Cunningham (1991) has described as a series of 'overlapping discourses' that occurred with what we might call an elective affinity. First, from the middle of the nineteenth century onwards there were unofficial, often religious, and certainly voluntary efforts made to capture the street child and win him or her into a life of order and moral certainty. The Ragged Schools can be seen as part of this movement, as can the later philanthropic and charitable initiatives of Lord Shaftesbury and Thomas Barnardo. Second, there were the more concerted and official attempts to contain child criminality which were manifested through robust criminal legislation and a relatively punitive sentencing policy: significantly larger numbers of people and particularly young people spent time imprisoned than in any other period of British history.

In Britain, the late modern private child, predominantly the city child, remains, we suggest, a victim of public space but is cast now in a significantly different relationship to it. For many children, especially those of the middle class, the big 'outside' is conceived as a dangerous place to be and the child is introduced to this risk only gradually and in company. There is always a discontinuity between the private and the public domains and this is due, in large part, to the successive enfeeblement of collective symbolism. The outside world is inhabited by strangers and the communicative form is a threat rather than welcome. Children are simply 'not safe' on the streets, a danger specified through the hyperbole of rapists, perverts and murderers and the mundanity of traffic. The disappearance of children from the street, documented by Hillman, Adams and Whiteleg (1990), is but one instance of this progressive reconceptualization of children and space. As Sibley notes, now

> the locality is more likely to be experienced from the car, necessarily in the company of adults, rather than alone or in the company of other children. The car then functions as a protective capsule from which the child observes the world but does not experience it directly through encounters with others. (1995: 136)

At the same time, however, for young people the city streets may remain enticing, its darker aspect being for them disguised:

> located at the heart of the urban system [the city streets] offer a number of consumer and entertainment possibilities: fast food outlets, restaurants, gambling arcades, cinemas and video stores, all with easy transport access. For young people these attractions are multiplied by the apparent lack of structure and schedule in these areas. (Connolly and Ennew 1996: 134)

However, recently the potentially malevolent space of the public world of the city has taken a finite and unexpected form: in Bootle in the UK during 1993 Jamie Bulger, a toddler, was abducted, tortured and murdered by two older children. The conceptual confusion of concepts of childhood that this peculiar event created is momentous, and has also had profound spatial implications (James and Jenks 1996). The predatory public space, hitherto understood starkly in terms of the adult–child dichotomy, is now seen to be made up of children too. Preconceptions about children are wavering, a disquiet amplified by other evidence that by far the majority of the physical, sexual and emotional abuse that any child is likely to receive will be from other children (Ambert 1995). Whether on the street or in the playground, bullying of children by children (Tattum and Lane 1989) adds to the 'danger to children' which the great outdoors now poses. Thus the space that childhood once occupied has now been transformed into the perimeter of children's privacy.

The extended case study of changes in childhood space in British society leads us to question more generally what sense can be made of the public domain in relation to the modern child. Though both complex and as yet uncertain, what appears to be occurring is in part a process of insulation, involving a further spatial segregation of the child. As ever with contemporary crisis management, moral and material, there is a convenient 'scapegoating', involving the searching out of something or somebody to blame. The targets identified in the outside space as threatening to children have been as banal as the unspecified causality of video games and their suspicious 'hyperreality', have been individualized in relation to the lack of discipline in homes and schools, and have been made personal through accusations about the decline in standards of morality. Variously invoked as external threats, all these are seen as key elements in the battle to recover the lost innocence of children and the perhaps missing space of childhood. Following the trial judge's remarks in the Bulger case, the British government's response has, predictably, been to exert further controls on children through schemes such as 'truancy watch', in which shopkeepers are enrolled to police the activities of children who, freeing themselves from the constraints of the classroom, may choose to spend their time in the street. In such ways, the global and public space of cities is increasingly under surveillance lest children be found in the wrong place at the wrong time. As Connolly and Ennew note, ' to be a child outside adult supervision, visible on city centre streets, is to be out of place' (1996: 133).

Childhood and Domestic Space

Notwithstanding the continued and voluble presence of children in many cities of the South and increasing numbers of homeless children on city streets in the North, the historical displacement of most children from the public world of the city, noted above for Britain, was accompanied by the growth of new attitudes towards the child. As Clarke notes, 'the specific interest in infant education was a new phenomenon in the early 1820s and has to be seen in the light of changes taking place within the middle-class family, in particular, the separation of spheres into male-public and female-private' (1985: 75). A new proximity thus signified the relationship between mother and child and defined the domestic space as 'home', which meant that childhood was destined for a new interiority. There was no need to ask what had happened to the now invisible *petit flaneur*; it was tied to its mother's apron strings, indoors! A significant pattern had been set. It is one which constitutes much in our current engagement with the space of childhood through its binding of the concepts of the 'family' and 'home' into 'the modern domestic ideal' (Allan and Crow 1989: 1).

As a conceptual and physical space within which the child is increasingly embedded, the domestic space of the 'home' is, in practice, of course not always an ideal space: the regulation and discipline of that space, like those of the school and the city, remain problematic for many children. Indeed, it is a paradox that in the haven which home may be said to represent, issues about surveillance, power and control of the child may come to be more strongly voiced. It is certain, for example, that the family home is most often the site for the sexual and physical abuse of children (Jenks 1996a), and indeed the onset of homelessness, the exclusion of the child from the home, may be precipitated by such abuse (Hutson 1995). The symbolic boundaries of 'families' and 'homes' may be breached by interventions from the state through police and social workers removing children to other places of safety. Somewhat ironically these are often 'children's homes', spaces embodying the safety and sanctity of idealized homes for children without homes or whose own homes fail to provide adequate comfort for the child. Thus the sanctity of the domestic space of the home as haven must be scrutinized more precisely to uncover the extent to which this refuge for 'the child' has in late modernity also become increasingly problematic.

Mapping out what he terms a geography of sensations, Sibley, for example, shows the ways in which the domestic space of the home, which as we have seen has become the child's centre, is constituted for the child through relations of power and control. Echoing the experience of schooling, space at home is bounded and constraining and in his discussion Sibley develops Bernstein's distinction between positional and personalizing families. The positional parent is one who has

> a rigid attitude to space and time in the home and anxiety over spatial boundaries. The practice of keeping children out of rooms or spaces decreed as adult spaces and a concern with the temporal regulation of children's activities would be typically positional. Keeping control means maintaining clear, unambiguous boundaries. . . . Only father sits in a particular chair, for example, and there is a fixed seating arrangement for meals . . . In the personalising family, all the distinguishing features of the positional family are reversed. Notionally, power is equally distributed between family members with the implication that the uses of space and time in the home are negotiable . . . toys spread across the living-room carpet would not be a problem. (Sibley 1995: 131)

In this formulation, for some children, the absence of autonomy both in the street *and* at home threatens to make contemporary childhood problematic (but see Solberg 1990). As Sibley notes, 'even in the most benign account of the home and family relationships, there are intimations of conflicting world-views, manifest in arguments over untidiness and bed times' (1995: 135).

There has been relatively little account of the ways in which domestic space is regulated for children, however, except through descriptions of childrearing practices which, offered by parents, yield an orderly view of the manner in which the home environment fosters (or impedes) the child's development. This lack in itself speaks to the privatizing of childhood in domestic space and the insulating role which the home takes on for children. Taken as a commonplace factor in accounting for delinquency, but more rarely in explaining success, the home, like the school and the street, offers a causality. This reinforces the suggestion made earlier that accounting for childhood social space must move beyond mere contextualization to a systematic exploration of its formative materiality. Glimpses of how this might be achieved through research which takes account of children's agency can be found in Hallden's discussion of the contrasting views of domesticity inscribed by Swedish boys and girls in their stories of family life (1992a; 1992b). The girls narrate stories in which the routine ordering of domestic space centres the girl-mother at the heart of the family, while in the boys' accounts a central male figure stands alone, distanced from domestic life. Thus we see the spatialization of children's acquisition of knowledge about gender roles.

If the home is thus more a female than a male space, a conception which McRobbie and Garber's (1976) early account of girls' bedroom culture documents, then what will happen to that domestic space if, as we have been suggesting, the external world poses an ever-increasing menace? Will it be, as McNamee's (forthcoming) account of children's use of computers suggests, that boys will increasingly colonize those spaces previously seen as part of the female domain? If this is the case, what space, if any, will be left for girls?

Childhood as a Subject(ed) Space

As we have seen, domestic space is policed by parents, paralleling the surveillance of the school and the street by the adult world. In conclusion we ask therefore if the only autonomous space left for the child is the interior, psychic space of the self? Or has this too now become subjected? Retracing our steps back to Foucault's discussion of the conditions of discipline, we can see that the control of childhood space functions through a combination of devices and that children are certainly subject to a fierce regulation mediated in relation to a time-scale. Usually that of their 'natural' development, the whole premise of adult interaction with the child, often even in pleasure, may seem to be one of control and instruction. The individual child, it would appear, emerges via the disciplined, spatial implementation of the timetable which instils a regularity and a rhythm in all the activities and tasks of children, including control of the material body through the performance of duty and style of life.

So, for example, just as soldiers are drilled persistently even beyond basic training, so children are required to eat, sleep, wash and excrete at specific and regular times. Within the modern conditions for discipline there is a further, internal spatialization for each activity. Periodized and subdivided into steps or stages for the individual, the learning of tasks is subject to a spatial and temporal division of labour leading to a more specialized and efficient functioning. By way of illustration, Foucault uses the example of children and the regimes used to encourage the mastery of handwriting – and here some of us might recall the achievement of a 'perfect page' of handwriting as a prerequisite to the issue of exercise books – while Walkerdine describes how, through the moral space of the school, girls and boys learn to take on radically different subject identities. Girls are rewarded for docile and nurturant styles of behaviour, to mirror the caring protectiveness of their female teachers, with boys being permitted to enact the 'naughtiness . . . expected, validated and associated with masculinity' (1985: 229). The disciplined environment of the school thus provides for children's self-realization in the same way that Durkheim's social actor became a viable subjective agency through the exercise of structural constraint.

Such a form of control, Sheridan notes, is 'not triumphant, excessive, omnipotent, but modest, suspicious, calculating. It operates through hierarchical observation, normalising judgment, and their combination in the examination' (1980: 152) . Distilled by Foucault into a single image – that of the 'panopticon', Bentham's perfect prison with its central tower, its maximally visible inmates and its unseen warders – this model of power captures the very essence of modernity's mode of control within a spatial, even concretely architectural, form. Modern power is refined, invisible, viscous and yet mobile. It is also rapid, accurate and considered. The panopticon's inmates do not know when they are under surveillance; they may be being watched constantly or they may not. The reality is that they are watching themselves. We have moved, then, from a collective to an individual space, with the public and external experience of shame and degradation transformed into the private and inner experience of guilt. Thus modernity's child, at school, on the street and even at home, becomes its own policeman.

This is a controlled subjection of the child as subject indeed. From the 9 o'clock watershed on TV viewing which in Britain postpones certain kinds of programme to later in the evening, when children are supposed to be in bed, through to the more rigid enforcement of legal age limits for entry into cinemas, the child gets to know 'its place'. Supporting this introspection, across all the domains which we have discussed are any number of child-centred teachers – and practices of continuous assessment, educational psychology and psychometric testing – school counsellors, educational welfare officers, parent-teacher associations, social workers and health visitors.

All these conspire tactically for the child's own good and represent the culmination of a nineteenth-century trajectory towards, finally, regulating the space within the child. Resonating with Jenks's (1982a) view that social theories of childhood are grounded in the visions of social order of adult theorists, Steedman's challenging analytic proposition is that accounts of childhood space relate most directly to lost or unexplored concepts of the adult self. In her discussion of nineteenth-century street children, Steedman places accounts of their state of being within an intentional interpretive frame. She states that:

> To some extent, the children that Mayhew (and other commentators) watched and reported on were seen through the conventions of melodrama, specifically in the meaning urban melodrama gave to children before the 1880s, as heightened embodiments of the suffering of the adults connected with them. In order to explore these relationships between melodrama, the means of representing working-class childhood, their history and the history of legislation concerning them, we need also to explore the relationship between the street and the stage, as the places where the child was most consistently watched. (1995: 114)

If the child is now to be constituted as a projection or an image that enables the adult consciousness to range through possible views of selfhood, then the private space that modernity illuminated is not just a concrete location. It is also an analytic dimension concerning the human interior, an understanding which, as Ivy (1995) notes, is emblematic in late twentieth-century American quests to recover the inner child. Here we reconnect with Foucault and his views concerning the shaping of the private self.

Conclusion

In an early paper Bernstein (1967) contributed to this question of childhood space with an analysis of the relative 'openness' or 'closure' of the social order in school. This work considered the quality of the child's learning experience according to the spaces that schools provide, spaces range from open-plan architecture to curriculum planning. Essentially, and prefiguring Foucault, Bernstein sees an old order, the domain of public symbolism, that is specified as closed and a new order, of private symbolism, that invites an openness. The forms of social control involve the transmission of common values and a fixed ritual order in the closed model, whereas openness requires personalized control, an appeal to individuals and a diminution of ritual orders. There is a consequent weakening of the symbolic significance of punishment. The transition from closedness to openness implies that changes will occur in the school's division of labour: institutions will become larger; teachers will perform an increasing number of specialized roles; and children are less likely to be held in groups according to ascribed status characteristics. The instrumental order of the school, that is the tangible spatial organization of teaching, will witness a shift from fixed structural units to a proliferation of groups. In this way time and space become less rigid and not regarded as fixed referents. Teaching becomes organized around exploring principles rather than the transmission of standard operations, and the authoritative teacher model of yesterday gives way to the problem-poser or facilitator. Curricula move from depth to breadth as teaching and learning have more to do with ideas and less to do with specific subject parameters. And finally the move towards openness makes for greater student choice and greater autonomy. The move to openness recommended by Bernstein as the achievement of modernity means that the boundaries containing childhood experience should be opening up. The spaces of childhood should be much less containing and constraining and Bernstein is entirely positive in concluding this thesis:

> None of this should be taken in the spirit that yesterday there was order; today there is only flux. Neither should it be taken as a long sigh over the weakening of authority and its social basis. Rather we should be eager to explore changes in the forms of social integration in order to reexamine the basis for social control. This, as Durkheim pointed out decades ago, is a central concern of a sociology of education. (1967: 353)

As we have explored here, Bernstein's optimism may have been misplaced.

4 The Temporality of Childhood

In exploring the ways in which social space works to constrain and contain children's lives the previous chapter emphasized structural and constructionist approaches to childhood. Here we suggest that age, generation and time are, similarly, important constraints on the form taken by childhood in any culture. However, significantly, they may also be ones through which the agency of children arises. Thus, developing our discussion of the range of theoretical possibilities which are now emerging within the new social studies of childhood, this chapter argues that one of the paradoxes that is childhood derives from its temporality.

Childhood is simultaneously our fond, adult rememberings of a time past and the immediacy of our own children's lives; childhood is united by the universal biology of human physical development and cognitive potential but, in the same moment, radically differentiated by the varied social contexts in which this growth can be culturally enacted in the life course. Thus, although the expectations and competencies of age may be thought to be generationally specific, at any point in time they turn out to be individually and momentarily negotiable.

This is the temporal shaping of children's experiences of being children and here we detail the sets of particular and particularizing temporal frameworks which together fashion the uniqueness of their childhoods. This focus takes us beyond a simple registering of the import which age status has as a variable in accounts of children's life experiences (see chapter 7) to ask about the ways in which broader temporal processes also configure the experiences and activities of children. Drawing on insights developed in recent sociological studies of time (Adam 1990; Bergman 1992; Hassard

1990; Gell 1992) it becomes clear, for example, that it is now not sufficient simply to argue that age categories – such as those of childhood or youth – are predominantly social rather than biological constructions, variously used in different cultures to account for the passing of time in the life course. Cross-cultural studies of childhood have by now rendered this indisputable, although perhaps not yet unproblematic (see chapters 6 and 7). Instead, to understand fully what 'age' might mean as a temporal constraint on children's activities we need to pay rather more attention than we yet have to the intersection between the structuring or ordering properties of time and its subjective experience (Hassard 1990). That is to say, we need to attend to the day-to-dayness of children's everyday lives as they unfold over time to instance different childhoods. Here we suggest, then, that childhood's temporal frameworks – those which give shape and pattern to children's lives and experiences – are therefore, in part, patterned by the temporal flow of children's own activities. In this sense, children themselves can be said to contribute to the structuring temporality of childhood.

Such a view leads to one of the central tensions in childhood studies explored through this volume: how far is it possible to achieve a creative theoretical alliance between those approaches which emphasize the importance of childhood as a structural condition of society and those others which stress the significance for our understanding of childhood of the experiential accounts to be gleaned from the changing biographies of young people themselves? If such an alliance is possible, what might this tell us, theoretically, about continuity and change in and through childhood or about the universality (or not) of children's experiences? The study of childhood time, we suggest, allows us to begin to explore these questions.

Although within contemporary Western societies childhood might be predominantly regarded as an age category, this chapter awards such a view of ageing few priorities. Instead, through emphasizing time as a qualitative rather than simply a quantitative measure, age as 'time passing' is seen as just one temporal dimension among many others through which children locate themselves or are positioned as persons in the social world. Distancing in this manner the inherent linearity and determinism of presociological and traditional theorizing about the child (but see Tesson and Youniss 1995) allows us room to examine the variety of other ways in which childhood is enacted as a temporal phenomenon. In this chapter, empirical debates about age and generation are situated in a wider exploration of the temporal frameworks around which different ideas of the child are strung and from which the enactment of any particular childhood can be said to take its cue. Two different, but as we shall see necessarily interlinked, time frames structure our thinking: *the time of childhood* – the ways in which childhood, as a discrete period in the life course, is embedded within the social fabric of any particular culture; and *time for children* – children's experience of and participation in the temporal rhythms of childhood through which their lives unfold.

Childhood in a Different Time

Cross-culturally the experience of time passing is variously expressed, voiced through a range of conceptual and symbolic means. Ecological time frames, common in predominantly agricultural and preindustrial communities (Evans-Pritchard 1940; but see Gell 1992: 15–22), link the passage of time in individual lives to the rhythms of the natural world, while in industrialized societies ageing is subjected to a precise accounting and measured regulation. But although, as Ariès (1962) remarks, the demands of bureaucratic, industrial economies make it hard for anyone in those societies not to know their 'age' – ages are constantly enumerated on the documents of their lives – more qualitative assessments of the passage of time may none the less threaten to intrude on these careful calculations.

In confronting the inevitability of death in European societies, for example, it is to the cyclical quality of time in the natural world that thoughts may turn. The linearity of human life, in which death represents an end point, may be translated into a continuous cycle of renewal through metaphors drawn from the natural world. Hope and the denial of death can be invoked through conjured images of children's youthfulness (Hockey and James 1993: 27–30). Such qualitative temporal judgements are, however, not brought to mind only through a desperate engagement with the finality of death. They permeate our more mundane thoughts and emotions. As Lakoff and Johnson (1980) have argued, that time has become metaphorically commodified in industrialized societies means we can run short of it, budget or waste it. Conceived of as a precious resource, this view of time extends to frame the life course in particular ways, yielding up as it does so particular timebound social identities. Lives can be squandered through risk or fecklessness, while other lives, carefully guarded, may be capitalized on. Young lives can be dramatically cut short through illness or accident. Mourned for their premature or untimely death, their value contrasts vividly with those who endure into deep old age to become seen as burdens on their kin for simply having lived too long.

This is powerful temporal imagery indeed and it extends beyond linguistic discourse to be enacted daily. Qualitatively translating the steady temporal flow of the life course, people comprehend and evaluate, rather than simply calculate, the passage of time in their own and other people's lives. Through this process identities are allocated and some people – the sick and infirm – may be denied their rights to citizenship (Hockey and James 1993) in the same moment as the child claims ascendancy in terms of its futurity (Jenks 1996b). Thus time, differently construed, works to shape rather than simply register the character and rhythm of the ageing process and it is on such a view of time that structural and constructionist accounts of childhood are built. Following the pioneering work of Ariès (and notwithstanding critiques of this work, see Pollock 1983; de Mause 1976; Wilson 1980) we take the claim that childhood in its present European form has not always existed and cannot therefore be regarded as an unproblematic description of the early part of the life course as our starting point. Evidence for this is drawn from seventeenth-century England when a Puritan concern for the potential sinfulness of children was reinforced through strict disciplinary regimes, an imaging of 'the child' which, in the following century, was displaced by a more tolerant and liberal focus on the vulnerability of children to the dangers lurking in the external environment (Hockey and James 1993: 63–72). In the twentieth century, Ennew (1986) argues, Western childhood has become a period in the life course characterized by social dependency, asexuality and the obligation to be happy, with children having the right to protection and training but not to social or personal autonomy.

To such historical observations of 'different' childhoods, social anthropologists have added evidence of the disparities which exist between the social experiences and expectations of children cross-culturally (see, for example, Briggs 1986; Reynolds 1989; 1996; Stafford 1995; and chapter 7). This underscores the suggestion that childhood is less a fact of nature and more an interpretation of it. That is to say, in any particular culture or at any specific historical moment 'the child' is a product of the ways in which the process of ageing is qualitatively, rather than simply quantitatively, accounted for.[1] Acknowledging this, while it renders the familiarity of life course categories momentarily strange, has the virtue of alerting us to the relativity of cultural constructions of childhood's biological base (but see chapter 8). Expectations of the nature and competencies of children and young people can no longer be tied so firmly to the temporality of physical, developmental change, and status positions such as 'child' or 'adult' cannot simply be regarded as an inevitable, naturalized effect of this passing of time. Thus, for example, among the Chewong of the Malay peninsular social personhood as an adult must be achieved rather than simply reached: the birth of a child signals the attainment of adulthood (Howell 1987). In Hausa society, by contrast, childhood effectively ended for a girl at ten years old when, betrothed to her future husband, she began to take on the social responsibilities of a wife (Schildkrout 1978).

What these two contrasting examples starkly remark, then, is that any account of what it might mean to be a child must be situated against the backdrop of the particular ways in which cultural conceptions of age and status are entwined and embedded in the particular structural arrangements of a society. As Turner (1989) notes, ageing and age groups are an important feature of social stratification. Furthermore, these examples remind us that the experience of being a child cannot simply and unproblematically be read off the immaturity of the body. Although chapter 8 will raise questions about social constructionist readings of the body, here we draw on one such account, Wright (1987), to show how at a particular historical juncture in English society the particularity of the young child's body became signified and redefined in its specificity as the body of a baby. In this sense the age category 'baby', used to describe the very early period in the life course, is itself temporally constrained by history: new ideas about 'babyhood' emerged out of a particular constellation of social, economic, scientific and political relations.

Wright contends that the condition of babyhood became redefined in England during the period 1890–1915 largely in response to wider changes sweeping the fields of medical science and healthcare practices. The rise of the germ pathogen model threw new light on the problem of infant mortality and, in particular, on new ways to combat common infant death, popularly thought until this time to be caused by 'summer diarrhoea'. Developments in medical knowledge combined with the professionalization of infant welfare practices and increasing intervention by the state in the lives of working-class families to reduce mortality rates and to place infancy on a new footing. Breast-feeding among working-class women was encouraged by a new army of health visitors, not simply as something which was 'natural' and hence desirable, nor yet as the appropriate expression of mothering and nurturance. More pragmatically, it became regarded as one of the more successful ways to avoid infant death. By the early part of the twentieth century the death of newly born infants was no longer seen as a natural and inescapable fact of life. It was something which was now not only undesirable but also preventable. Wright notes: 'like a gestalt shift, the change utterly transformed babyhood and made it hard indeed for those who had shifted to understand how others might see things differently' (1987: 197). Thus the social construction of babyhood during the later nineteenth century provides us with one detailed illustration of the historically contingent nature of life course categories.

Childhood as a Time in the Life Course

The above account of the birth of babyhood as a new kind of infancy in nineteenth-century Britain underscores the importance of structural approaches which examine just how the 'time of childhood' is given form in any particular society at any historical juncture. As Armstrong (1983) shows, one of the consequences of the growth of medical knowledge in the twentieth century has been the proliferation of different types of 'child', differentiated into categories of perceptual difference from some notional model of the 'normal' child (see chapter 8). Although clearly childhood can be seen as a permanent feature of any social structure, the particular social and cultural parameters which define and regulate that conceptual space of 'childhood' and the efficacy with which they are shored up, are all temporally – that is generationally – situated. Any account of the unfolding of 'childhood' in children's lives must therefore acknowledge the effects of such historical, temporal structuring.

Within the sociology and anthropology of childhood such a perspective is gaining increasing acceptance as new theorizing about socialization shakes off the shackles of a biological determinism that once seemed necessary (James and Prout 1990b), and even within developmental psychology, recent writings are beginning to emphasize the contingent nature of childhood categories. Pioneering work by Bradley (1986), for example, asked us to reconsider the childhoods presented by key figures within the child development tradition. Questioning the visions of infancy presented in various accounts, Bradley argues, in part, for our recognition of their temporal specificity. Not only are the childhoods these scientists present a reflection of their particular predispositions towards the subject, they are inevitably a product of the historical social relations in which they, as scientists, worked and wrote (see chapter 9). More recently, the arguments put forward in Stainton-Rogers and Stainton-Rogers (1992) comment directly on the temporality of thinking about 'childhood'. Addressing what they describe as shifting agendas of child concern, they depict the variety of ways in which childhood as both social institution and life course category has been differentially 'knowledged into being' through scientific and popular discourses (p. 15). These stories of childhood are, they argue, not only particular cultural productions: importantly, they are produced at particular points in time (see also Burman 1994; Morss 1990).

Whether or not such a perspective still remains a minority viewpoint within the discipline of developmental psychology (Richards and Light 1986), it is clear that this body of work has contributed a great deal to sociological insistence on the contingent nature of childhood categories. In particular it has helped disinvest childhood of not only its universality (Woodhead 1996) but also its timelessness (James and Prout 1990a) by distancing childhood from an unremitting biological determinism. While chapter 8 will consider the ways in which the child's body might be best restored in considerations of childhood, these insights from recent work in child development have allowed a measure of agreement to be reached over the temporality of concepts of childhood. It is now certain that the 'time of childhood' contextualizes the precise form and manner in which any particular children are enabled to live their lives as children. The previous chapter explored the spatial detail of this cultural zonality. Here we pursue further its temporal dimensions.

Childhood and Generation

A first step is to explore generational aspects of 'the time of childhood' and to acknowledge its power as a temporal classification. Steedman's account of the elusive child figure of Mignon, for example, directs us towards a consideration of how ideas of 'the child' and ' childhood' work at particular historical moments to reflect wider social concerns. Mignon (who was never a 'real' child) appears first in Goethe's *Wilhelm Meister* (1795–6) as a motif of childhood. Of uncertain age and gender, the mysterious Mignon provides a symbolic focus for childhood itself, and subsequently, throughout the nineteenth century, versions are to be found across a wide diversity of cultural arenas. In Steedman's view, Mignon's power is her representation of the adult's search for the self in childhood, for a 'past that is lost and gone' (1995: 174).

For Bromley (1988), similarly, the widespread and popular appeal of autobiographical accounts of childhood experiences in the early part of the twentieth century – for example, Rose Gamble's *Chelsea Childhood* (1979) or Winifred Foley's *A Child in the Forest* (1974), and there are many more – needs some explanation. This he finds in the ways in which such autobiographical rememberings choose to represent childhood: it is a 'generalized and generational childhood' in which the inequalities and harsh realities of social class are sentimentalized and thus the inequities of childhood's history and the diversity of children's experiences become temporally blurred. Written for a postwar generation, such prewar childhoods are, he suggests, rendered timeless. They become motifs of 'the child' in every person's past.

Though the powerful seductiveness of such homogenizing and synthesizing childhoods in their imaging of an eternal child (James and Prout 1990a) lies in their reflection of many of the themes already noted in presociological accounts of childhood, as Steedman and Bromley explore, each mythical 'child' is a product of a specific generational perspective. It is a temporally particular childhood, situated within particular structural constraints. Following Schwarz (1976), then, a focus on the time for childhood allows us to explore how historically variable concepts of childhood allocate particular temporal or, more usefully, generational identities to children both in the past and for contemporary generations of children.

In thus partially resurrecting Eisenstadt's (1956) concept of generation here, we are mindful of the functionalist frame within which it was developed. None the less, we would argue for its continued utility, for the notion of 'generation' reminds us of the easily forgotten relational dimension of childhood: the child is a child only in relation to its adult counterpart, identified both through its difference from adults in general and through kinship links with pairs of particular adults (Jenks 1982a). And that relationship of difference and particularity is, in essence, generational: to speak of 'my child' is to acknowledge the temporal discrepancy of child and adult identities, to acknowledge the different and particular qualities of the 'time of childhood'.

In O'Neill's recent discussion of the liberal culture of child risk, the generational position of children is clearly articulated with respect to its political and policy implications. He argues that liberal theories of society centred on individual agency fail to acknowledge adequately the intergenerational position of children. Working with what he describes as a 'thin concept of the necessary institutional framework of individual agency', such theorizing underplays the fact that a child's birth marks both an intragenerational event, for the parental couple, and an intergenerational event with respect to the family (1995: 5). But this staking out of temporal identities is neither value free nor apolitical. He notes, for example, that liberal theorists espouse the belief that all children should have equality of opportunity, while at the same time acknowledging that children are born, not as equal citizens, but as embodied subjects whose 'familial bonds delimit and enable political conduct' (p. 4). And yet, to overcome the inequalities of birth, liberal contract theory, which finds expression in the complex history of social and welfare practices in Western societies, must necessarily subscribe to the potentially dangerous cultural fiction that, at birth, all children are equal. For O'Neill, the risks for contemporary children, which he sees as ever increasing, arise out of this fundamental contradiction: 'only by overlooking the child/family bond can we imagine the child's political equality whereas the child's equality is a myth to which it is committed to "save" the inequality within and between families' (p. 7). Recognition of and research into the details of children's generational experience – for example, the contesting discourses of children's and parents' needs which are played out through everyday life – may, O'Neill suggests, be one way in which to begin to solve this paradox and to put an end to the political mutism of children.

A recent change in the British legal system – the 1989 Children Act – would seem to exemplify such a move and provides us with a second illustration of the generational nature of childhood and the historically situated context of children's lives. Ostensibly designed to give 'voice' to children and to allow children some rights in law which have previously been denied to them, the Act potentially heralds a decisive shift in contemporary notions of childhood. Riches, for example, states that for many in the health and welfare services, the new Act was envisaged as 'revolutionary ... with significant implications for families, children and many many different professions' (1991: 3). Pressure for legislative change concerning the protection of children, combined with a growing demand for children's rights during the 1970s and early 1980s, had paved the way for an Act which, in principle, sets out to restore the balance between children's rights and those of their adult carers such as parents, teachers, social workers and medical practitioners.

Although still in the main focusing on traditional areas of concern such as child protection, the Act attempts to redress the balance between the state and the family, following the much publicized mistakes made by health and welfare workers in cases of child death and abuse in Britain during the 1980s. Thus, for example, the notion of parental rights, which at times may work against those of the child, is replaced with that of parental responsibilities, and the foundations are laid for social structural changes in the ways in which children are treated by parents, educationalists and health and welfare workers. Above all, the Act champions the 'best interests' of the child. This, we suggest, represents a significant conceptual shift in contemporary notions of childhood, although, as Carlton (1991) points out, this late modern version of childhood still fails to adequately acknowledge the diversities in children's everyday experiences, derived from gender, ethnicity and health status. It still does not take into account the plurality of childhoods (see chapter 7). None the less, since 1989, for a new generation of British children their intergenerational position as children has become viewed in a different light.

Although now enshrined in law, some would argue that this changed perception of childhood has not dramatically affected children's experiences since the Act may prove to be unworkable. Others disagree and see the Act as making it possible for children to become political actors (Alderson 1993: 46–51). Miles and Harvey, for example, citing examples from the health field, note that the Act ensures that 'a child with sufficient understanding to make an informed decision' can refuse a medical examination or assessment, and that

> when a child is brought to a doctor because of a suspicion of abuse permission must always be obtained for a medical examination to take place; this can be obtained from the parents or guardians, but older children must always be asked for their permission. This still applies to older children even when a court has asked for an examination; the parents cannot refuse, but if the child refuses, the doctor is not entitled to do the examination and the reason for this should be explained to the court. (1991: 38)

For critics of the Act, on the other hand, the immeasurable difficulties of establishing when a child is thought 'old enough' to understand questions or of deciding whether any particular child has sufficient understanding to give informed consent beg the question of the extent to which, in practice, children's rights will be increased and their political participation made possible.[2]

However, notwithstanding such debates, what the Act has irrevocably done is to envision 'the child' in a potentially new light at the end of the twentieth century. No longer marginal, 'the child' is positioned as a social and political actor, a person with opinions, a decision-maker. But rupturing as it does the perceived passivity of children's traditional ideological placement, it is a vision of 'the child' which, now spilling over into populist discourse, threatens to make out of the contemporary generation of children a new 'folk devil'. In this sense it may be less than empowering.

Writing in a national newspaper, Bennett (1994), for example, points to a doubling in the number of accusations concerning physical and sexual abuse made by children against teachers since the passing of the Act. In 1991, 71 members of NASUWT (the teachers' union) were accused of abuse; by 1993 this figure had risen to 158. But only nine teachers were taken to court, something which Bennett regards as proving the unreliable and dangerous aspects of children's testimonies. That children are speaking out against their teachers she attributes directly to the enlarging of children's rights, of which she disapproves: 'if you give children rights, children will use them.' Do we yet know, Bennett asks, whether extending children's rights will empower children? Might it not disable them and extend their subjugation further by denying them their childhood? By the latter Bennett no doubt intends to convey the kind of mythic happy and innocent childhood belonging to an earlier generation of privileged Western children which Ennew (1986) has described.

It is in such debates, we argue, that the generational aspect of childhood can be seen displayed, giving 'the time of childhood' for any particular children the particularity of its form. In the context of the developing world and the globalization of Western concepts of childhood (Boyden 1990 and see chapter 7) this generational dimension of childhood gains a new and starker potency. This is illustrated by Rival's (1993) account of the impact of formal education on the Huaorani of Amazonian Ecuador. Since its introduction in the 1970s, schooling has produced radically new social divisions in the traditional structure of the long house – there are new status groups, children (those who work mentally and are dependent consumers) and parents (those responsible for food production). In addition, it has effectively deskilled children as competent Huaorani. Children who now spend their days in school learning literacy skills have little time left to acquire traditional knowledge of the forest and its resources. Both of these are central to the Huaorani way of life. Thus, Rival argues, a new generation of adults may be emerging for whom the indigenous Huaorani culture is being rendered marginal. The twin aims of its nation-state – to render the population literate and to protect indigenous cultures – are revealed as incompatible.

The Age of Children

It is against such broad pictures of childhood in any culture or historical period, brushed in through ideas of the life course and generation, that the temporal rhythms which help enact ideas of 'the child' in society must be seen. Against this background, as we shall describe later, the precise patterning of the time of childhood gives form to children's own temporal experiences of childhood. First, however, let us consider what that pattern reveals about the nature and competencies of models of the child in any particular society, for it is with these expectancies for the 'self' that children themselves must engage.

Clearly, concepts of age, defined as the registering of time passing in an individual's life, are central here. Traditionally, accounts of age and ageing have distinguished between those societies in which 'age' provides a structured and organizational status system of age sets or classes for groups of individuals and those in which the ageing process is individually remarked by movement through status categories or 'grades' of person, such as those of child, adolescent and adult (Baxter and Almagor 1978; Bernardi 1985). In the former kind of social organization – a notable contemporary example being that of the Masai of Kenya – age sets provide an explicit structuring system: coeval children are born into, and remain in, an age set, all of whose members progress together up a hierarchy of political power, economic responsibilities and social duties. Bonds of obligation and reciprocity provide continual social links between members of an age set, while differing ties to the social structure and polity mark out one set's uniqueness from the other. This confirms the operation of gerontocratic power. Growing old together, members of a set die one by one, to be replaced at the bottom of the hierarchy with a new constituent membership for that named set. In such systems every man, though not necessarily every woman, belongs to an age set whose responsibilities change, over time, vis-à-vis the other sets in the system. Thus, as Evans-Pritchard noted in his classic monograph on the Nuer of East Africa, 'an age-set group changes its position in relation to the whole system, passing through points of relative juniority and seniority. This mobility of age-set groups is peculiar to the system and is a necessary characteristic of it, for it is an institution based on the succession of generations' (1940: 256).

It is clear that while age-set systems require grading – some recognition of the ageing process – age grades can exist without setting (Baxter and Almagor 1978; Prout 1987). This latter case would appear to characterize the position in most contemporary Western societies. Lacking a formal set system at the level of the polity, emphasis is placed on the individual's movement between status positions in the life course, with adulthood being seen as the pinnacle to which children and adolescents aspire and as the position of power from which older people find themselves gradually displaced. Thus stereotypes of ageing – thrusting youth and senile decline – trace out an elliptical, rather than hierarchical, path for the life course in Western cultures. As Hockey and James observe,

> passage through the life course – from birth to death – involves the wielding and attribution of personhood at different times and . . . power is asymmetrically wielded as individuals move between marginal and central social positions, between different conceptions of personhood. Parents, for example, are persons in a way which small children are not; adults are persons in ways which 'the elderly' no longer are. And in each relationship, power is unevenly exercised. (1993: 45)

The infantilization practices carried out by some carers of very elderly people are a function of this asymmetry, remarking parallels in the status positions of young children and old people. Both are positioned as powerless dependants.

What these contrasting cultural examples of conceptions of ageing and the life course indicate is that the temporal, structural position of children must be understood as by turns relational and cultural. Children are children in relation to other age grades, grades which themselves bear historically and culturally distinctive markers. This much Eisenstadt (1956) acknowledged in his suggestion that the generational cultures of children and young people, often marginal and subversive in their style, are functional responses to structured movement within the life course. As transient and transitional cultures they enable a smoothing over of the troubled passage between child and adult status.

These twin aspects of generation have been well documented in the literature on youth cultures, seeming to imply that a kind of age setting is also to be found in Western contexts. However, as Hebdige's (1979) work demonstrates in contrast to Eisenstadt, youth subcultures represent timebound rather than timeless generational cultures. In this important sense they are different from those age sets of young men to be found in traditional societies which act 'as socially therapeutic channels for [their] aggressive activities' (Baxter and Almagor 1978: 3). Although perhaps seeming to share a number of characteristics, they differ in two critical ways. First, young men pass out into adulthood not as set members but as individuals, a movement clearly documented by Willis (1977). Second, and perhaps more importantly, as cultural markers of identity these youth subcultures can only be understood in terms of the specificity of their response to the shifting relations between generations of adults and children: different subcultural styles encode the oppositional responses of different generations of young people to their experiences of belonging to a particular peer group in a particular era.

To illustrate this temporal structuring of childhood we turn again to the example of the school curriculum (see chapter 3), for it is in the school system of European and North American societies that we find age taking on set-like qualities: children progress with their same-aged peers through a structured sequence of hierarchical class positions, gaining in seniority as they go (James and Prout 1990a). For example, in Britain at five years old – seven in many other parts of Europe – children enter the world of the school and they progress with their same-age peers through a fixed series of educational stages linked to an established, spatial hierarchy of classes. Each of these carries differing obligations and duties in relation to levels of educational attainment, the demonstration of social skills and adoption of responsibilities. It is an age-set charter laid out through curriculum design.

The consequences of this narrow banding of calendar age, which is tied to qualitative judgements of academic achievement and social maturity, are for some children severe. Unlike traditional age-set systems, where lifetime membership is guaranteed, the age-set system of a school throws up anomalies for expulsion: those who fail to meet the expectations of their age grade – children with special educational needs – or those who surpass them – gifted children – may be labelled as different and declared to warrant a different kind of educational provision. They are threatened with summary removal from their class as classificatory anomalies. In this very literal sense, then, these different childhoods are simply the outcome of a particular conceptualizing of the time of childhood.

The finesse with which this age-set system is orchestrated can therefore clearly work to disempower as well as empower any individual child. As Pollard and Filer (1996) note, a child's school career is a recursive learning process, dependent not only on individual capabilities and competencies but on the learning challenges, learning resources and learning contexts in whose spaces and times, as children, they are enmeshed. In their exhaustive and detailed three-year study of the lives of five primary school children at home and school, Pollard and Filer show that although they are all members of the same age set, each child's educational experience is unique. Their learning outcome is contingent on the opportunities to learn which their social relationships and environment facilitate. That is to say, the same institutional structures and spaces – schools, classes and homes – afford different children different opportunities at different times.

For example, each of these five children had very different access to assistance with learning. Sally, hard-working and successful, was always confident enough to ask the teacher for help if in doubt. Hazel, seen by her first teacher as stubborn and uncooperative, only gained in confidence in Miss George's class where her artistic talents were finally appreciated and encouragement was given. On the other hand, James's school career, which had begun badly, simply deteriorated during two years at school, his initial caution becoming translated by later teachers into signs of stubborn reluctance. Heading for educational failure rather than success, it was James's position in an age set – one which he shared with the more successful Hazel and Sally – which would provide the ultimate source of judgements of his competence.

The Structuring of Time for Children

The above discussions of age, generation and time make it clear that children's social experiences cannot be regarded as simply a function of either their biological age or their social status position. Rather, complexly interwoven account must be taken of the ways in which both these processes shape children's own experiences of time passing. Graphic illustration of this can be found in descriptions of childhood offered by those children for whom time is limited by the prospect of imminent death, or for whom hospitalization and serious illness have placed a premium on time itself (Bluebond-Langner 1978; Alderson 1993).

For doctors and many parents it is the future adult represented by the child who must take precedence in decision-making about medical treatment, a model of child welfare evident in social policy legislation since at least the end of the nineteenth century (Parton 1985). As James and Prout (1990a: 225–8) note, this image of the child means that children's everyday activities risk judgement, monitoring and assessment in terms of their consequences for later adult life. Whether in relation to education, work and employment, or in respect of their spiritual, physical and mental well-being, children are judged, nurtured and protected with the future adult in mind. But, as Alderson's (1993) discussion of children's consent to surgery shows, this positioning of children may be at odds with children's own perception and experience of time passing.

That children themselves may prefer to view the world more contemporaneously, rejecting such future-orientated perspectives as distant from their current concerns, is illustrated in Alderson's account of Tina's attitude to medical treatment. Tina refused painful leg-lengthening surgery on the grounds that she wished to remain as she was, a decision which ran the risk of being judged as incompetent and of being seen as evidence for the confirmation rather than refutation of her immaturity. Alderson depicts the competing temporal frameworks through which the decision about surgery was negotiated:

> Tina wanted the right to choose and to safeguard her present identity. Tina's mother . . . wanted to safeguard the rights of the adult Tina, and Tina's interests as she might perceive them then, in preference to her present perceptions. A further pressure was that the innovative treatment might not work. Her mother would then have to try and undo any damage done to Tina's self esteem by persuading her that she would be better if she were taller, and show that she was loved and accepted for herself. (1993: 39)

For those children who are dying and have no future as adult citizens time takes on an even more highly charged significance, as

Bluebond-Langer (1978) describes in what is one of the first pieces of research to take account of children's own perspectives on the social world. Denied the knowledge of their own death, she relates how children in an oncology ward in the United States learn to read subtle cues from the adult world about the stage of their illness and about the time they have left to live.

For children who are sick or disabled, the qualitative structuring of daily and yearly time may be especially poignant for it has dramatic and powerful consequences for their personal experiences of childhood. But it is not just sick or damaged children for whom time takes on particular qualities. The interweaving of conceptions of children's biological age and generational position works to pattern all children's lives with special temporal rhythms. As Prout (1992) has observed, schooling imposes complex temporal schedules which, through their intersection, structure daily, weekly and yearly cycles and create, for children, different spatial and temporal constraints and possibilities in relation to their schoolwork which must be negotiated with parents and teachers. Similarly, family routine imposes mealtimes and bedtimes, while welfare and educational legislation dictates the broader temporal rhythm of childhood itself as it is enacted in the life course. And through this patterning of time, children's access to and participation in a diversity of social arenas becomes proscribed: children's time is inextricably linked with the social space of childhood, as we have already demonstrated in chapter 3. Primarily, this is achieved through the setting of various age limits to – to list just a few – school attendance, access to work, voting rights, TV and film viewing, leisure activities, geographical mobility, financial transactions, sexual intimacy, property ownership, independent decision-making, criminal blame and personal responsibility.

Studies of children's experience of these temporal restrictions are illuminating for the insight they provide into children's social lives. Though as yet few accounts exist (but see chapter 5), initial findings suggest that children's culture emerges in and through the temporal, as well as spatial, interstices of adult social structures. Amit-Talai, for example, shows how the temporal structure imposed by the school system on the lives of young people works to shape their experiences of friendship. Taking a group of North American teenagers as the focus of her study, she argues that 'disjunction and distinction are . . . less the outcomes of teenage peer relations than the conditions in which North American youth cultures often develop' (1995: 145). Those anxious about the temporary and impermanent quality of adolescent friendship might do well to explore the cultural conditions of its engagement before seeking a psychological cause rooted in the angst of the adolescent experience. For the teenagers she studied, friendship could only develop in the times, few and far between, when they were allowed to congregate in their peer group. Organized during the school day into age-grade cohorts of one year's span, they found friendships with older or younger teenagers difficult to establish because, quite simply, they rarely met.

But even within an age cohort it was not easy to find the time – quite literally – to make friends:

> School interaction was . . . tightly compressed by the strictures of the school day and a constant subtext of adult apprehensions. So long as students remained on school property, they were subject to supervision. Staff monitored the halls, bathrooms, cafeterias and school grounds during recess and lunch-time, as well as during class periods, a monitoring edged with an undertone of anticipating suspicion. Lunchtime presented an ongoing determination of students to cluster and the equal determination of staff to disperse them. Pupils were not allowed to linger too long in the cafeteria. Once they had finished eating, it did not take much time before the teacher came to hasten them out. The daily washroom gatherings of girls as they attend to their hair and make-up, conversed, smoked or munched a slice of cold pizza were regularly interrupted by the arrival of a teacher who would usher them out. (Amit-Talai 1995: 151–2)

Young people's control over their leisure time was also limited through the temporal rhythms of the household:

> Only a small number of students, of either gender, regularly invited their friends into their homes. They might go with a friend for a walk around their residential block, meet just outside the front door and go on to a movie together but they did not often venture inside the home. If they did invite friends over, they tried to do so when their parents were not there. Home and friends did not easily mix, while the varying and often conflicting hours of part-time jobs created scheduling problems as well as limiting spare time altogether. (Amit-Talai 1995: 151)

For these teenagers, Amit-Talai argues, peer sociability and contacts emerge in spite of, rather than because of, the competing temporal demands of the home and the school. While recognizing, as Willis (1977) does, that the narrow age setting of the school system and the temporal demands of the school day may foster peer group cultures through compressing and intensifying social relations into small windows of time, Amit-Talai argues that social intimacies are difficult to maintain. Not only are clusterings of peers spatially policed by teachers (and parents) and by themselves, but the small amount of time available for peer sociability at school tends to limit self-disclosure. Trust takes time to develop, time together which young people may not have. Thus, she argues, discontinuity of friendship should not be taken as a sign of adolescent pathology: 'the reconstitution of peer relations is not an inevitable element in adolescent transitions; it is an aspect of a very particular construction of adolescence' (1995: 162).

That peer group culture partly emerges out of the temporal demands laid on children and young people by the institutional structures through which their growing up is regulated and controlled is well documented in Corrigan's (1979) account of the oppositional culture of a group of working-class boys in the north-east of England. 'Carrying on' or 'mucking about' in class, an activity which earned the boys their delinquent label, was, Corrigan argues, often simply the continuance of external modes of normal behaviour, such as talking or eating, into the internal space of the school classroom. That is to say, normal behaviour became abnormalized through an implicit questioning of who – boys or teachers – could regulate the activities taking place during lesson time.

Children's Experience of Time

That children are often reluctant to detail their age, preferring to obfuscate rather than elucidate its numerical value, might tell us something about their experience of time. Replying through ritual, formulaic devices to questions about age – I'm as young as my hair but older than my teeth – or with a precision uncalled for – twelve-and-a-half, thirteen-and-three-quarters – suggests that age might be seen by children as a restriction on their activities (James 1983). The patterning of children's time described above confirms this suspicion through suggesting that children's experience of time passing can only be understood in relation to the social and institutional structures through which their access to and control over time is managed. However, studies of children's experience of time are relatively rare in the literature, with just a few notable exceptions.

Solberg's account of children as the new home-stayers provides a clear illustration of such an approach. Drawing on fieldwork with children in Norway, she argues that an implicit negotiation over age takes place within families as parents and children organize the temporal pattern of their everyday lives. In Norway, as compared to Britain, ten years old is regarded as an age when children can be left alone, unsupervised, for short periods of time, and Solberg's account of children's use of this time reveals a skilful manipulation of their parents' perception of their independence and competence. From the children's point of view, time spent alone in the house after school and before parents return from work is valuable time – the home has much to offer in the way of free food and entertainment – and the children are assiduous in making sure that their control over this time (and space) is maintained.

> The house represents an important asset for children in this respect. Knowing the time when mother or father is due home enables the children to prepare to 'hand it over' to them. This sometimes means stopping doing things they know their parents would not appreciate and covering up any traces of these activities before their return. (Solberg 1990: 132)

The effect of this careful time management by children is twofold. Not only do the children gain control over daily time, they also massage upwards their claims to age. As Solberg puts it, such demonstrations of temporal competence encourage parents to 'experience their children to be "growing" older socially with respect to their biological "age"' (1990: 134).

Solberg's study has wide-reaching implications because, as O'Brien (1991) notes, we have relatively little knowledge of whether time spent alone is seen by children in a positive or a negative light and whether the corresponding lack of time spent with parents is detrimental or beneficial to the well-being of the child. Rather, harnessed to a range of political agendas, debates within the field of social policy have been based solely on an adult perspective. Arguments have centred on the possible harmful effects which the increase in women's full-time participation in the workforce might be having on the social, emotional, physical and educational development of the child. If a child-centred perspective were adopted, such as that offered by Solberg, we might achieve a more balanced view. It is surely possible that the emergence of various forms of community childcare services to fill the void left by working mothers might be of benefit, rather than detriment, to the child. Working solely from an adult perspective, as yet we simply do not know.

Christensen's focus on tempo in her account of the social construction of help among Danish schoolchildren offers us an important insight into just how much we have yet to learn about children's experience of time (see also chapter 8). In exploring how children help one another when they fall sick at school she argues that time and tempo are both important considerations, since children and adults may work with different temporal frameworks. She starts with the observation of an adult paradox: children complain to teachers about feeling unwell, symptoms which moments later magically disappear. Teachers are perplexed for 'recovery is constituted by a time frame which, from the adult's point of view, does not correspond to the original presentation' of the sickness episode:

> A frequent adult response to a child's claim of being sick or feeling unwell is: 'Go and sit down for twenty minutes and let's see if you will feel better.' From the adult's point of view 'time' is an indicator which reveals whether the condition is a momentary expression of the child's undefined sensations and thus is supposed to prove whether the child is 'really' sick'. (Christensen 1993: 497)

From the adult viewpoint the 'reality' of the sickness is the key issue. Sickness must be demonstrably evident through bodily breaches – blood or vomit – or through symptoms enduring for a length of time. Only then can it be regarded as 'sickness'. Only then will comfort and assistance be provided. Young children's conception of sickness is, by contrast, primarily an experience without time limits: whether of short or long duration, it is the event of sickness itself, with its associated dramas, which is important. Thus minor changes in the body – the bruise or the scratch – and more dramatic playground accidents are undifferentiated by children with respect to their demands for adult help and interest. Such is the tempo of young children's lives that both are constituted as sickness episodes, both are events worthy of report. It is this dissonance in time frames, Christensen argues, which is both problematic and endemic in adult–child relationships.

Conclusion

The above examples of children's experience of time are suggestive of an important, still missing, dimension in the questions we ask about age, time and generation in childhood. To explore fully how the time of childhood is experienced by children in their daily lives – whether as the social consequence of the age category 'child' at the level of the state and social policy, or as the mundane imposition of bedtimes by parents within the home – we need first to be cognizant of the possibly different temporal rhythms through which adulthood and childhood are shaped as both generational and relational experiences. We need to explore points of intersection between these temporal frameworks, noting the outcome and consequences of any mismatch, in relation to the social policies and more implicit cultural rules which regulate the lives of children. Second, we need to pay attention to the structural and experiential contexts of childhood time. Third, we need to ask how it is that, over time, children learn to take on a more adult rhythm to their lives. This is surely not simply the outcome of biological ageing. Might it not reflect, instead, the gradual synchronizing of two social contexts – childhood and adulthood – whose distinctions, marked out through cultural symbols of temporal and generational difference, are so commonplace as to be unremarkable. If so, we cannot as yet give a full account of the precise ways in which this meshing of temporal frameworks occurs in and through the temporal flow of children's everyday lives.

5 Play as Childhood Culture?

The unitary symbolic category of 'the child' is, as we have shown, being called into question by the new social studies of childhood. Structural and constructionist approaches reveal a diversity of childhoods, spatially and temporally fractured, while those adopting child-centred perspectives demonstrate that children's experiences of childhood are both fragmented and fragmentary. Studies of the social lives of children, for example, show how their everyday social experiences shape their particular local cultural identities as children (James 1993; Mayall 1996 ; Solberg 1994; Song 1996) while simultaneously raising questions, for children, about their engagement with and containment within the more global category status of 'child'.

Previous chapters have detailed some of the complexities of this diversity, both in space and over time, largely through consideration of the institutional structuring of childhood. Here we examine the empirical staking out, remarking and rejection of those differences by children themselves in an exploration of the everyday social relations through which children constitute their childhoods. And in doing so, we tackle a thorny question in contemporary childhood studies: the epistemological status of 'children's culture' and its empirical role in what is traditionally termed 'peer group socialization'. The impetus for Hardman's (1973; 1974) pioneering work within the anthropology of childhood in the 1970s, the concept of 'children's culture' is now being questioned by new sociological approaches to childhood.

Our discussion will chart a wide-ranging and discursive intellectual journey. First we ask whether it is possible to speak of a separate cultural world of childhood and, if so, how it might best be accounted for? Is it sufficient to suggest, as some do, that 'the culture of childhood' is to be found expressed in a set of distinctive cultural forms called 'play' – children's games and verbal lore – material argots of a youthful subculture which children swap with one another? Or rather, following more common sociological and anthropological approaches, should 'children's culture' be considered more properly as the everyday contexts of children's social lives among their peers, the 'whole way of life' specific to a particular generational group? But if the latter approach is adopted, how far is it sensible or indeed credible to argue that children's daily lives can be understood as separate from, for example, the lives of other family members, or analysed in isolation, as if untouched by the constraints of an 'adult' world to which, in the end, they must inevitably subscribe?

Clearly both approaches to 'children's culture' are problematic because in their different ways they play down the social context of children's lives *outside* of their relationships with their peers. As Mayall (1995) argues, the proposal that children constitute a group with its own separate and insular children's culture denies the empirical reality that children's childhoods are largely constituted within the family through adult–child relations, rather than child–child relations. But if we reject the pioneering 'separate and other world' approaches exemplified in the model of the 'minority group' and 'tribal' child (see chapter 1) to explain the cultural peculiarity of childhood, what alternatives remain? Might we not be forced to retreat to some more presociological and traditional notion of 'the developing child', with its combined and persuasive emphasis on the determinism of cognitive and biological immaturity? And if this is the last resort for theoretically accounting for the obvious, very distinctive social relations through which 'childhood' is daily enacted by children, then the outlook for the new sociology of childhood is bleak.

However, by teasing out the theoretical ramifications of this questioning through a series of empirical examples, this chapter begins to resolve the impasse. In sum it argues that the vexed question of the theoretical status of 'children's culture' can be fruitfully addressed as the temporal site of cultural reproduction. Although it is true to say that socialization takes place throughout life and does not end with childhood (Mayer 1970), none the less it is children who, in occupying the particular temporal location in the life course that they do, are necessarily the main vehicles of culture into succeeding generations. That children 'learn' about culture and become socialized (or 'fail' to and become deviant) is the main theoretical thrust of functionalist accounts of socialization ; precisely how they do so is less certain. What this chapter argues for, then, is careful and detailed analysis of children's social relations which will allow us to explore empirically the dynamics of the processes of both continuity and change in social experience which constitute cultural reproduction (Jenks 1993).

In short, we argue that the particular cognitive, emotional, social and material relations of children's childhood – those attributes of children's social lives variously documented by researchers and shorthanded in the literature as 'children's culture' – simply represent particular instances of the day-to-day process whereby children become socialized, distinctive in symbolic form but not in kind. Their analysis reveals the particular temporal, social positioning of children who, individually and collectively, are learning to 'do' culture. Taking note of children's cultural worlds allows us, then, to glimpse the ways in which processes of cultural reproduction are taking place. In this sense, following Geertz (1975), children's culture is not to be seen as a causal power but as a context within which their social relations can be described. Far removed from the concept of passive cultural fashioning, critiqued in chapter 1, a focus on the socializing 'culture of childhood' highlights children as active contributors to, rather than simply spectators of, the complex processes of cultural continuity and change within which they learn to live out their present and future lives. In this way we demonstrate that the structural contexts in which children find themselves not only constrain their action (see chapters 3 and 4) but also enable it. The 'culture of childhood' thus remodelled turns out not to be an obsolete and redundant concept but instead to provide further evidence of the contribution which childhood studies can make to central issues of social theory (see chapter 10).

A Play Culture of Childhood?

The seminal works of Iona and Peter Opie would at first glance seem to offer sufficient evidence of a separate culture of childhood for the debate to be rendered hollow. The exhaustive collection of child lore and games which they documented over a period of thirty or more years stands as eloquent testimony to the existence of cultural forms unique to children. Similar collections by Rutherford (1971) plus the large corpus of literature on children's games (Sutton-Smith 1977) would seem simply to underscore the point that children inhabit a separate, enduring children's culture:

> The folklorist and anthropologist can, without travelling a mile from his door, examine a thriving unselfconscious culture (the word culture is used here deliberately) which is as unnoticed by the sophisticated world and quite as little affected by it as is the culture of some dwindling aboriginal tribe living out its helpless existence in the hinterland of a native reserve. (Opie and Opie 1977: 22)

Indeed, for Hardman it was reading the Opies' works which spurred her into thinking that children might be regarded as a muted group in society and childhood its cultural context. Rather than simply dismissing the two volumes (Opie and Opie 1977; 1969) as interesting folklore, Hardman was drawn to the Opies' introductory comments. They pointed to traditions circulating from child to child and described a secretive children's world external to the home and family. These observations, she felt, required more anthropological comment than the 'reductionist interpretation' given by the Opies (Hardman 1973: 85). Thus she was led to argue that the linguistic and playground games of children could be studied as indices of a child social life which was independent of the adult world, and to suggest that talking to children directly would permit account to be given of what that minority world-view looks like from the child's perspective. Children were to be their own informants. Arguing against previous traditions of child study – developmental psychology, functionalism, the culture and personality school – she proposed a radical alternative:

> those anthropological fields concerned with children, which I have mentioned, view them to a greater or lesser extent, as passive objects, as helpless spectators in a pressing environment which affects and produces their every behaviour. They see the child as continually assimilating, learning and responding to the adult, having little autonomy, contributing nothing to social values or behaviour except the latent outpourings of earlier acquired experiences ... My proposed approach regards children as people to be studied in their own right, and not just as receptacles of adult teaching. My search is to discover whether there is in childhood a *self-regulating, autonomous world* which does not necessarily reflect early development of adult culture. (Hardman 1973: 87, emphasis added)

For the Opies, and later Hardman, the concept of 'children's culture' appears relatively unproblematic. It slips in easily to describe what seems to be another world heard from, an otherness or difference characteristic of being a child, and in doing so takes up an enduring theme in literary and biographical accounts of the forgotten, tribal or marginal world of childhood. But in thus validating more populist imagery, this sociological affirmation of children's culture was to set the stage for later social concerns about its potential disappearance (Postman 1982), for what Stephens calls 'discourses of lost, stolen and disappearing childhoods' and the imaging of 'the domain of childhood as threatened, invaded and "polluted" by adult worlds' (1995: 9). However, although difference and separation between the worlds of adults and children would seem therefore to be thematic, if not emblematic, in defining these life course categories (see Jenks 1982a), accounting theoretically for those 'different worlds' is proving less tractable. Early on in the emerging debate about childhood, V. Reynolds for example noted that empirical research does reveal 'a completely different world, so different that we seem to be confronted by a different order of being' (1974: 34). Yet, as Munday (1979) retorted, it must also be acknowledged that – somehow or other – those same child inhabitants do eventually become recognizably adult. How, then, to explain this paradox, if not through recourse to the traditional developmental models against which the new sociology of childhood had made its stand?

More recently, the debate has broadened through the assertion that children possess not just one culture which is different from that of adults, but two, which are gendered. Noting the frequency with which this model of 'different worlds or cultures' is invoked by researchers studying the social experiences of boys and girls – boys' play and girls' play (Lever 1976), boys' language games, girls' language games (Grugeon 1988; Corsaro 1979) – Thorne (1993) argues strongly against it. Her reasons are twofold. First, she suggests, the different gender cultures model obscures the fact that girls and boys are often together – in families, at church, in neighbourhoods; second, the rigidity of this dual classification as a heuristic device works to fix something which is fluid, always moving and subject to change. To these latter points we shall shortly return.

Here, however, we consider the characteristics of this gendered model of children's culture. Drawing on field material gathered in the United States, Thorne summarizes this as follows: 'boys stress position and hierarchy, whereas girls emphasize the construction of intimacy and connection. Girls affirm solidarity and commonality, expressing what has been called an "egalitarian ethos" ' (1993: 95). For Thorne, not only does this model fail to account for her own empirical field situation, but it is, she suggests, a very particular cultural model of boy–girl relations:

> when I searched through my field notes to see how they related to patterns put forward in the literature, I found that much of the supportive evidence came from my observations of the most popular kids in Miss Bailey's classroom. This tips off one central problem with the separate-and-different worlds literature: not everyone has had an equal hand in painting the picture of what boys and girls are like. (p. 96)

In Thorne's view, much of the childhood literature is riddled with what she terms 'the big man bias', a perspective derived from observations of the activities of flamboyant (often working-class) groups of boys which display a stereotyped superhero masculinity; the experiences of 'being a girl', by contrast, derive largely from researchers' engagement with the concerns of articulate white, middle-class girls. Thus, in her critique of the separate-and-different worlds argument for the gendering of childhood, Thorne implores us to note within-gender variation as well as 'crosscutting sources of division and commonality like social class and ethnicity' (1993: 97). To overcome this dualism it is necessary, she argues, 'to start with a sense of the whole rather than with an assumption of gender as separation and difference' (p. 108).   ·

However, while Thorne's account is a useful and necessary corrective to much work on childhood which may fail to acknowledge the diverse experiences of boy and girl children and which is often methodologically unreflexive about the cultural seduction of the ethnographer by particular groups of children (chapter 9), it does not offer a solution to the basic paradox with which this chapter is concerned. In Thorne's account, children are a political 'minority', if not a 'tribalized' group, constituted (unproblematically) as separate and different from adults. Our question has simply become compounded: how do we best account for 'children's cultures'?

Contextualizing the Culture of Childhood

The vibrancy of many recent ethnographic accounts of children's social lives in the playground or on the street may unwittingly invite an exoticizing of childhood as 'another culture heard from'. Narrating 'childhood' as it unfolds from children's mouths – smutty jokes, ritualized insults, jeers and sparring – and as it is displayed in their actions – vivid games of make believe and chance – researchers within the new sociology of childhood are able to document a whole way of life seemingly at odds with the dulled lives that adults lead (James 1979; 1986; 1995b). In thus providing a fixity of form for the patterns of behaviour through which children conduct their lives among their peers (Geertz 1975), the sheer vitality of its difference tempts us to reify this social action as 'culture'. Yet, as noted, being in the company of their peers is but a small part of children's everyday experiences; for the most part they are at home or in the company of adults, and accounts of children's family lives present a stark contrast. Though until recently rarely conducted from a child's perspective, such studies of the life of children at home focus largely on their engagement with 'adult' problems: divorce, single parent households or health and illness. In such accounts of children's lives the sense of their otherness and difference is much diminished. No longer exoticized, children are revealed experiencing and confronting the problems of their parents in ways which are familiar to us as adults. Their competence is clear, their methods of coping far from strange, despite the fact that the material and emotional resources at their disposal are often far fewer. There is, it would appear, little evidence for the 'culture of childhood' at home. What, then, accounts for this difference?

A first clue can be found by considering the spatial location of recent empirical, ethnographic work with children (see chapter 9). Whether exploring children's language, concepts of the body and of gender, play or racism, the majority of studies working with a 'children's culture' perspective draw on fieldwork conducted in school playgrounds or other spaces occupied predominantly by children (see chapter 3). This is an unsurprising discovery, for these are places where researchers can most easily locate their subjects. However, the notion of a separate and autonomous 'children's culture' may, we suggest, be in part a product of the specificity of these research contexts, making the concept of 'children's culture' an artefact of the research process itself. Recognizing this danger is not, however, to refute the the notion altogether or to argue for its abandonment. Indeed, it is rather the reverse. It suggests that something which could be called 'children's culture' exists only in the spaces and times over which children have some degree of power and control: in the private domestic space of a teenage girl's bedroom (McRobbie and Garber 1976); in the playground at playtime away from teacher's eyes (Slukin 1981; Pollard 1985); among groups of young boys in the evening in the street (Corrigan 1979); in the times left empty by the timetables of an adult world (Solberg 1990). It emerges in those interstices of temporal and spatial orderings.

Thus, in agreement with Thorne, we would argue that 'the culture of childhood' can be characterized by fluidity and movement. Indeed, this may be its essence: a form of social action contextualized by the many different ways in which children choose to engage with the social institutions and structures that shape the form and process of their everyday lives. Such a conceptualization of children's culture, with its emphasis on contextual agency, goes some way towards explaining the diversity of children's childhoods noted by James and Prout: 'some children become highly skilled and flexible social actors while others are less skilled, less flexible and, at the extreme, become trapped in one mode of action which at times, but only at times, maps onto their social situation' (1995: 91).

But if children's culture might minimally be described as the context within which particular forms of social action can be interpreted and described, then it is clear that this context is not simply, or even necessarily, spatial. Recent anthropological analysis of children's linguistic culture and conversational styles explores the internal dynamics of what could be described, more formally, as a generational or temporal peer group culture. Drawing.on two examples of British fieldwork taking place during a ten-year period in different parts of the UK, James (1995b) notes the many similarities in linguistic play between these two groups of children studied. These, she argues, stem from a generational 'culture of childhood' which both shapes and is itself shaped by children's passage through the life course. As one group of children is poised to enter the 'cultural world of childhood', older children may be beginning to relinquish membership of the category 'child'. But united in their marginality from central social (adult) institutions, all these children share temporarily a common, generational culture, while clearly adopting different cultural stances to it with respect to their individual biographical locations.

Thus, for example, traditional rhymes and jokes facilitate the sharing of sexual knowledge. Learned by younger children listening to the repartee of their older peers or gleaned from half-heard conversations, these language games constitute both a corpus of cultural knowledge and, most importantly, a particular way or (*pace*

Hebdige 1979) style of knowing – whether to admit ignorance or feign accomplishment, how to brag and when to boast, whom to name-call and when to do so. Thus it is culture as contextualized social action, not ossified cultural forms (jokes, games and childhood lore), which passes between generations of children in defiance of adult restrictions on what children 'should' or 'ought' to know. In this sense, as the previous chapter argued, the 'culture of childhood' is both timeless – its inherent conservatism partially explained by this mode of transmission – and, in the same moment, temporally located. These are the twin features which remark the special generational experience of being a child and belonging to 'the culture of childhood'.[1]

However, that children's culture is in truth a generational culture inevitably raises the question as to whether it can or indeed should be construed as a subculture. Paradigmatic of the work carried out by the Centre for Contemporary Cultural Studies in Birmingham during the 1970s and early 1980s, youth subcultures were portrayed as oppositional, ritualized cultures of resistance against dominant class structures. Derived largely from the study of white working-class boys, subculture in Hebdige's (1979) hands became a performative style and for Willis (1977) the way in which working-class boys learnt to labour. Despite the industry of criticism which grew up in response to the work of the Birmingham school (see Brake 1987; Jenkins 1983; Wulff 1995), for our purposes the emphasis given by Hebdige and Willis in particular to the theme of the appropriation and transformation of culture by young people remains particularly pertinent. Not only does it give prominence to the idea of agency, but it is also suggestive of the ways in which 'children's culture' or 'youth subculture' might be conceived of as sites of cultural reproduction. That is to say, it suggests that how children and young people learn about the social world is through a creative, often transformative engagement with the social and institutional structures of which it is composed. In this sense, children's socialization and their part in processes of cultural reproduction involve no passive mimicry, something noted by Margaret Mead (1978) in her earlier concept of cofigurative culture:

> Her notion of cofigurative culture can in fact be seen as a kind of cultural agency. Because of some social change the parental post-figurative culture is not useful for the younger generation to take over as it is. This is when members of the younger generation have to develop their own cofigurative culture together. (Wulff 1995: 9)

Hinging debates about the performative distinctiveness of 'children's culture' on approaches which focus on agency and social action allows us to progress a great deal in our reformulation of the 'culture of childhood'. It enables us to explore the ways in which the differences which are said to characterize 'the child' are socially engendered in and through the particular social structures they encounter, and to investigate the resulting and varied forms of agency adopted by children in their everyday engagement with those structures (see chapter 10).

Working with this formulation, then, children's culture is not a 'whole way of life' nor yet a body of esoteric lore; rather it is a form of social action, a way of being a child among other children, a particular cultural style, resonant with particular times and places. Cross-culturally, therefore, children's culture should take on different forms, reflecting the position and status which are accorded to them. However, those few child-focused studies there are drawn from contexts outside Europe and the US point to the absence of any well-developed 'children's culture', for in these contexts children's and adults' worlds are less socially divided and culturally distinguished.

Child's Play?

Long a key area of childhood research for developmental psychologists and early socialization theorists (see Burman 1994), the study of children's play and games has also provided a rich vein of ethnographic material for the new sociology of childhood. Precisely because the status identity of 'child' is, in Western societies at least, predicated on a particular conception of children's action – that, as we shall discuss in the following chapter, 'children play while adults work' – the study of play and games continues to provide a key arena for exploring many different aspects of children's social lives. Play, it would seem, is what children do. But understanding just how children 'do' play, as with how they 'do' culture, is far more problematic.

Along the historical trajectory of Western societies the binarism of the work/play distinction became progressively mapped on to the adult/child dichotomy, both symptom and cause of the growing conceptual and practical separation between the social worlds of adults and children. By the end of the nineteenth century, the series of Factory Acts in Britain, for instance, finally removed children from the world of adult work and fixed in law a difference in the spheres of social action for children and adults. This difference in turn marked out the distinctiveness of the status positions 'child' and 'adult' in the life course: play became the prerogative of children and work that of adults. By the late twentieth century both these marks of identity have become increasingly fixed attributes of child or adult status, serving both to stigmatize adult unemployment and to lament the labour contributed by children.

But though play rather than work has become a form of social action synonymous with childhood, children's social activities, as chapter 6 will suggest, are not simply constituted through play nor yet is their work necessarily always to be regretted. Here we eschew the term play as a cultural evaluation of children's social actions in order to engage more directly with the intentions and motives of children as social actors. This is not to deny that children play games, be they games with rules or those more formless activities of fantasy. Rather, it is to allow us to dispense with more functionalist explanations of the 'purposes' of play which seem to unduly preoccupy the adult world, and for which, as yet, few convincing accounts exist. For while it is clear that play provides the opportunity for children to rehearse future adult roles and thereby learn to take on 'societal affective and cognitive systems' (Schwartzman 1978: 330), how this occurs is less well explained. Of play and games Sutton-Smith writes: 'the implicit assumption that these phenomena [are] socializing has simply precluded the need to prove the connection' (1977: 234). For him, children's play can be seen to be as much about nonsense as about sense, as much about experiment and transformation as about mimicry and repetition. Thus, although children's play might be regarded as one context within which children learn about future adult social roles, it may be through novel or innovative forms that this knowledge is acquired. Following Sutton-Smith, socialization should only be seen as a function of play in as much as it 'potentiates responses, rather than prepares them' (1977: 236).

This notion of play as 'adaptive potentiation' is persuasive in two respects. First it permits a child-centred focus on children's activities, exploring what play might mean to children as a form of social action, rather than simply following adult definitions of play. Second, it facilitates seeing the agency of the players. It allows us to account for how, within the particular temporal trajectory of any individual child's life course and in conjunction with a variety of people (friends, siblings, parents, teachers and strangers) and across a variety of experiential domains, 'childhood culture' is the shifting context within which children integrate and share their social experiences.

In Thorne's account of play as integral to processes of gender formation this process can be clearly seen. She argues that child's play, in the adult tongue a metaphor for that which is trivial or easy to do, disguises the serious intent which 'play' as social action has for children. In the social construction of gender or, more properly, in the process of children's learning about gender difference, play is as much about inaction as action, as much about spontaneity as ritual, about power alongside weakness, and freedom combined with control. Thorne writes:

> I am troubled when the full range of children's actions and feelings get compressed into the 'play' side of our cultural dichotomy between 'work' and 'play'; the dichotomy falsifies the full reality of everyone's experiences. Observing on school playgrounds, I saw not only play but also serious and fateful encounters; I witnessed anger, sorrow, and boredom, as well as sport and jest. (1993: 5–6)

This challenge to concepts of child's play is taken further in Connolly's account of racism and sexism among British children. He demonstrates the continual conceptual slippage between something which adults might call 'play' and the more serious workaday social relations between children where knowledge of the social world is appropriated and exchanged. Through physical forms of play such as football and kiss chase with the girls and then in the linguistic play of competitive sparring, the five-year-old boys with whom Connolly worked demonstrated a dominating masculinity. As witness, five-year-old Stephen claims to have one hundred girlfriends, despite the disbelief of his peers that he could ever 'sex' them all: 'I'll pull all of them on top of each other and when I've done one – put her over there, then when done another one put her over there, then another one put her over there, then over there and over there and over there' (1995: 185).

But in this sexual/gender 'play', Paul Connolly argues, are combined other social codes. Through play the boys articulate their ideas of class and race, revealing an eloquent, generational engagement with their particular cultural locales of home, neighbourhood and social class. In the play of these little children Connolly shows us the ways in which broader processes of cultural reproduction are taking place as children socialize each other and socialize with one another. It is, for example, through their demonstration and articulation of these wider discourses that these boys become 'constituted as aggressive hard and sexual' by their teachers (1995: 191). At five years old their class, gender and ethnicity is literally confirmed and reproduced.

A parallel example can be found in Steedman's *The Tidy House* where she presents a story written by three working-class eight-year-old girls recounting the life and loves of two families. Writ large in the children's own words is their understanding of their own futures as working-class wives and mothers, of women bearing the brunt of domesticity and child care. Written as a play, the storyline is a blunt acknowledgement by three young girls of their own futures and, Steedman suggests, 'served the children as an investigation of the ideas and beliefs by which they themselves were being brought up' (1982: 1). *The Tidy House* is valuable in providing us with a rare children's account of growing up in conditions of poverty and, through the text of the play, shows how they 'critically confront the way things are and dimly imagine, out of those very circumstances, the way they might be' (p. 157):

> the having of babies out of rivalry, the persuasion and cajoling of children into life, the passive pressure of men by women to become fathers, the conflict over differing theories of child-rearing and the disintegration of those theories when a child cries or the chimes of the ice-cream van are heard in the street outside the tidy house. (pp. 21–2)

That performative styles such as these, which illustrate strategic processes of cultural appropriation and transformation by children, are often simply termed 'play' underscores the suggestion that integral to the identity status of 'child' in Western cultures is the devaluation and disempowerment of children as competent social actors. Thus a crucial site of cultural reproduction – the social, emotional and material space within which a child's identity as this or that kind of child is engendered – has often been missed or undervalued simply through its denigration by the use of the term 'play' and the conception of play as just imitative rather than creative social action. Most notable in traditional socialization studies, the problem also pervades more subtle and theoretically complex accounts of social and cultural reproduction (for example, Bourdieu 1986; see also chapter 8).

Children and their Peers

Traditional accounts of children's socialization make much of 'peer group culture' as the site of cultural reproduction. Children's peers are seen as the sounding board against which individual children judge themselves and are judged, with group culture not infrequently cited as problematic rather than beneficial to a child's social development (see Musgrave 1987). There is, for example, a deal of conceptual slippage between work on subcultures (seen as disruptive if not downright oppositional) and the peer group as a status body to which blame for deviance or delinquency can be attached. Within the literature the 'peer group' is a potentially dangerous collectivity of children, its communal influence damaging to the individual child. Children's friendships, on the other hand, must be encouraged. Indeed, within the huge body of research on children's friends, which stretches back well into the 1930s, one recurring theme is adult anxiety about those children without friends. It is a refrain which asks anxiously, what is 'wrong' with those children who do not spend time with their peers? Here is a curious irony indeed.

It is, however, explicable as a product of the discourses within which each research tradition is centred. Traditional socialization theory, based as it was on social psychological models of child development (see chapter 1), assumed a unidirectional flow of cultural information from competent adult to incompetent and passive child. In such a model there was little conceptual space for the possibility of child-to-child socialization and any socialization 'failure' was thus effectively pathologized in relation to individual children. But when the peer group did come to be seen as a socializing context, most research developed as part of the previously noted subcultural tradition of the 1970s. Thus explorations of peer group socialization became effectively part of the contemporaneous discussion of deviancy, with but little attention being given to the role of the peer group among ordinary children.

The study of children's friendships, with its longer history, was similarly centred on an implicit developmental model. A child's grasp of the concept of friendship was assumed to progress through a series of stages, ageing providing the mechanism through which children learnt to take on more 'adult' types of friendship. The net effect of such a model was, however, to problematize those children who 'failed' to progress up the conceptual ladder and who became stuck in friendship relations inappropriate to their age (Bigelow and

La Gaipa 1980). Neither did it reveal much about the quality of those relationships. We still knew little about how children experienced friendship relations of particular kinds and calls were made for more qualitative and ethnographic accounts of children's friendships (Gottlieb and Leyser 1981; Putallaz and Gottman 1981).

The parallels between these two traditions – socialization and friendship research – are noteworthy, for what the new social studies of childhood have done is to bring them together. Through a focus on children's agency, characteristic of the minority and tribal group approaches, a more positive role has been assigned to the peer group. It is becoming clear how children's friendship networks help facilitate processes of cultural reproduction, for it is largely with their peers that children play, tell jokes and swap ideas. And by abandoning sequential, developmental perspectives, the 'type' of children's culture which this activity brings into being can be seen as fluid and contextually produced rather than structurally predetermined.

An illustration of the new perspective which a child-centred focus has made available is provided by James's (1993) account of friendship among young children in Britain. This reveals that the meanings which young children attach to the word 'friend' may be different from those which adults understand. For example, durability, an important feature of adult friendship, is often absent from the friendships of young children, a factor which by turns has provoked concern for children's psychological well-being as well as confirmation of their social immaturity. Such adult-centred perspectives, James argues, miss the point. They judge friendship in adult terms whereas it is clear that young children, newly entered into the social world of a British primary school, may be neither distressed nor euphoric about the constancy of friendship relations. Only slowly do their friendships become adult-like. At first, simply 'having friends' to enumerate is important; the value of 'being friends' over a period of time emerges as a secondary feature, as children become more enmeshed in the social world of childhood. Learning to be friends involves learning the subtle processes through which 'friendship' is enacted by children through their peer group culture, a 'culture' marked by conformity and individuality, equality and competition:

> Friendship is not simply a cognitive relationship of affectivity. It must be affirmed, confirmed and reaffirmed through social action. This explains how the emphasis on 'sameness' and conformity in children's social relationships – wearing the same clothes, eating the same food, liking the same football teams – works to mitigate the

significance which any differences might have. It represents one visible demonstration of friendship, for it is through such public performances that children evaluate and acknowledge their friendships with one another: being friends must not only be experienced but be seen to be experienced. (James 1993: 215)

Thus belonging to children's 'culture' is part and parcel of the ways in which children learn, or fail to learn, to interact and make friends with their peers.

In Corsaro's early ethnographic research on nursery children's friendships in the United States can be found one of the earliest illustrations of the valuable insights into children's social relationships which are to be gained by conjoining work on peer group socialization with that of friendship. Writing in the late 1970s he noted that much previous work on children's social competence and socialization concentrated simply on how adults instructed children, and he insisted that of more importance was the study of children's peer group interactions when adults were not present. For him, the contextual complexity of the interactions which take place when four-year-old children attempt to join in the games of other children constitutes a different child's social world. In effect, Corsaro argues, they describe a children's culture:

Many of the children's access strategies in peer interaction appear to be quite different from adult rituals. These strategies do, however, involve the children's developing awareness of the functions of access rituals, a central feature of competence. In this sense, many of the children's early strategies for gaining access in peer interactive settings may be precursors to adult access rituals and merit careful analysis on that score alone. In addition, the study of children's access rituals is important for understanding the organisation of the child's world on its own terms. (1979: 317)

It is in this sense, then, that children's culture can be seen as an emergent property of children's active engagement with the spatial and temporal structures which constrain them (see also Corsaro 1985).

Children's Childhoods

It was noted earlier that much of the research into children's culture has taken place in schools, a function both of methodological constraint and the bare fact that it is the school which contextualizes the greater part of children's social lives with other children in Western societies (see chapters 3 and 4). Educational ethnographies have provided us, therefore, with a valuable insight into the social worlds of children (see for example Pollard 1985; B. Davies 1982; Whyte 1983). Though many are directly engaged in exploring children's experience of school for the purposes of pedagogic research, the ways in which the schooling process itself works to contextualize other dimensions of children's social lives can be clearly glimpsed.

In Pollard's (1985) account of British primary school life he details the ways in which the learning contexts within which children find themselves shape patterns of social interaction between children. In his study the children themselves made clear and named distinctions between three different groups, distinctions which drew on levels of academic achievement and children's willingness or unwillingness to participate in and adhere to the rules of school life emanating from adult teachers. Similarly Corrigan's (1979) research among adolescent boys in northern England details the sharp divisions drawn by the boys between high and low academic achievers. It becomes clear how the process of schooling provides, through children and young people's engagement with it, an emergent cultural framework which, in turn, works to structure the social lives of children at school. This process is clearly demonstrated in B. Davies's detailed account of children's attitudes towards friends and friendship. For the Australian Aboriginal children with whom she worked, Davies notes that

> they are less concerned with consistency of action from individuals than they are with consistency within given situations. They are not bothered, for instance, if a friend's home behaviour is different from his school behaviour, or if friends display non-friendly behaviour when the situation requires it. (1982: 113)

And it is the schooling process which, Davies argues, explains this variation:

> This detailed awareness of the definition of the situation and its power to dictate appropriate behaviour may well be associated with the fact that schoolchildren experience frequent and regular changes of situation over which they have little control. They must pay close attention to the requirements of any one situation such that within its own terms it becomes predictable. Once a situation is predictable, then competent appropriate behaviour becomes possible. (p. 113)

This close reading of social structures, spaces and times is, for Davies, fundamental to children's patterns of social action, a style of acting in the world which is both fluid and creative. For her there is no doubt that 'children's culture' exists as a contextual frame of reference for children which emerges through their engagement with the adult world, creating what she terms the double world of childhood. Of children's humour she writes:

> The laughter arose through the trisociation of these worlds, or frames of reference. They have collided the different agendas, roles and realities in which they habitually participate. They have used their knowledge of the adult world (of which they are partial members), their knowledge of their own world (of which they are full members) and their knowledge of the interactive patterns between these worlds, to create an explosively funny situation. They cannot be adults but they can play at being adults and use the adult world as a source of fun. (1982: 170)

If children's culture can therefore be said to be emergent in children's direct engagement with the structures of the adult world through which childhood is defined – the family and the home, the school and the legal system – then it is through exploring how children negotiate their social interactions in and across these domains that greater insight will be gained into the culture of childhood for expectations of 'the child' will clearly shift in and between these differing contexts (James and Prout 1995; 1996). In exploring the ways in which children manage to make sense of their diverse encounters it may be possible to see how their strategic use of particular cultural styles of performance leads to a way of being and belonging which we gloss as 'children's culture'.

At present, however, few studies address this directly for rarely does research cover both home and school contexts. Mayall's British study is one of the few to attempt this. She argues that although the parents of children of primary school age exercise power over them at home, they are also keen to encourage a competent independence in relation to self-care. In school, by contrast, children's competence is diminished by the demands of the curriculum, so that 'children's own ability to negotiate an acceptable social position and way of life is conditioned by the relatively highly reified models of children and of adult behaviours' (1996: 82). In these settings, then, the children must work with two rather disparate versions of 'the child', which may potentially lead to situations of conflict in both or either (see also James 1995a). At home, for example, care for the body is encouraged by parents, with decisions over washing and teeth-cleaning gradually becoming the responsibility of the child; at school that same child will be denied the opportunity to watch over his or her body, its use and forms of expression being strictly regulated by the demands of schooling for 'docile' and well-ordered bodies (see chapter 3).

A comparable perspective of children's positioning by the constraints of an adult world is offered by Pollard and Filer. In their account of the social world of children's learning they clearly demonstrate, through detailed case studies, the precise ways in which the schooling process in Britain intersects with the home and community environment to structure the learning experiences of children. What any individual child experiences and achieves is, they argue, a result of the complex interweaving over time of sets of different interactions in these environments, interactions which not only shift and change but, through their intersection, can both facilitate and hinder learning:

> For each pupil within a cohort, in other words, classroom contexts are both the same and yet are different. They are the same in that pupils may well all be present at identical times, adjust to similar expectations and often engage in similar curricular activities. However, they are different because each child experiences the classroom in the light of their particular structural position, learning stance, interests, strategies, identity and cultural background. The way in which each child interprets the classroom setting, acts and learns is bound to reflect this differential positioning and to lead, in consequence, to differential experiences and outcomes. (Pollard and Filer 1996: 281)

Conclusion: Lessons for the Culture of Childhood

This chapter has moved well beyond its initial concerns. We began with the suggestion that the culture of childhood might be seen in the linguistic and playground games of children, a collective culture, enduring and separated off from the adult world. We end with the suggestion that this 'culture', though evident in such cultural forms, is contingent, emergent and partial, barely graspable to fix in a more solid form, that the individual child is only temporarily and tenuously part of a more collective experience which we can call 'childhood'. Children are in this sense empowered by the structures which constrain them.

This change in gear is, we suggest, not surprising for such a shift parallels current debates in the social sciences about how best to account for culture. In recent social anthropological writings holism is no longer thought an appropriate medium through which to account for culture, with dissenters arguing instead for a view of cultures as partial, fragmented and multivocal (Clifford and Marcus 1986; Rapport 1993). The arguments for an autonomous children's culture are, as we have shown, also beginning to be questioned, with a shift being made towards seeing this culture as a context of action and interaction which may only at certain times be seen to be in any sense collective (see chapter 10). And yet the achievement of this recognition has been through the championing of children's rights to be heard as cultural brokers and informants, ideas currently being taken up within policy arenas with respect to specific issues of development and a more general practical focus on forms of social and cultural reproduction (Johnson et al. 1995; Save the Children Fund 1995). It is a curious irony, therefore, that at the precise juncture when there is a potential sociological retreat away from the idea of there being a separate and distinctive world of childhood, the independent rights of children are being loudly championed in the adult world. And nowhere is this clamour being more strongly heard than in relation to working children, the topic to which we next turn our attention.

6 Working Children

Whatever the place of children is thought to be in industrialized societies, it is not usually regarded as 'at work'. What children are supposed to do is play and learn – but that is not generally recognized as work. If they are seen to be working (either in paid employment or in household domestic or caring work), the reflex is towards constituting this as an aberration or an outrage – a social problem premised on children's vulnerability and need for protection. But at the same time, precisely because children do not work, they are again rendered problematic: through their demand for adult time they constitute a countervailing pressure to adult success in a flexible and increasingly global labour market; or they represent obstacles to the participation of women in the labour force because of the expectation that it is their mothers or other female carers who will take the main burden of attending to children's needs.

Thus in mainstream sociological writings about work children are virtually invisible (see, for example, Grint 1991). Though more noticeable in historical accounts of early industrialization, children here are represented as the victims of super-exploitation who were rescued from the predations of capitalism by the combined influences of social reformers and moralists and by certain economic transformations which shifted demand away from unskilled towards more skilled and educated labour (Cooter 1992). With this, children were relocated in 'childhood' – an idealized and romanticized state – and sheltered from the competitive sphere of market relations and the public domain (Zelitzer 1985). Even the conspicuously competitive and public world of schooling, into which children were shifted as a part of their exclusion from paid employment, is reconciled within this ideological positioning by a language which

CARL A. RUDISILL LIBRARY
LENOIR-RHYNE COLLEGE

decouples children's activities in the schoolroom from the adult 'world of work'. Schooling is thought of not as work but as a preparation or mere analogue for it. What children do there is dealt with, therefore, as the sociology of education, not that of work.

This invisibility of children in the sociology of work is particularly surprising when we consider the sophistication achieved in discussions of what constitutes work. Sociological writers have long ago ceased to conceptualize work in essentialist terms. If, for example, the definition work is confined to paid employment, then what of the myriad unpaid tasks (often performed in households and by women) which are essential to the production and reproduction of the conditions which make it possible for anyone to engage in employment (Morris 1990)? How do we account for the widespread self-provisioning indexed by do-it-yourself activities or gardening and which are arguably essential to at least some household economies (Pahl 1984)? How do we categorize exchanges in kind between households and individuals or account for the apparently successful informal economy which takes place outside of official reckoning for tax and other purposes of governance? And if work is to be defined by its subjective qualities, being experienced as a non-discretionary use of time or not enjoyable, then how do we understand occupations such as farming where life and work intermingle, or the position of those such as professional sportsmen and women who are paid for doing what others do as a discretionary leisure activity?

Such discussions, which expand rather than restrict what might be seen as work, would seem to open up possibilities for recuperating some children's activities as work. And yet it is only recently that social scientists have begun to take a more systematic interest in children's activities as forms of work. However, questions are now being asked about the extent to which children are engaged in paid employment; about the social and historical contexts of this work and its place within labour markets and household economies; about the conditions of children's work and its significance to children and others; about children's contribution to household and caring work; and, most radically of all, about the status of schooling as a form of work.

Thus children and work promises a topic of extreme diversity and complexity, one which this chapter argues is comprehensible only through the combined and multiple frameworks of analysis identified in chapter 1. Structural approaches can ask questions about the location of children's work within the political economy of particular localities and their connections into regional and global systems of production, exchange and distribution. In this, the changing relationships between household and economy are of especial interest, as are questions about how prevailing discourses of childhood intersect with economic issues. Such a focus promises an understanding of how labour markets are segmented and therefore how work activities are distributed through the life course. The second kind of approach, though much less well developed in the literature, is child centred and focuses on agency in the social organization of children's work. It can ask how children's work takes place and how it is negotiated and made meaningful, with a commitment to a much fuller attention to children's own accounts and a respect for their competence in making decisions about their lives and futures.

The North–South Divide

One notable exception to the more general trend of excluding children from discussions of work must be recorded at the outset. There *is* a longstanding acknowledgement of children's work in societies outside the industrialized 'North', recognizing its wide variety and complex character: domestic work such as cleaning the house, preparing food and taking care of younger siblings; subsistence work in fields or workshops which provides goods that can be exchanged on the market; work as apprentices living and working in other households while learning a trade or craft; as slaves or bonded labour, sold to others and put to work for their benefit; as beggars working the streets on their own behalf or as part of a collectivity, be it a family, clan or gang; as labourers earning a wage in the fields, workshops or factories.

However, notwithstanding these observations, it is clear that North–South divisions are both crude and problematic. There is no absolute distinction between the developing and the developed world; developing countries are not all alike and the picture changes according to the principle by which nation-states are grouped (Sklair 1991). Furthermore, nations are socially divided and what is true for rich inhabitants is not true for the poor and the poorest. And in the developed world child labour has certainly not disappeared. But, against this, children at work are much more visible in the societies of the South; their participation in productive work is more commonplace and its significance is somewhat different from that in industrialized countries. Dogramaci (cited in Boyden 1991: 19) makes a telling observation of this everyday presence:

> Child workers are highly visible . . . not only at the market place but at almost every street corner; from shoe shine boys to newspaper hawkers, from cigarette vendors and all manner of peddlers to messenger boys, from waiters in virtually every restaurant and coffee house, to helpers in all sorts of shops and establishments. They can be seen guarding parked cars, collecting garbage, transporting materials at construction sites, working at automobile repair shops or gas stations, sweeping floors in office buildings. Even more significantly, they work in many places less obvious to the public eye: in the myriad of small factories or industries tucked into back streets or alleys of the cities . . .

So unremarkable are these sights that in the 1980s the Egyptian tourist authorities used a picture of a child picking cotton as part of their promotional literature, even though statute law forbids the employment of children under twelve in the agricultural sector (Abdalla 1988: 31). According to census returns at the time, children between ten and fourteen represented 11 per cent of the total workforce.

Current estimates of the number of children working worldwide are difficult to make and unofficial figures can vary from official ones by a factor of ten or more. In India, for example, official records show 10 million child workers, but trade unions place the figure at 100 million. This lack of reliable information, due in part to official indifference and obstructionism, also indicates that agreed definitions of what counts as work and who counts as a child are lacking. Nevertheless, it seems reasonable to assume that the number of children working worldwide greatly exceeds 100 million (Fyfe 1989). And the vast majority of these are to be found in the economies of developing countries, with the greatest number working in the agricultural sector.

As we show later, detailed local studies (Bequele and Boyden 1988; Boyden and Myers 1994) are essential to understanding the circumstances of these working children for, as immediately becomes clear, the content and meaning of children's work is highly dependent on its social, cultural and economic context. Attempts to theorize from not altogether commensurate contexts in order to produce analytical frameworks to enable children's work to be more generally understood remain theoretically weak and have moved little beyond trying to classify the surface appearance of different types of work. But even this has proved a difficult task: the sheer empirical complexity of the phenomenon means that classificatory dimensions tend to proliferate. While the identification of the factors which shape children's work is useful in guiding further research, the schemas themselves tend to underscore the often highly moralized priorities, assumptions and concerns of the classifiers, rather than help explain the phenomenon of child work itself. In each case, a few dimensions are highlighted, with the basis for this choice often left implicit and without authority.

Rogers and Standing (1981), for example, include categories of work as part of a whole range of children's activities. They suggest ten areas: domestic work; non-domestic work; non-monetary work; tied or bonded labour; wage labour; marginal economic activities; schooling; idleness and unemployment; recreation and leisure; and reproductive activities. Although broad (and therefore able to capture something of the wide range of children's activities) these categories appear quite ad hoc and arbitrary. Nor are they mutually exclusive. UNICEF, on the other hand, is perhaps too parsimonious and is consequently rather reductionist, distinguishing only three main types of children's work:

1 *Unpaid work within the family*   This is further divided into domestic work, agricultural or pastoralist tasks such as planting, harvesting and herding livestock, and handicrafts or cottage industries such as woodworking or leather work.
2 *Work within the family but outside the home*   Included in this are agricultural or pastoralist work (which may be full-time or seasonal, local or migrational); domestic service (when a child is taken into the family of relations but is expected to do household work); construction work and employed or self-employed work in the informal economy.
3 *Work outside the family*   This may involve being employed by others, a situation that includes bonded and slave labour, apprenticeships, skilled trades, commerce, industrial and similar unskilled work in mines etc., and domestic work. It may include begging or prostitution and pornography. Children may also be self-employed in the informal sector in a variety of different tasks such as shoe shining and car washing.

As is immediately apparent, the key distinction employed here is whether or not the work takes place within a family context. The assumption seems to be that children working in a family will face less risk of harm than in other contexts, a point of view which is extremely contentious. It implies that household production tends to be associated with agrarian settings and non-waged labour. In fact neither of these need be true. Neither is it obvious what the term 'family' should mean. This leads to the elision of important distinctions between family, kinship and household and, as White (1995) implies, it is by no means clear in any case that children working for or with kin are at lower risk.

Those struggling to understand the situation of children at work within a given locality are forced to wrestle with numerous and diverse factors: whether the location of the work is urban or rural; whether the work is paid or unpaid, in money or kind; whether the children are employed by others or self-employed; whether the work is part of the formal economy, recognized and included in official economic statistics, or whether it forms part of the informal sector; whether children are enmeshed in forms of slavery or bonded labour; and what content the work has – in agriculture, commerce, industry or the domestic sphere. Each of these factors shapes the character of work and intersects with the others to form a complex picture.

These analytical problems are further compounded by the fact that children's work activities are most commonly discussed in terms of child protection. Drawing on presociological discourses of childhood as a time to be protected from adult responsibilities, discussion is often underpinned by an individualized, biological and psychological developmental perspective. This assumes that work contradicts the very essence of childhood, its existence being most frequently explicated in terms of economic necessity:

> In the South, the only way the urban poor can survive is by putting as many members of the household as possible to work. Where there are no State welfare payments, and where self-employment and low, unstable incomes are widespread, the labour of children is crucial. This is especially the case where the household head is unemployed . . . [In Bombay] the children were paid only one-half to one-third of adult incomes, yet in more than half the families they augmented domestic income by up to a quarter. In just over one-third of the cases, the child's earnings increased the family income by as much as 50 per cent . . .' (Boyden 1991: 117)

There is obviously a great deal of truth in this view. However, authors such as Boyden who have a practical knowledge of the everyday realities of children in the 'South' are careful to point out that economic compulsion does not tell the whole story. Her research in Bangalore, for example, showed that many parents thought that learning a trade early was the best way to endow their children with the means for future survival. Similarly Schildkrout, drawing on her research with children in Islamic northern Nigeria, argues that their work is crucial to social and cultural reproduction. To understand contemporary child labour, she suggests, entails looking 'in more detail at the nature of the specific cultural and social contexts in which it occurs . . . child labour has to be evaluated in relation to the total life experience of the child, particularly . . . future occupational opportunities' (1980: 481).

Apparently simple solutions to the 'problem' of working children, such as legally enforced abolition, are thus found increasingly wanting. Forcing children out of the labour market can lead to much worse outcomes (such as displacing them into prostitution). Thus many campaigners, especially those closest to the lived reality of poor children's lives, now focus their attention on improving the conditions of their work and ensuring its proper regulation by, for example, arguing for health and safety provisions and the right to exercise collective bargaining (Bequele and Boyden 1988).

This perspective shades into a more radical one which takes as its starting point children's right not only to protection, but also to participation. This view sees children as being excluded from work by adults, the implication being that children's right to employment should be extended as a way of improving children's social and economic status. In one sense, this stands as a criticism of, for example, labour movement lobbies in the industrial world who regard working children as a threat to their own employment as adults. As White (1995) has argued, campaigns such as the US Harkin Bill which seek to boycott the importation of products unless they are certified as 'child labour free' concentrate on child labour in the export sector, despite the fact that in these industries conditions are sometimes better than those generally prevailing elsewhere and that child workers see such employment as preferable to unpaid work in the household or on family farms. This protectionist framework thus attends to children's voices in a highly selective way. It counterposes, for example, children's right to education with their engagement in work but fails to acknowledge that for most of the world's children, it is work which makes schooling possible. More generally, it ignores the claim from children that, for a variety of reasons, working can make a great deal of sense.

Child Work versus Child Labour?

One result of the common location of children's work within a
protectionist discourse is that distinctions in the literature are often
made between 'child work' and 'child labour', inscribing the difference between them as a central analytical one (Nichols 1992). Fyfe,
for example, argues that:

> we need to make a basic distinction between 'child work' and 'child
> labour'. This has led to much confusion and failure to focus and
> mobilize significant attention to real priorities within the field. Clearly
> not all work is bad for children. This view commands almost univer-
> sal agreement. There is little doubt that many children welcome the
> opportunity to work, seeing in it the rite of passage to adulthood and
> a positive element in the child's development. Light work, properly
> structured and phased, is not child labour. Work which does not
> detract from the other essential activities for children, namely leisure,
> play and education, is not child labour. Child labour is work which
> impairs the health and development of children. (1989: 4)

Organizations concerned to protect children from abuse and exploitation mobilize the child labour/child work difference in order to
classify some of what some children do as harmful. The designation
of these kinds of activities as 'labour' enables them to create priorities for intervention, as well as drawing a line beyond which certain
forms of child work should be abolished and the abolition enforced.

In one sense this is very useful. The distinction captures a strong
sense of children's particular vulnerability to certain forms of work,
especially that which is intrinsically dangerous and where children
suffer particularly high rates of ill-health or injury (see for example
Salazar 1988; van Oosterhout 1988). It also focuses attention on
forms of enslavement such as bonded labour, now illegal in India
but still practised (Whittaker 1985; Karp 1996). Here debts incurred
by a family have to be paid off by labour in industrial enterprises,
with the brick-making industry a widely quoted and persistent
example. In practice, through low wage rates and deliberate fraud,
debt repayment becomes an almost impossible task and the debt is
transferred to children whose entire lives can be spent in endless toil
and spiralling indebtedness. In such examples, labour might seem
to be an appropriate term to use.

However, although most countries of the world place controls on
the work children are legally allowed to do, in practice these labour

laws are widely ignored. In part this is because children's work is simply too diffuse. Normalized by its ubiquity, child work is rendered invisible. Consequently, working children who do come to the attention of the state may be seen less from a humanitarian perspective than as a problem of social order: 'young street workers engaged in retailing or services are not recognised as workers but are instead brought before the magistrate as vagrants, abandoned or perpetrators of anti-social acts' (Boyden 1990: 204). On the other hand, a substantial proportion of working children are not likely to come under scrutiny: the majority of child workers are to be found in the rural sector, away from official regulation, and often working with other members of their family. Others are kept in conditions designed to minimize outside contact, such as the child labourers in Thailand who are virtually imprisoned and whose letters home are censored (Boyden 1991: 124). These children often work in small workshops doing work subcontracted from larger businesses who can, knowingly or not, deny that they employ child labour.

In part, controls are evaded because there are widespread social and economic interests in so doing. Officials can be bribed to turn a blind eye to illegal labour practices which may be highly profitable, although it is also the case that for some industries, for example carpet-making in India (Kanbargi 1988) or leather tanning in Egypt (Abdalla 1988), the low pay that child workers receive ensures their survival in competitive world markets. At the same time parents may actively resist state regulation of their children's work. This was certainly the case in the United States and Europe as progressively tighter controls were introduced in the nineteenth and early twentieth century (Stadum 1995). From the perspective of the poor families in the contemporary world, the harm that child labour may do to an individual child has to be weighed against the survival of the household as a whole.

The humanitarian impulse to protect children has, as noted earlier, therefore to be tempered by the realization that in many circumstances it is unrealistic and even undesirable that children should be excluded from work which helps their household to survive. The more grounded policy developments in this field are attempting to combine the abolition of the worst abuse of children with broader policies for improvement at the level of the household economy and beyond. As is often the case non-governmental organizations have been at the forefront of new thinking in this respect (Boyden and Myers 1994). Rather than focusing on children's work in isolation, they have adopted a broader approach which focuses on issues of both structure and agency. Household income as a whole is addressed by generating securer employment for adult members; increasing the appeal of schooling to poor families by gearing the curriculum more to their practical needs and adding in school meal provision as a way of redistributing wealth as well as increasing enrolment and attendance; and organizing alternative employment for children in cooperatives which offer training as well as income and which can foster children's sense of participation and agency. As Boyden has pointed out, such an approach is crucial since 'under present economic conditions, greater access to education for children may mean an increase, rather than a reduction in children's work responsibilities: many children work in order to pay school costs' (1994: 38).

However, although the distinction between child labour and child work may be useful in determining priorities for social policy and practice, it is far less helpful as an analytical term. Indeed, here we have used these interchangeably – a somewhat unusual practice. The reason for this is not hard to see: what is claimed as an analytical distinction is primarily a moral one. It invites a judgement about the value of children's activities in terms of what promotes or undermines 'childhood', 'health' and 'development', assuming that these can be treated as though they were self-evident universals of an obvious and unproblematic kind. In fact there is a wide diversity of views about what work children should do, the conditions under which they should do it and the balance of its various costs and benefits to individuals, groups and societies. All condemn gross violations of children's well-being, but beyond that there is rarely agreement. As White argues:

> It is indeed impossible to draw a clear and unambiguous line between 'child work' . . . and 'child labour' . . . Most attempts to draw the line are too general, vague and circular to be of use, or if they try to be concrete and specific, too contradictory and illogical, and out of line with the views of children. (1995: 13)

By making the distinction between work and labour turn on moral judgements about what promotes healthy development for children, writings on child labour often fail to make specific distinctions between different forms of labour. For example, attention is not drawn to the crucial differences between children's waged labour on the market and 'unfree' or forced labour, such as chattel slavery, serfdom and debt bondage (Archer 1988).[1] As Wallerstein (1974)

notes, unfree labour is a fundamental feature of contemporary capitalism despite the overall context of the production and free exchange of goods on a world market. Children, who in general have
little status compared to adults, and especially the children of poor
families would seem therefore to be especially vulnerable to forced
labour. However, though there is a scarcity of definitive research, it
is certain that relatively *little* child labour takes these unfree forms.
But it is symptomatic of the analytic confusion about child labour
that the examples most often cited by campaigners are precisely
those which either fall into categories of unfree labour or share (like
the instance of imprisoned child labourers in Thailand given above)
some of their characteristics. While waged labour undeniably also
has exploitative characteristics, it would seem that the campaigners'
need to induce moral outrage overrides the need for analytical
precision or even straightforwardly accurate description. Sawyer
(1988), for example, uses the term 'child slavery' quite indiscrimi-
nately to cover virtually all circumstances where children are at
work.

The consequences of such a slippage amount to much more than
analytical infelicity. Solutions to the very real degradations of unfree labour offer little practical purchase on most of children's work.
Indeed it is arguable that inappropriate responses make the problems faced by children worse rather than better. One such example
is the disastrous consequences which followed the dismissal of
child workers from the Bangladesh garment industry in the early
1990s. In contravention of the legal position, about a tenth of the
three-quarters of a million workers in clothing factories were children under the age of fourteen, mostly girls doing tasks which were
not very physically demanding such as cutting loose threads from
garments and distributing garment sections to machine operators.
Their dismissal was a response by employers to the threat of an
international boycott of their products on the grounds that they
were manufactured using child labour. The result, shown by a
follow-up study, was that the dismissed children continued to work
– not one had restarted school – but in far more risky conditions
in the informal and street economy (including prostitution). They
had reduced earnings, worse nutrition and poorer health compared
with the minority who had retained employment in the garment
industry. The children themselves argued, some of them in a peti-
tion to the press, that light factory work combined with attending
school for two to three hours a day was the best solution to their
poverty. The result was a new scheme in which employers linked

re-employment with schooling and future employment prospects (Boyden and Myers 1994).

When we turn to industrialized societies the labour–work distinction also proves quite unhelpful. Fyfe (1989), for example, is unable to sustain the distinction in charting the historical events and circumstances that have led to the regulation of children's work and its marginal position in the formal labour market. He moves seamlessly from children's factory work during the industrial revolution to surveys of children's contemporary involvement in paper rounds, housework and babysitting without ever drawing on the distinction he claims to be so central. This elision hides another important possibility: the distinction made at a structural level between paid employment outside the home and domestic work may be one that does not make sense from the point of view of children.

It also relies on the problematic division between public and private spheres, strongly critiqued in the literature on women's work, which has drawn attention not only to the 'double shift' that the combination of paid employment and domestic work creates for many women but also to the contribution that 'private' household work makes to the 'public' economy. Though children are made invisible in this debate – the assumption being that they are the objects of work, not contributors to its accomplishment – it is clear that children also engage in such work (Goodnow 1988), although as Brannen (1995) and Song (1996) show for the UK, there are important differences of gender and ethnicity. Contributions to general household work may be a point of contest between parents and children but the gradual accomplishment of 'self-care' by children also makes a significant contribution to the public economy through releasing women from mothering tasks (Mayall 1996). More poignantly, when a parent is sick or disabled, children take on major caring responsibilities which otherwise would have to be shouldered by the state (Aldridge and Becker 1993).

In one important respect, however, Fyfe's account makes a centrally important point: the notion that children's paid employment no longer exists within the economies of the industrialized world is an illusion. The turning point for children's participation in the UK labour market was between 1900 and 1920. During this period the practice of children devoting the majority of their daytime hours to schooling became established and fourteen years old was encoded in law as the minimum age for employment in factories. The current legal position in Britain is defined by the 1973 Employment of

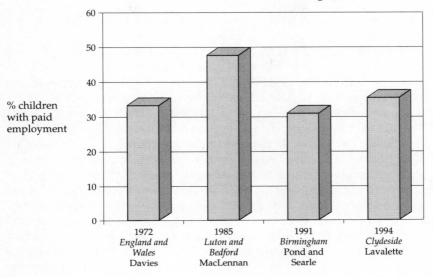

Figure 1   Proportion of children working by year, locality and study

Children Act. Building on and clarifying the confusion of local and national legislation inherited from the 1930s, it limits the hours during which children are allowed to work (they cannot work before 7 a.m. or after 7 p.m., or before the end of the school day, or for more than two hours on Sunday) and in general forbids the employment of children under thirteen. In addition, those in employment have to be registered. In practice, however, the 1973 Act remains virtually unenforced and is widely broken. Over the last decade a series of surveys in different localities have demonstrated a significant proportion of children – one-third or above – with paid employment (see figure 1 and Davies 1972, MacLennan 1985, Pond and Searle 1991 and Lavalette 1994). Levels like this appear to persist even when differences in definition and methodology are taken into account. European data from Holland and Germany show a similar proportion (Hobbs et al. 1992).

The data in figure 1 represent the incidence of children working at a point of time. Studies which have asked for previous experience of employment increase this proportion to 66 per cent (Clydeside) and 62 per cent (Luton and Bedford). There is also consistency across the studies in the type of jobs children do: milk, newspaper and other deliveries, sales jobs, especially door to door, and table waiting were the most frequently reported, with some gender differentiation. Boys are more likely to be found in delivery jobs and girls in sales and waiting on tables.

Much of this work is undertaken illegally. Sometimes this is because of the type of work or because hours worked are longer than those permitted by the 1973 Act, but most frequently because the children are not registered as required. Pond and Searle (1991) estimated that 72 per cent and Lavalette (1994) 92 per cent fell outside of legal requirements. Typically the work is low paid: Pond and Searle found that 40 per cent of children earned £1.50 an hour or less. Some work raises health and safety concerns: children doing milk rounds were found to be getting up every day to start work at 4 a.m. and then going on to school. Because most of the work is illegal it tends not to have any official recognition and is therefore very loosely regulated. One result of this is that while there are regulations limiting the weight of the load an adult postal worker is allowed to carry, there are no such limits for children: newspaper delivery boys and girls have been found to be carrying much heavier loads.

Hobbs, Lavalette and McKechnie argue that, taken together, these studies suggest that the pattern of child labour in the UK (and possibly other industrialized capitalist economies) cannot be explained as the result of the poverty of particular families (although this is the case for some children). Neither can it be explained in terms of a particular form of labour reserve which expands and contracts according to the point in the economic cycle. Rather, they suggest that such an economic perspective has to be supplemented by a broader view of the social segmentation of the labour market: that child labour is a permanent and structural feature of capitalist economies, with children occupying a particular, rather marginal, insecure and low-status segment of the labour market:

> children's labour market activities are affected by an interaction of politico-legal, ideological and economic factors . . . The ideology of childhood labels particular experiences, including certain forms of employment, as ideal for children and allows them to combine education with the invigorating and disciplining effects of work. While the availability of various marginal economic activities meets both children's demands for work and employers' needs for a cheap source of labour power, together these features identify particular types of jobs and particular employment experiences as ideally suitable for children. (Hobbs et al. 1992: 98)

Although it is certainly the case that child labour is less central to the functioning of the economies of industrialized societies than in developing countries, and is less visible, a series of studies show that children's paid employment is far more widespread than is generally recognized. One might go so far as to say that the predominant pattern for teenage children is still to combine schooling with paid employment for at least some of their final years of school education.

Invisible Work and the Demographic Transition

It seems, then, that what appears at first sight as a stark divide disguises a number of continuities between children in the North and those in the South. Though there are, of course, important questions of life circumstances (see chapter 7) which cannot and should not be denied, it is simply not the case that children in industrialized societies are excluded from work activities. However, their involvement is certainly less visible, they have greater discretion over that involvement and their work is less central to the economies of the households they live in, and still less to survival. How, therefore, might we understand these differences?

One suggestion is to argue that children's work is not inherently invisible but is rendered so. Morrow sees this invisibility as an effect of:

> the social construction of childhood as a period marked by dependency and an absence of responsibility [that] prevents us from knowing about those cases of children working and taking responsibility. An analysis of children's everyday lives outside school reveals that children have continued to work, but their labor has been made invisible behind a conception of the child as dependent, nonproductive and maintained within the family unit. (1995: 226–7)

This stereotypical sequestration of children within the family is intimately connected with the pattern of social changes which occurred (unevenly and at different paces) in Western Europe and North America during the nineteenth and twentieth centuries. This included changes in the economy, such as the shift from household and local to national and international scope, from predominantly agricultural production to industrial and service economies, and from manual to non-manual labour. Concurrent shifts in the family involved a move from complex agricultural households, through the predominance of the nuclear family (with a male breadwinner, a female homemaker and two or three children) to a contemporary pattern which is more fragmented but which includes a large group of dual income families, together with more diversity of forms (such as lone-parenting and reconstituted families).

As Wintersberger points out, although many of these changes have affected adults and children alike, there is one remarkable difference: 'while adult's work has not only retained but generally increased its economic value, children's activities have entirely lost it' (1996: 1). His point is an important one, even if a little overstated. Children are no longer seen as productive and any work-like activities are rendered invisible: their employment for paid work is seen by adults as marginal, their contribution to domestic and household work largely denied, and schoolwork is discounted as work altogether.

Much traditional research on children and the economy, we suggest, draws on and reinforces the invisibility of children's work contribution by giving almost exclusive attention to calculating the cost of children. There are two basic methods. The first defines a list of goods and services needed to meet children's needs. Often, especially when the underlying purpose of the research is to establish poverty rates or levels of welfare benefits, this involves calculations of the minimum required. As with debates about absolute and relative poverty (see chapter 7), the tendency is to work with notions of an income which allows for participation in social life rather than mere physical existence, centring the discussion around political and moral negotiations. The second method, known as the equivalence scale approach, involves comparing the differences in expenditure between different kinds of households – primarily between married or cohabiting heterosexual couples with and without children. It is then calculated what additional income a couple would need in order to maintain their standard of living after the birth of a child (or a second, third one etc.). The application of this approach is again caught up in a number of complexities, the most important being that it runs the risk of systematically underestimating the cost of children because the empirically observed expenditures are determined primarily by the budgetary constraints. The theoretical cost of a child in this approach tends therefore to be higher than that observed in actual households.

It is important to note, however, that these discussions about the cost of children have almost entirely been concerned with the costs borne at the household level. There has been little interest in the cost of children to society as a whole – as Wintersberger (forthcoming) puts it, 'public budgets are according to a functional and not a generational logic.' Preliminary research in this area suggests that in most industrial societies the preponderance of social spending on children is in the twin areas of schooling and child allowances paid to families. Only a small part is accounted for by health and social services and, indeed, as has recently been suggested (Thompson 1989), welfare policies involve systematic biases against children and young people. They tilt the balance of benefits towards adults, especially the elderly, and create inequities in intergenerational exchanges and distributions. More detailed examination, however, suggests a more complex and uneven picture. In some societies (notably the UK and the US) children are more likely to be at risk of poverty than elderly people (defined as those of pensionable age), but in others (for example, Australia) the reverse seems to be the case. The picture is even more complex when non-cash benefits, such as health and education, are taken into account. In general terms these tend to narrow the gap between children and elderly people and their relative positions depend on a complex series of interactions between demographic trends, labour force participation and unemployment, earnings levels, income tax and transfer policies and the value of non-cash benefits (Kennedy et al. 1996). Furthermore, the impact of all these varies according to factors such as family structure, the number and ages of children and family income (Bradshaw et al. 1993).

In relation to discussions about children's work and contribution to societal wealth, these questions about intergenerational wealth flows have prompted Qvortrup (1995b) to suggest a radical reformulation. This draws on the work of the Australian demographer Caldwell (1982) who argues that processes integral to industrialization, especially the demand for a more educated labour force and the consequent introduction of mass compulsory schooling, shifted the relationship between individual households and the economy as a whole. The main consequence was that the balance of advantage at the household level shifted away from the need to have as many children as possible and towards a reduction in family size. This accounts for fertility decline as societies make the transition from preindustrial to industrial economies.

Thus in preindustrial society children's work (whether in domestic work, household production or on the labour market) contributed directly to household wealth, also producing benefits such as the promise of future care for the older generation by socially obliged kin. The balance of intergenerational wealth flows at the household level was in favour of parents. From the point of view of each household, survival and prosperity depended on maximizing the number of children and optimizing their productive activity. After the introduction of mass compulsory schooling, intergenerational wealth flows were reversed and children came to be seen as a cost not a benefit at the household level.

Clearly this economic imperative helps our understanding of the different position that children's work occupies in contemporary non-industrial (or currently industrializing) societies, but there is, Qvortrup argues, an important limitation to this argument:

> wealth flow is only explained at the level of the family . . . Therefore he [Caldwell] is bound to conclude, rightly given his own terms, that children eventually become an economic burden for parents. But does this necessarily mean that they have become a burden for adults as a whole or for society? (1995b: 58)

It is from this perspective that Qvortrup raises an intriguing possibility – that children by means of their school labour are part of the societal division of labour. He develops this idea by suggesting that children's work at school is part of what is termed the diachronic division of labour: children in industrial societies are compelled to work in ways which produce themselves as the embodied form of societal investment, what in Bourdieu's (1986) terms might be seen as forms of capital, but ones which are not immediately marketable. There is therefore a time gap between the work of schooling and its realization through employment.

This is a radical departure. It raises important questions for the sociology of childhood in general and for understanding child work in particular. It opens up the possibility of theoretically reconnecting schoolwork with the other forms of work which children do, making it possible to transcend the disjunction between different forms of child work at any given point. It recognizes, but does not analytically reproduce, the differences between societies which we have noted but found, through this chapter, to be increasingly unconvincing. It allows us to see that children across societies do both manual and school work and contribute to both family economies and national ones – with the proportions, meaning and significance of each varying. Qvortrup's analysis therefore suggests a way in which children's work, even that which has been render-ed invisible, can be usefully compared, employing theoretically coherent categories rather than those which are arbitrary or policy driven.

The Meanings of Work

So far, our discussion in this chapter has drawn far more on what we identified at the outset as structural approaches in the new social studies of childhood. In part this is because there is relatively little existing research on children's work which asks how they might have agency within its organization and accomplishment or about the meaning which such work might have. This in itself might be seen as part of the invisibilizing of children's work – or the making visible of it only as a problem. As Grint argues, which activities count as work is always contested and the attribution of the label to an activity always tells us something about the social relations in which it is embedded:

> Where the self-description of agents' activity implies that their activ-ity is conceived by them as work, we should take note, but the point really is not whether this or that activity is actually work, but what such activities involve, whose interpretation of the activities carries most weight, and why this should be the case. (1991: 32)

Just as up to the mid-1970s it was assumed that domestic work fell outside the purview of the sociology of work, so it is noticeable that much of this research is still dominated by the (adult?) assumption that what children do is not real work. Serious attention, for exam-ple, is not given to health and safety in children's legal paid employ-ment in industrial economies because it is held that such activities are really more akin to leisure or harmless character-building endeavours. A similar assumption pervades the sociological litera-ture on schooling. As Prout has pointed out (1992: 137), what children do at school conforms to almost any definition of work which extends beyond paid employment. Certainly it is not at all unusual for children themselves to see it as work. But the literature on schooling has been generally unwilling to recognize this: for example, Sharp and Green's (1975) account systematically distin-guishes between work (what children will do in the future) and 'work' (what children do at school which looks just like work but cannot be given equivalence with it).

We have remarkably little research evidence on how children themselves understand the different activities in which they are involved: how they handle and use categories of work; which of their activities they understand as work and how this might shift between contexts; what their motivation for engaging in different types of work is; how involvement in work affects and is affected by their kin and other social relationships, and so on. The very act of posing questions in this way suggests that studies of children's work could pay rather more attention to how it is involved in the construction of children's lives as a whole. White, for example, has highlighted the link between children as workers and children as consumers:

> Ideas on lifestyles now travel around the world very fast and reach not only the metropolitan cities and elites; directly or indirectly they reach the villages and shanty towns of the world's poor. All over the world . . . it is increasingly important for children not only to have sufficient food and clothing . . . etc. . . . but to have certain kinds of (non-traditional) clothes . . . to consume certain kinds of foods and beverage, and to engage in certain kinds of recreational activity which are considered attributes of 'proper' people. The majority of the world's children . . . do not have access to all these things but this does not mean that they are not aware of them or free of the need for cash. This is in turn one important and growing . . . cause of the decision of children with or without their parents' approval or consent, to enter the labour market . . . [A]longside the cases that are better known and publicised – of children forced into labour by parents or unscrupulous labour recruiters – there are many children, all over the world, who simply decide they need to earn money. (1995: 4–5)

Such a perspective suggests a need to develop our understanding of the variety of children's motivations to work – going beyond the generalizations of the macro structural or historically constituted trends we have explored so far and beginning detailed work on how children in their relations with their peers and with adult society constitute a sense of their own needs and wants.

In one of the relatively few studies of this kind Solberg (1994) draws attention to the possible implications which children's work has for the negotiation of age and its meanings. Her observation of children's everyday involvement in the Norwegian fishing industry, where children work alongside adults in the casual work of baiting long fishing lines, she noticed that the status of 'child' was frequently overridden by their acquired but temporary position as a worker. This was not a question of children being forced to work – involvement was discretionary for everyone – but once in the work setting children's attempts to make their age relevant to the completion of the task were simply ignored. She suggests children in this situation socially 'grow', taking on competences and other psychological attributes sometimes denied them in other contexts. In contrast, Song's (1996) account of children's labour in Chinese families' take-away businesses in Britain reveals how their work is embedded within discourses of family and goodwill which oblige children to work under the guise of 'helping out'.

Morrow's (1994) account of why children work explores the meanings which work has for children more explicitly. Citing evidence that much child work in Britain is done by children from relatively affluent families she argues that children's work cannot simply be understood in relation to family poverty, although in some families in Western Europe and North America the contribution made by children to family income is undoubtedly as important as it is for many families in developing contexts (Nieuwenhuys 1994). However, as Morrow points out, children living in poor families may often have fewer, rather than more, opportunities to work: travel to and from places of employment may be difficult and the local area may offer few opportunities for children to undertake babysitting, car washing, newspaper deliveries and so on. The reasons why children work must be sought from children themselves, Morrow argues, and she suggests that participation in the new teenage consumer markets may be an overwhelming factor. Although some children saw work as offering them confidence and experience for future adult work, for most it was the opportunity to purchase luxuries not financed by parents which was their reward for working.

Conclusion

Such studies highlight the need for much broader enquiry into the ways in which work, among other factors, affects how children and adults negotiate and renegotiate their identities and relationships.

Similarity the effects of working need to be understood within a life course perspective. What, for example, do children themselves see as the costs and benefits arising from work? It is clear that children (as well as parents and other adults) sometimes see working as a means of developing skills which will help them in their later lives. In the instance given earlier, children opposing their mass dismissal from the Bangladesh textile industry saw the benefits in combining work with schooling partly in these terms. At the other end of the spectrum of privilege, Allatt (1993) has suggested that when middle-class English children take part-time work while they are at school it is seen by their parents and themselves as a means of accumulating social and cultural capital – of enmeshing themselves in social and economic networks, making contacts, learning skills of interaction, etc. – that can at a later point in their life be transformed into economic rewards.

It is perhaps understandable that a field of study such as children and work, which has found a place on social science agendas only recently, seems to place a premium on classifying and quantifying the phenomenon it addresses. Mere counting, however, inscribes the picture with a static quality. While there are undoubted benefits to measuring child work, one of the major costs is that its processual aspects tend to be lost. These are well illustrated by Glauser's analysis of the process by which some Paraguayan children in Asuncion come to live and work on the streets apart from their families. As he has observed, this rarely occurs all at once but happens in a series of steps: a child might visit the city for short periods in the day, for example to sell vegetables from the family plot; they might then find that sales are better in the evening or at night-time; they miss transport home and drift into staying on the streets for longer and longer periods. He suggests there is a notional threshold and once it is crossed children find that it becomes more and more difficult for them to re-establish contact with their family: 'Crossing the threshold seldom occurs because of a sudden conscious decision but is usually the outcome of a long process during which families, including children, struggle to maintain themselves. Often those involved are not fully conscious of the direction that events are taking' (Glauser 1990: 153). Not only does this give a crucial new dimension to understanding these and other local processes of children's lives but it is undoubtedly useful in thinking about how to help children avoid the worst and most detrimental consequences.

Given the complexity, reliance on problematically moralized

categories (such as the work/labour distinction discussed above) risks creating more confusion than clarity. Much of the attempt to map and quantify children's work comes from agencies intent on its reduction, control or elimination. The politics of such an endeavour often turns on a process of moral shaming in which governments, employers, consumers, etc. are pressured to make themselves appear progressive in relation to others. This may be politically and morally worthy (though this is usually more ambiguously the case than its proponents often like to admit) but it does not help to generate well-grounded understanding of the phenomenon. The result, as we have seen, are analytical frameworks which lack the theoretical sophistication and breadth required for a productive relationship with sensitive empirical enquiry into complex local variations of children's work. Developing structurally focused theoretical frameworks which measure up to the task – Qvortrup's is an excellent example – is therefore a necessary condition for real advances in understanding. At the same time, studies focusing on the meanings of work – which are, as we have suggested, multiple and include the meaning to children themselves – are also essential. In both cases the crucial element is that children are understood as social actors who are not only shaped by their circumstances but also, and most importantly, help shape them.

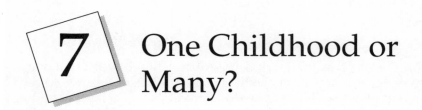

7　One Childhood or Many?

Attempts to develop a comparative understanding of children and childhood across diverse societies undoubtedly face a large number of problems. Often there is a fundamental lack of data or of data in a usable form: in many countries children are not used as a primary unit of analysis in the gathering of social statistics. Information on households, for example, has to be reconfigured and reinterpreted to obtain even a preliminary view of what childhood might be like. But even where specially collected data do exist, problems of commensurability and comparability may remain. Not only may categories be defined and interpreted differently, as we saw in the previous example of working children, but sometimes categories that make sense in one situation do not readily translate meaningfully into another – or, at least, translations are only achieved by committing gross symbolic violence against local meanings and constructions.

These latter problems are well known to anthropologists, who have perhaps the longest tradition of comparative research in the cross-cultural study of childhood and child-rearing (Whiting 1958; Whiting and Whiting 1975). Methodological difficulties of sampling, data quality, coding and categorization pose so great a problem that, for many anthropologists, such comparative methods can never substitute for immersion in ethnographic work (La Fontaine 1986). Attempts at large-scale cultural comparison are viewed with scepticism or rejected altogether in favour of methods which can grasp the ethnographic complexity of particular cultures or milieux and permit local knowledge and meanings to be understood in their own terms. Explicit comparisons are only undertaken with a careful consideration. Thus generalization takes place, not statistically, but theoretically: the accretion of case studies constitutes a permanent dialogue, a process which leads to the gradual refinement of theoretical concepts over a prolonged period and at the level of the discipline as a whole.

For the concerns of this volume these issues have a profound importance. Not only do they raise questions about method (see chapter 9) but, perhaps more fundamentally, they confront social constructionist approaches to childhood with a central conceptual challenge: is it ever possible (or desirable) to speak meaningfully about 'childhood' as a unitary concept? If, as we saw in chapter 1, recent sociological approaches explore childhood as imminently and irrevocably contextualized by culture then under what circumstances can or should comparisons between children's experiences be made? And if such comparisons are to be made, how might they be theoretically and conceptually grounded to avoid beating a retreat to presociological theorizing or recourse to some notion of the 'natural' child? In sum, what the question of childhood diversity raises is the extent to which recent sociological approaches to childhood are constrained or enabled by their insistence on the relativity of concepts of 'the child'?

Our discussion of the substantive issue of working children set out some of the practicalities: what is a child and what is work varies across different childhood times and spaces. Here we extend this argument, beginning with the responses to the analyses of the important collaborative European project 'Childhood as a Social Phenomenon' (CAASP). A key objection was lodged, namely that its participants utilized the term 'childhood' in the singular. One of the project's leading figures, Jens Qvortrup, defends this usage on epistemological grounds. Exploring childhood as an undifferentiated phenomenon – as, in his words, *'the* childhood' of a society – allows, he argues, consideration of what it is that all the children in a given society have in common about their relationship with the rest of that society. It facilitates comparison through envisaging childhood as part of the social structure, as a category like old age or youth. Critics, on the other hand, insist that it is always necessary to speak of plural 'childhoods' (see chapter 10). This draws attention to the ways in which childhood is cross-cut by other social divisions such as North–South inequalities, social class, gender and ethnicity. Its usage acknowledges the complex, plural realities contained under its rubric.

Qvortrup sets out the grounds of this debate as follows:

In a sense this is true. Who can possibly claim there to be only one childhood when it is so obvious that children lead their life under a variety of conditions, depending not least on the socioeconomic background of their parental home? On the other hand this view would, if followed to the end, constitute an unsurmountable obstacle to any generalised insight, because it indicates the preponderance of what is unique over what is common. (1994: 5)

In addressing the question of 'one childhood or many', this chapter therefore draws attention not only to the question of childhood diversity, but at the same time furthers theoretically the different epistemological and methodological approaches to the study of childhood which we identified in part I as characteristic of contemporary sociological thinking.

Childhood in Social Structure

To begin our exploration of diversity through focusing on childhood as a part of social structure has the advantage of potentially placing childhood within a long and well-established sociological tradition of mapping and explaining patterns and regularities in social behaviour through the use of large-scale statistical and survey methods. It allows for certain questions to be asked: what are a given childhood's characteristics; what are its continuities and changes over time; how does it compare with childhood in other societies? This comparative task is an important one and, notwithstanding the conceptual and methodological problems entailed (to which we have already alluded), we can turn our attention to the practical task of answering these questions.

Immediately we do so, however, it becomes apparent that, given the vast amount of social information collected in the modern world, it is surprisingly difficult to assemble a clear, still less a comprehensive, picture. This is true when one is speaking of research about a particular society (developed or developing) and even more so when the task of comparison is attempted. Qvortrup reports that when the CAASP researchers looked at the data available in Europe:

It was a surprise to most of us to learn to what extent children were not covered in available research, statistics, government reports etc. In most cases they were virtually absent; while on the other hand we

could find information about adults who one way or another sur-
rounded them . . . the best that could be done was to make a patch-
work of bits of information which, in most cases, was not collected
with the purpose of telling about children, but in which children
were somehow involved. Children were, in other words, split up into
categories that were not really relevant for our understanding of their
life conditions; they were actually described according to adult
categories. (1993: 33)

Elsewhere Qvortrup (1990) demonstrates in a series of examples
how different the social world looks through the lens of official
statistics if children, rather than some other base such as households
or marriages, are taken as the unit of account. For example, it is
often claimed that the number of children without siblings has
steadily increased: in Denmark, for instance, from 43 per cent in
1974 to 49 per cent in 1985. This comparison is based on the method
of calculation which counts the number of families with children in
them and then looks at the proportions with one, two, three or more
siblings. However, when a child, rather than the family, is taken as
the unit of calculation it becomes obvious that many children have
older siblings who have left the household, with the result that the
proportion of nine-year-olds without siblings plunges to 16 per
cent. Similarly Hernandez (1994) shows that when figures for those
living in poverty in the US are collected on the basis of the number
of adult parents, 18 per cent are calculated to be countable in this
way. But when children are looked at, the figure rises to 27 per cent
living in poverty.

Such discrepancies entitle us to ask why it is that children are so
seldom employed as the unit of account in social research. One
reason may be the adult-centred practice of the social sciences:
studying children has had low status and has not been seen as a
successful strategy in building an academic career (Ambert 1986).
But the problem of children's invisibility is more generalized than
this and includes, for example, their obfuscation in official statistics:
children are stereotyped as economically non-productive (but see
chapter 6) and therefore do not appear as a unit of accounting in
discussions of work and employment. Children also lack extensive
means of participating in decision-making processes, ranging from
adult–child power relations in families and households to children's
lack of political expression.[1] Account is rarely taken, therefore, of
children's social and political roles in wider structural changes.
Only in certain arenas of public policy – those connected with

children's future roles as citizens and children as carriers of futurity – do children feature centrally. To these we will return. First, however, we explore childhood and social structure by looking at those comparative approaches which take the specificity of childhoods as their starting point.

Childhood as a Diverse Structural Phenomenon

Most comparative discussions of childhood in different societies emphasize difference and this is especially the case in relation to children in developing countries. There are, of course, great methodological difficulties in such an enterprise; as noted in chapter 6 there is no absolute distinction between the developing and the developed world. The situation of Brazil or Malaysia, for example, is very different from that of Burkina Faso or Mozambique: while the first two might be thought to be newly industrializing and establishing a presence on world markets, the second pair remain economically marginalized. A further problem is that there are huge differences within countries: income and wealth can be extremely unequally distributed. In many countries the growth of a (usually somewhat insecure) urban middle class has gone hand in hand with the growth of both urban and rural poverty. Economic growth has brought social polarization, instability and destitution as part of an increased gross national product. UNICEF, in its report on the state of the world's children, argued what had long been known: 'as disparities in the share of national wealth enjoyed by different sections of the population may in some cases be extreme, so per capita GNP may conceal more than it reveals about the condition of the poor' (1989: 75).

In Brazil, for example, it is estimated that the poorest 40 per cent of households accrue only 7 per cent of the total GNP, giving an annual per capita GNP for each poor person of $287. This compares with 22.4 per cent in the Netherlands, which has the most equitable distribution, accruing $5,141. But GNP statistics simply do not differentiate between children and others in the population so that comparisons between the specific socioeconomic positions of children in different countries are extremely difficult to make.

For these reasons UNICEF has developed a series of indicators which directly or indirectly show how children are faring. These include mortality rates for those under five years of age; the infant

Table 1 UNICEF basic indices for children grouped according to under-five mortality rates (columns 1–3 1987, column 4 1984–6)

Group by U5MR	Under-5 mortality rate (annual deaths per 1000 live births)	Infant mortality rate (annual deaths under one year per 1000 live births)	Life expectancy at birth (years)	% of population below absolute poverty line (urban/rural)
Very high U5MR				
Median	209	129	48	50/68
Burkino Faso	237	139	48	no data
High U5MR				
Median	123	84	59	32/44
Peru	126	89	63	49/no data
Medium U5MR				
Median	60	45	67	20/34
Brazil	87	64	65	no data
Low U5MR				
Median	13	10	75	no data
UK	11	9	76	no data

Source: Adapted from UNICEF, *The State of the World's Children, 1989* (Oxford: UNICEF/ Oxford University Press, 1989), pp. 96–7, by permission of Oxford University Press.

mortality rate for those under one year of age; life expectancy at birth; percentage of the appropriate age group enrolled at primary school (for boys and girls separately). Table 1 shows a selection of these, grouped according to their under-five mortality rate. These figures paint a stark picture of the gross disparities in the social and economic conditions of children around the world. Children in the least developed countries are twelve times more likely to die within a year of birth, and sixteen times more likely to die under five years of age, than are children in the most developed countries. At birth, children in the most developed countries can expect to live over half as long again as children in the least developed. To this we can add a raft of important dimensions that, by accretion, create entirely different life chances, so that children in the developing world are more likely to be born with a low birth-weight; to suffer from moderate or severe malnutrition before the age of five; to have their height and weight growth restricted; to receive less than the total calorie intake required for full functioning; not to have access to pure drinking water; not to have access to health services; not to be immunized; to lose their mother because of death in childbirth. They are less likely to complete primary schooling; and far less likely to complete secondary schooling. In short they are liable to live lives in a constant struggle with poverty.

It would be comforting to imagine that world economic development, combined with aid from the industrialized countries, was gradually ameliorating this situation. The opposite appears to be the case. In 1989 UNICEF summed the situation up as follows:

> For almost nine hundred million people, approximately one sixth of mankind, the march of human progress has now become a retreat. In many nations development is being thrown into reverse. And after decades of steady economic advance, large areas of the world are sliding backwards into poverty. (1989: 1)

In the 1980s most of Africa and Latin America saw average incomes fall by 10–25 per cent. Government spending has been cut back by large proportions (50 per cent on health and 25 per cent on education). The average weight-for-age of young children is declining in many countries and the proportion of six to eleven year olds in education has started to decline.

In sum, what these accounts point to is that it is quite misleading to think about childhood in the developing world as homogeneous. Not only are there differences between nations, but there are also important cleavages within any given society. Being a child of a prosperous middle-class, urban family in Rio is not the same as being a child of a poor, share-cropping family in north-east Brazil. But neither is it the case that simple distinctions can be made between the developed and the developing world. As approaches focusing on the structural diversity of childhoods show, industrial societies are also divided ones and, arguably, are becoming more divided in recent years than in general they have been since the Second World War.

Child poverty here again provides a comparative focus. Though notoriously difficult to define – as indicated above, special problems to do with the form in which statistics are collected come into play when the question of child poverty is raised – none the less an important distinction can be drawn between absolute (sometimes called primary) and relative poverty. Absolute poverty is used to indicate circumstances which lack the basic resources for the continuance of life. Although, as we have seen, this remains a pressing problem for many in the developing world, left-wing social scientists argue that this indicator is no longer appropriate for understanding poverty in the industrialized countries, while right-wing politicians eagerly exploit the term to suggest that the problem of poverty has been overcome. The notion of relative poverty addresses both these objections by suggesting that what counts as poverty should be measured in relation to the position of others in the society, especially against some measure of what is thought necessary to live in an acceptable manner. Perhaps more variable, and certainly more sensitive to social norms, such a concept includes a range of needs which extend beyond those of physical survival. It includes factors such as the ability to maintain links with kin and others (for example, by using transport) and to participate in social, economic, political and cultural life.[2]

But the very relativity of the concept makes comparison problematic: different measures of counting who is poor produce different results, a problem simply compounded for international statistics. However, the best estimates of the most comparable data show a substantial proportion of children living in poverty (Duncan 1994).

Similar data show that within each nation child poverty is concentrated in certain population groups and over different periods of time. Huston, for example, suggests that in the US in the 1970s there was an important differentiation according to whether poverty was a permanent state or not:

> Race is the most striking and disturbing distinction between families whose poverty is persistent and those for whom it is transitory. Black children have a much higher chance of living in chronic poverty than do white children. The average black child ... spent 5.5 years in poverty; the average non-black child spent 0.9 years in poverty. (1994: 9)

Others have shown that child poverty in the US is also concentrated particularly among children in single-mother families, children of women who were unmarried or in their teenage years at the time of their birth, and poorly educated mothers (Duncan 1994; Furstenberg et al. 1987). The position in the UK is comparable: black and ethnic minority families and lone-parent families are the most likely to have low incomes, putting their children into poverty (Blackburn 1991: 17–19).

Not only are substantial proportions of children living in poverty across the industrialized world, but it seems that there has been a substantial rise in their proportion during the last twenty years. This is the case whatever definition or measure of poverty is used. In the US in 1949 about half of children were defined as poor, a figure which fell markedly and steadily over the next two decades. By the end of the 1960s it had reduced to 16 per cent. During the 1970s, however, rates began to rise again and, with some dips during economic expansions, have continued that upward trend. In 1985 , 20 per cent were counted as poor (Duncan 1994: 23–4). In the UK the upward trend began at the end of the 1970s and accelerated during the following period (Blackburn 1991: 14–15), a trend which, Bradshaw notes, was particularly marked for children:

> During the 1980s children have borne the brunt of the changes that have occurred in the economic conditions, demographic structure and social policies of the UK. More children have been living in low income families and the number of children living in poverty has doubled . . . There is no evidence that improvements in the standard of living of the better off have 'trickled down' to low income families with children. (1990: 51)

Given the emphasis put by presociological discourse on the child as future citizen (see chapter 1) it is not surprising that much research around child poverty and deprivation, whether in developing or developed countries, has concentrated on the long-term effects of early childhood experiences. To this end prospective, longitudinal studies have been conducted which examine the effects of the social conditions in which children live on their later adult life. In the UK alone there have been three major studies of such cohorts, starting in 1946 (Atkins et al. 1981; Wadsworth 1981), 1958 (Fogelman 1983) and 1970 (Osborne et al. 1984). These studies take a cohort of children born during a defined period and follow them through their development over the following years. Though employing a methodology fraught with difficulties – not least the tendency for cohort members to drop out – it is strongly argued, none the less, that childhood experience of poverty has an adverse impact on children throughout their subsequent lives: higher rates of infant and childhood mortality; higher rates of childhood disease and poorer health; lower height and weight; lower educational achievement; and higher delinquency (Wadsworth 1986; Bradshaw 1990).[3]

Thus, in these kinds of approaches towards childhood and social structure, it is the specificity of childhoods which emerges as a predominant theme through comparative analysis. Emphasis is laid on differences between childhoods in terms of the empirical positions which children find themselves living in and with respect to the differential outcomes for 'childhood' as a preparatory stage in the life course which this diversity inevitably engenders. Children are seen as a future resource, with concern centring on the quantity and quality of children as a form of human capital. Consequently amelioration of children's social conditions or interventions are promoted and evaluated purely in terms of some future, usually economic, pay-off.

Childhood as a Unitary Structural Phenomenon

A second, radically different approach towards childhood and social structure is that exemplified by Qvortrup et al. (1994). This stresses the importance, for comparative analysis, of stressing childhood as a unitary rather than diverse phenomenon. Indeed, one of the great achievements of the CAASP project was the bringing together of statistical and other survey data about children in Europe, covering topics such as demographic trends in birth rates and fertility; social and geographical mobility; mortality and morbidity; educational achievement and disadvantage; divorce; housing; and the distribution of wealth. In addition, a variety of legal and social policy matters were discussed and their impact and shaping of childhood examined (Qvortrup et al. 1994), enabling the researchers to suggest some social trends which childhood in the countries under study seemed to have in common.

The first of these they term 'institutionalization'. This indicates a trend towards children spending more and more time together in organizational settings specifically designated for them (schools and nurseries, for example, see chapter 3) and is seen as part of the creation of a separate world of childhood. At the same time a second process, and one only partially in opposition to the first, can be glimpsed: the increasing identification of children with the family to which they belong, a trend marked by parental acknowledgement of children as a cost for which they have to take responsibility. In research and policy-making, as well as everyday understandings, children's activities and identities are increasingly being submerged within the family. On the other hand, and somewhat in contrast to these trends, childhood is subject to what the CAASP researchers term 'individuation' and 'individualization': the trend towards treating children as separate beings (on whom, for example, schools and agencies keep personalized records) with a right to a participative voice.

Within this stimulating set of ideas are captured some of the paradoxes of contemporary European (or North American) childhood, processes which are not unidirectional, but cross-cutting and contradictory. As Brannen and O'Brien argue:

> The complex interaction [between them] . . . does not appear to serve children very well . . . [W]hile the individualisation of children means that children have or can make choices, the opportunities for choice are increasingly standardised in modern societies. Providing children with specialised institutions . . . whilst also stressing children's individuality, has unintended consequences . . . (1995: 732–3)

However, notwithstanding the important theoretical and empirical contribution made by such an approach for an understanding of contemporary childhood, it can readily be objected that dealing with childhood as a whole and across many different local (including national and regional) circumstances, produces a rather abstract and schematic account. On the other hand, though the details of diversity may be less clear, a focus on one childhood rather than many childhoods does offer a broad perspective from which to address processes of comparative childhood structural change.

Children in their Localities

As a counterbalance to the structurally focused and longitudinal studies so far described, other approaches take the agency and specificity of children's own diverse experiences of childhood as their central focus. This offers a rather different slant on questions of comparison. The former, Huston notes, assume a social policy framework which is largely adult-centred, one which her own child-centred approach seeks to counter:

> Children's healthy development is conceived as a goal in its own right . . . [It] leads one to ask about the direct outcome of policies for children, not just for their parents. It leads one to examine a broad range of developmental outcomes that go well beyond the typical economic criteria of dollars earned or hours worked. (1994: 4)

For example, it is often assumed that child poverty will be overcome by raising the income of households, that is to say of adult members or heads of household. But this is merely an assumption with no guaranteed outcome. Similarly, in many cases the underlying rationale of policies (and related research) on children is, as we have seen, not focused on the present lives of children, nor are children party to the discussion. The concern is with their adult future. This was recently noted by a leading children's voluntary organization which suggested to the UN Summit on Social Development that

> children become the subjects of policies made without any reference to them . . . In environmental planning, for example, settlements and neighbourhoods are usually designed without asking children their views. The resulting developments are likely to be unfriendly to children, leaving them without space to play and socialise, but exposed to dangers from poor design, dangerous traffic flows and unsafe public spaces. (Save the Children Fund 1995: 39)

Counter-examples would be the children's ombudsmen created in some European states or the participatory strategies of some voluntary agencies working in the field of child labour, but these are on the whole exceptions to the general picture.

Instances of how questions of diversity might be explored with the child as a social actor placed centre-stage in regard to comparative social policy are, then, rather rare. However, recent research from Nepal (Johnson et al. 1995) illustrates how it is possible within a local study to capture some of the complexity of children's lives. It centres children as social actors but at the same time recognizes both the importance of social and cultural differences between children in the locality and the impact of broad social and economic changes. The researchers spent eighteen months in the Sindhuli district of Nepal, and using a variety of participatory approaches – listening to children's song, interviews with children and adults, and observation of everyday life (see chapter 9) – attempted to understand the children's roles in the household, how these were shared with adults and how the relationship changed in response to socioeconomic and environmental change. One of the most striking differences between this research and most comparative statistical work is that it places the lives of children in context, looking at the complex interactions of their lives in detail. It makes no attempt to speak for 'the world's children' as a whole nor does it strive to use standard categories of 'the child' or 'childhood' into which local understandings must be squeezed. Instead it looks at the concrete conditions of a locality, showing how detailed local investigation can yield more and different understandings than is possible using measures established to apply across a wide diversity of societies.

The villages where the children live, the climate, seasonal fluctuations, farming methods, land tenure and political systems all form an essential framework within which to understand children's lives. Particular attention is drawn to environmental degradation and change, especially deforestation and irrigation schemes, during the last decade. The effect of irrigation, for example, is shown to bear on the lives of children through a series of linkages that are simultaneously social and technological. In 1969 an irrigation canal was built which made an increase in production of grain possible. Although this has enlarged the income of families and enabled the children to go to school, it has also increased the work the children have to do, especially at certain times of the year. Deforestation has had a more straightforwardly negative effect on children. The clearing of the forest through slash-and-burn agriculture twenty years ago has caused long-term destabilization, escalating landslides caused by floods which were previously contained and dissipated by forested areas. The effect of these changes feeds through to the lives of children: forest depletion means they have to spend more time foraging for fodder and firewood; this in turn means that the children cannot engage in waged work which brings income to the family and, consequently, some children may not be able to attend school; less fodder means that fewer livestock can be kept, and fewer livestock produce less manure and crop yields drop; more chemical fertilizers have to be bought which are expensive and not so good for the land, which in turn becomes less productive; stock animals become more vulnerable to pests and more die. The children become less well fed, have more work and less schooling.

In this study children are not dealt with by the researchers as a unitary category. They are complex persons caught up in and experiencing the dimensions of significant social and cultural difference and change. Ethnicity, wealth and gender are the major social divisions. The majority of people are ethnically defined as Tamang (that is of Tibeto-Burmese origins) but there are minority ethic groups partially overlapping with caste divisions. Some households have large landholdings and employ others to work on them, some work their own land, and the poorest are cash-croppers, renting land and paying for it with a proportion of their produce. Finally, the status of women and girls is lower than that of men and boys throughout the area: the birth of boys is preferred to that of girls; patrilineal inheritance means that land passes from fathers to sons, being equally divided between brothers; and sons stay in the parental home, while girls leave home on marriage. These divisions intersect with those of age so that while all children share certain experiences, other experiences change and modify them through ethnicity and caste, wealth and gender.

The researchers draw a threefold distinction between 'assistance', 'work' and 'labour': some tasks were seen as helping in the household but children were not expected to take overall responsibility for them; some work was crucial to the livelihood of the household and a child might be expected to be responsible for it; finally, employment outside the home, usually according to a contract of some kind, was seen as labour. The main division, however, was between children who went to school and those who did not. This distinction is not the same as school enrolment (the figure reported by UNICEF): many children who are enrolled in school do not actually attend. School-attending children did more assistance than work or labour; children not attending school did more work and labour than assistance. Gender was also crucial, in part because girls were far less likely to attend school than boys. The education of boys was seen as an investment in the future of the parents and the household, but girls were seen as more valuable for their present work and (after the age of twelve) labour for the household because they would leave to get married. Girls, therefore, had an extra burden of work, additional to collecting fodder, such as cooking and cleaning dishes. This work boys were not expected to do.

However, as Johnson, Hill and Ivan-Smith note, these general patterns are affected by ethnicity, caste, wealth and a number of other conditions of life (such as the state of the local job market or the geographical location of the school). For example, while Tamang people were committed to schooling for boys but not girls, some Magar and richer Sunwar families wanted to educate girls as well as boys, a decision not determined by wealth alone. Even in the lowest occupational castes both boys and girls may actually attend school, in which case the men have paid employment and the bulk of domestic work falls to the adult women, including daughters-in-law, and to the younger children of the household. On the other hand, among Tamang families the wealthiest are less likely to send their daughters to school and more likely to send them to work in carpet factories, their domestic work being compensated for by the other children in the house.

The researchers link their findings directly to development policy, both for the locality and in terms of general lessons, arguing that addressing what looks from the outside like a pressing need can reduce the overall quality of life when the interconnectedness of people's lives is taken into account. Children have small voices and are likely to be drowned out by other more powerful ones; development policies which do not attend to children and childhood are likely, they suggest, to strengthen the powerful at the expense of the weak. To this end they outline a number of steps which might begin to overcome the invisibility of children in development. Thus the unitary problem of childhood diversity is, through this child-centred study, partially redrawn as a diverse problem, but one with a potentially unifying strategy of amelioration.

Children as Social Actors

As we suggested in chapter 1 of this book, seeing childhood as part of social structure tends to predefine the sociology of childhood as taking place at or towards the end of the sociological spectrum that can be characterized as concerned with 'structure' rather than 'agency'. Although something of a caricature and a divide, this perception has its uses. An understanding of how children deal with their circumstances (including the changing formations of childhood described in chapter 4) requires, for example, studies which foreground their agency in social action: the lifeworlds of childhood, the daily lived experience of children, their experiences and understandings, their interactions with each other and with adults of various kinds, their strategies and tactics of action. Such a task clearly requires detailed attention to localities and settings but that is not sufficient in itself. Attention must also be paid to the structural connections between different arenas of action, how they mutually influence each other and how children move in and between these positions. As James and Prout suggest,

> children might employ a variety of modes of agency within and between different social environments ... the possibility [exists] that children locate themselves flexibly and strategically within particular social contexts and that, through focusing on children as competent, individual social actors, we might learn more about the ways in which 'society' and 'social structure' shape social experiences and are themselves refashioned through the social action of members. (1995: 78)

Just such a linking of the the 'global' with the 'local' is found in Frones's (1995) work on schooling in Norway. He starts by pointing out changes in the distribution of educational and occupational success in Norwegian society (an observation incidentally which could be made of several other postindustrial societies): women are now more successful than men at almost all levels of the education system and are emerging as statistically dominant in a number of traditionally male professions such as the law and medicine. For Norway this represents a very rapid social change which has been accomplished in something like twenty years. While recognizing that this has its roots in many different social and cultural phenomena, Frones argues that the processes by which this occurred depended on some features of childhood in Norwegian society. In particular, the reorganization of schooling meant that children experienced those years within relatively bounded cohorts imposed by the education system. A school, for example, could experience a complete turnover over a three-year period. What was a 'pioneer activity' (for example, girls aspiring to the medical profession or the law) at the year of entry could become a norm within a very short space of time.

What matters about this example for the purposes of this discussion is not whether the explanation is empirically correct or complete, but its general form. Instead of mapping the state of things at a point in time and seeking explanations within a synchronic data set, Frones attempts to trace the diachronic process by which the outcome has occurred: social structure and large-scale social change are not separated from the activities of the boys and girls and of men and women in the localities or at the so-called 'micro' level. Each is the outcome of the other, each implicates the other.

Diversity and the Social Construction of Childhood

Early in this chapter it was suggested that questions of childhood diversity might be counterposed with some notion of 'the childhood' of a society. Undoubtedly productive though this idea is, we have seen that it is open to a number of objections. But the greatest challenge comes from the social constructionist view of childhood. This rejects any idea that childhood rests on some pregiven essential nature and contends that notions of childhood, indeed the very term and concept itself, are a way of looking, a category of thought, a representation. The idea of childhood, in this view, came into being through discourses that created their own objects. The plural is important here because it is also held that childhood can be constructed in diverse and shifting ways. Hendrick (1990), for example, in a brief survey of constructions of the child in recent British history describes ten different models, ranging from the child of the nineteenth-century Romantic movement to contemporary versions of the psychological child. If this is the case, one of the main intellectual tasks of a sociology of childhood is to uncover the conditions of the discursive possibility of these different versions of childhood (see chapter 10).

The structural view of childhood, which emphasizes its diversity as childhoods, leaves such questions largely unexamined, or, at the very least, renders them side issues. Instead, as we have seen, the task becomes to insert childhood into a picture of social structure without asking too many questions about the underlying assumptions that make it possible for a society to think that childhood *is* a significant category. It would seem, then, that a structural approach runs the risk of basing itself on, and leaving unexamined, the everyday assumptions about what childhood might be. Of course, there may be some point in doing this. It certainly makes a comparative sociology of childhood between European and North American societies possible and it may be useful to assume that, in executing such a comparison (notwithstanding some methodological problems), there is some roughly comparable phenomenon present in each society. But this narrows the comparative task a very great deal. It potentially excludes many children outside of advanced industrial societies: though we might speak about 'childhood', 'children' and 'the child' in a general way that gestures towards the generational relationship between younger and older members of a society, in so doing we always risk smuggling in unacknowledged assumptions about what precisely these terms might mean in particular localities. In other words, we risk drawing on some standard model of what 'childhood' is which may be quite unfounded in the specific local circumstances.

Save the Children Fund makes exactly this point in its document to the UN Summit on Social Development. Drawing on the work of Boyden (1990), it argues that much policy assumes what it calls the 'standard model' of childhood, an observation which echoes Ennew and Milne's stark account of media stereotypes in the developing world: 'Third World children are all non-white, malnourished and lacking in identity . . . The child of the First World . . . is essentially

an individual . . . encouraged to a "full and harmonious" development of his personality . . . in an atmosphere of love and understanding' (1989: 11).

The point here is not that these stereotypes are inaccurate – though
indeed they are extremely misleading. It is, rather, that the second
image of childhood is taken to be 'proper' childhood. Childhoods in
the developing world are, by contrast, cast as unfortunate, even
outrageous, violations of some universal, natural childhood. In such
a game plan Western childhood acts as a normative basis, the spring-
board for remedial action elsewhere. As Boyden (1991) argues, such
assumptions were encoded in the Convention on the Rights of the
Child, sometimes against objections from locally knowledgeable
child welfare agencies, with potentially damaging effects on poor
families and their children:

> The beliefs of welfare and rights practitioners about the activities and
> experiences suitable for child life may differ radically from those of
> parents and children . . . Under these circumstances the children, and
> consequently, their families, are considered legitimate targets for
> state intervention. From the point of view of the former, children
> present in public spaces . . . and absent from the school or the home,
> and children at work or living in the street all signify family or
> personal dysfunctioning. But the perceptions of parents and children
> may be that these are not pathological behaviour patterns: on the
> contrary, the development of precocious mechanisms for survival is
> seen by many as integral to normal socialisation. (1991: 208)

Implicit here is a challenge not only to the specifics of the Convention but also to its embeddedness in the universalist psychological model of the child which in chapter 1 we identified as an
example of transitional theorizing. As Burman (1996) argues, this
model has been treated as if it represented context-free, abstract
truths about children, rather than seen for what it is: a model
composed of potentially highly problematic and certainly historically located constructs. Even attempts to make this more culturally specific (Myers 1992) ultimately do so, Burman suggests, only
at the cost of reducing the social context of child development to
the interpersonal zone of parent–child interaction. This effectively
ignores vast tracts of economic, cultural and social change which
cannot but shape how children are raised. The danger of neglect-
ing, indeed not even being able to contemplate, a whole series of
questions and realities about the diverse social worlds of childhood therefore still remains.

Conclusion: the Global, the Local and their Connections

While an emphasis on studies which highlight children as social actors in their local circumstances is, as suggested, a useful corrective to the attempts at global, structural comparison, it cannot be considered adequate in itself. In merely counterposing the global and the local through structural and agency approaches the character of their interconnectedness is overlooked. As we have seen, only rarely do accounts explore both. More important, however, is that the distinction between what is global and what is local is marked by instability and indeterminacy. Globalization is not necessarily a one-way process in which societies are transformed and modernized in a Western mould; it is a more complex series of multilevel and multidirectional transactions. Nor is globalization to be confused with scale. For example, is UNICEF local or global? On the one hand, it is actually a relatively small-scale organization concentrated in a small number of localities, although it has extensions out into many other localities. On the other hand, UNICEF creates, through its reports and policies, a large-scale phenomenon by gathering together and centralizing material from around the globe.

Prout (1996) has argued that metaphors of distance and connectedness give a useful handle on the problem of accounting for childhood diversity in a global context. Following Cooper and Law (1995) and Lee (1995), he utilizes the distinction between 'distal' and 'proximal' representations of childhood. This concerns not the literal spatial distance of observer and observed (or of social researchers from the object/subject of their analytical concern); rather it seeks to understand a set of research practices which produce the effect of distance and proximity. It is suggested by Lee that the distal represents social phenomena as a fait accompli:

> the stability of their boundaries and their functionality are taken for granted . . . [testifying] to the being of divisions and the integrity of the divided, as if time had come to a halt just prior to the analysis . . . The distal view often carries a love of stability and closure for their own sake, or for the sake of an analytic parsimony. (1995)

This might be used to characterize what we have identified as comparative research which works with a unitary notion of childhood. Questions of variation and difference are bracketed for the purpose, with more or less awareness of the dangers and in more or less theorized ways. It also would encompass those other structural approaches for which the specifics of childhood diversity constitute stable differences between children.

On the other hand the proximal view traces through an apparently static phenomenon in order to reveal

> the flux of events that compose it, revealing it as the product of its implications; temporally generalised because it sees no slackening of the pace of becoming (the entity remains open to the future); ontologically generalised because it recognises the heterogeneity of the elements that compose [it]. (Lee 1995)

This characterizes the 'close-up' complexity of more ethnographic comparative research such as that in Nepal discussed above.

The interesting point is, why should comparative research on childhood tend to favour the distal over the proximal? This question directs attention to the processes through which knowledge production takes place, in essence the alliances of interest in which researchers enrol and are enrolled by groups such as policy-makers. Proximal representation of social life as unfinished, tangled and in process have little immediate appeal as panoptical devices and therefore do not promise to function well as instruments of governance. As we have seen, the childhood is in part constituted through regulation (see chapters 3 and 4). The very format of distal presentation, on the other hand, reflects these demands: the 'executive summary' and the 'table of results' distil (almost certainly at the cost of reduction) complex realities into forms which can be taken in at a glance, and ordered and controlled. Distal knowledges present a neat and tidy outline: they can be acted on. To use Bauman's (1987) phrase, they offer themselves as 'legislative' rather than 'interpretive' accounts of social life which seem to have a special and readily understandable appeal to policy-makers. This is especially the case for those who control and deploy resources of all kinds: those who are at the top of hierarchies and have discretion over (relatively) large-scale resources are also, usually, remote from the localities to which their decisions pertain.

But like all translations, distal reductions are a treacherous guide to complex proximity. Things which seem well defined and clear in one location fall apart in another. These points are well demonstrated in Judith Justice's work in Nepalese health and development (1986). She has shown how the perspectives of international agencies (such as the World Health Organisation), political institutions in Nepal, regional, district and village health posts are each driven by local (often different and sometimes contradictory) social and cultural saliencies. Her analysis looks at each of these as a locality with its own processes and imperatives. But (and to give a particular spin to her work) to say that somewhere is local is not to say that it is isolated. Each locality is connected (partially and differently) with others. The operation of these connections plays a crucial role in the formation of knowledge. It is not so much that planners in the WHO in Geneva are simply in a different geographical location from the villagers in Nepal; it is the character of the connections between them which is problematic. She shows, for example, that whereas sometimes the connections are simply not made at all, most often they work to create a gradient which facilitates a flow from Geneva, filtered through Kathmandu, to the villages. It is rarely the other way round. There are, to use a mechanical metaphor, plenty of pumps in the circuit between Geneva and the villages but the circuit has many one-way valves and filters. The meanings and practices which constitute social life in those localities are remote from policy-makers and the connections which could translate them into the worlds of policy-makers are poorly made.

The wider context of children's participation and the diversity of their lives, as suggested by Save the Children Fund, require therefore that we ask questions about the ways in which children's perspectives as social actors are being translated into new policy directions. Given the strategic advantages that adults have in exercising power over children in an adult-centred world, it is always possible, indeed likely, that the processes by which children's preferences enter decision-making will themselves shape the effect they have. In some cases this translation is obvious: children are either not taken into account at all or views are given on their behalf by adults who claim the right to know what is in children's interests. Sometimes this is because it is assumed that, having once been children, all adults know what it is like to be a child. This is of course highly questionable. At other times, articulating children's interests becomes a matter of a claim to expertise in relation to educational, medical, welfare, policing matters and so on. But such knowledges are always, as Foucault has taught us, bound up with the exercise of power. They are not neutral but imbricated and express discourses about society which are themselves expressions of the practices of professional groups. For example, it is well documented that interventions in child abuse cases often revolve round competing claims by different professionals to have a special understanding of the situation (Taylor 1989). These understandings do not necessarily coincide: legal and welfare frameworks, for example, often construct the child in different ways while they each make claims to speak in the interest of the child. The result can be that children slip between the spaces of these competing claims to knowledge.

In these circumstances, then, theoretical and methodological decisions or preferences deserve consideration in terms which recognize that what might appear as technical choices are always imbued with social implications. Representing children through the distal and the proximal are both productive. There is always a moment when researchers, if they are to speak at all, are compelled to fix the phenomenon. Nor can policy-makers hold off decisions because the processes, complexities and fluxes of social life have not all been explored. Geertz gets close to the sense of this dilemma when he writes of the need for 'a continuous dialectical tacking between the most local of local detail and the most global of global structure in such a way as to bring them into simultaneous view' (1983: 69). But to engage in this dialogue means examining closely how the connections between localities are actually made: who and what are included in the flows between them and how do the connections actually operate? It hardly needs saying that children are among the least well connected in such circuits. Whether in the developed or the developing world they face the most obstacles in making their local reality felt and are the most mediated by others in the process. How are their realities to be represented in the circuits of knowledge of childhood research? How are children's different life circumstances to be addressed, understood and ameliorated? How are old circuits to be modified? Or are new circuits needed?

8 The Body and Childhood

One of the main propositions being furthered through new sociological approaches to childhood is, as we have seen throughout this volume, that childhood should be understood as a social or cultural construction; that it cannot be straightforwardly 'read off' from the biological differences between adults and children such as physical size or sexual maturity. In this sense, social constructionism has proved a most useful language in which to frame opposition to the presociological, naturalistic orthodoxies which, as chapter 1 described, characterized past approaches to the study of childhood. While this theoretical shift was perhaps necessary to combat biological reductionism and determinism, this chapter argues that by now it needs re-examination and modification in the light of current debates in social theory. Our focus for this here will be on childhood bodies.

Just as for childhood studies, social constructionism became something of an orthodoxy, though a disputed one, for studies of the body – and for much the same reasons. In both cases it seemed to provide the most secure defence against attempts to read social relations as epiphenomena of nature. But in both cases the theoretical costs of this manoeuvre have become more apparent. Broadly speaking it might be said that social constructionism stands in danger of replacing one reductionism with another: in brief, the body and the child appear as effects of social relations, leaving little room for the body/child as a physical or corporeal entity. In the social constructionist version, the body/child becomes dissolved as a material entity and is treated as a discursive object – the product not of an interaction between 'nature' and 'culture' but purely an effect of discourse. Drawing lessons from recent developments in the sociology of the body, this chapter argues therefore that a refocusing on the material bodies of children could enable us to explore childhood as both a construct of discourse and an aspect of children's lives which shapes social relations as much as it is shaped by them. In this way we want to underline a very necessary insight about bodies and children which social constructionism risks undermining: that social action is (generally speaking) embodied action, performed not only by texts but by real, living corporeal persons.

A second set of issues is also addressed, and they put a somewhat different gloss on the question of childhood diversity which was our previous topic. Social constructionist writings about childhood often contain implicit and unresolved reservations about the extent to which the materiality of childhood can be dispensed with, and these are at their most noticeable when it comes to childhood bodies: to explaining age, physiological change and growth. James and Prout (1990b), for example, already sound a note of caution in their suggestion that discourse theory is not without its problems, acknowledging that the (material) body should be understood as at least a limit or constraint on the possibilities of infinite and diverse constructions of childhood. But if childhood is in this sense unified by biology, what weight should be given to it?

Finally, there is, we suggest, a lack of clarity about the status of the body in much of the work in new sociological approaches to childhood. On the one hand the body as a material entity is simply bracketed out and discourses of childhood are the focus; on the other, it is constantly present as an empirical phenomenon, especially in those child-centred ethnographies which attempt to apprehend the experience of childhood from children's own points of view. As we shall see, in children's own accounts of the body its size, shape, gender and other characteristics loom large. This lack of precision about children's bodies may therefore be something of a missed opportunity: while these new approaches to childhood research make great play of children as active agents in social life, they often fail to appreciate the importance of embodiment in the processes through which children participate in social life. In our critique may be found a way in which to begin to move such an account forward.

Foundationalist and Antifoundationalist Accounts of the Body

It is now widely agreed that an adequate social theory must account for the body and the part it plays in social relations. For a long period this was difficult because sociology and biology operated around mutually exclusive definitions, with the boundaries of each discipline drawn in a way that legitimated a convenient but ultimately misleading division of labour. Biologists were, perhaps, less reticent about claiming explanations for social behaviour – most notoriously through the reductionist simplification of sociobiology. With some notable exceptions, sociologists on the other hand tended to define the scope of their interests as the non-biological. So, for example, as we have already seen in our discussion of transitional theorizing (chapter 1), the concept of socialization not only tended to place children in a passive relation to culture but also drew on a notion of culture that was posed in distinction to nature. This both limited the field of legitimate expertise of the social sciences in relation to childhood and society, and also, perhaps more importantly, left the legitimacy of the biological sciences unchallenged.

For some social theorists, for example B. S. Turner (1984; 1992), the cause of this split was the frequently cited mind–body dualism that was said to have framed much of Western thought since the Enlightenment. Social science placed itself on one side of the mind–body dualism such that society and culture were defined primarily in mentalist ways, that is to say, society was constituted through non-natural, even non-material entities such as beliefs, ideas and norms. Whether or not this is the real root of the problem has been disputed; most recently Shilling (1993) has suggested that the body has been not so much straightforwardly absent as an absent presence in sociology. It has been assumed but not clearly theorized or problematized. Whatever the case, it is clear that the problem for the social sciences is to bring the body and society into a different sort of relationship with each other, avoiding, on the one hand, a collapse into biological reductionism and, on the other, a dissolving of the body as a material entity into a set of insubstantial meanings.

Contemporary sociological thinking about the body is divided, Turner (1984) has suggested, between what he terms 'foundationalist' and 'antifoundationalist' approaches. These mirror the twin reductionisms considered above and involve contradictory ontological and epistemological assumptions at every level. While he argues that both 'foundationalist' and 'antifoundationalist' approaches are inadequate in themselves, and that some theoretical synthesis or transcendence of them is required, Turner's characterizations make a useful starting point for examining how these different assumptions have been applied to childhood bodies.

Foundationalists, Turner argues, take the view that the body is a real, material entity which is not reducible to the many different frameworks of meaning to be found cross-culturally, such as the representations of the body to be found in the anatomical textbooks of European and North American biomedicine or the chakras of Ayurverdic medicine. At their most basic, foundationalists assume that there is something out there, so to speak, which functions independently (if not fully so) of the social context in which it is found. The body is an entity which is experienced and lived. What is prioritized in this perspective, therefore, is largely phenomenological, the task of sociologists being to document and analyse how the body is interpreted and experienced by different actors in different social and cultural contexts.

The dangers of a foundationalist view of the body are well illustrated by much of the psychological research on children's developing body awareness. While these studies (for example, Gellert 1962) give some insights into how children come to learn about the body, they make the mistake of simply taking current biological and medical versions of the body for granted. Children of various ages are asked to draw the human body and indicate where different organs are to be found. Inevitably, children's knowledge appears as an incorrect or faulty version of the supposedly 'correct' (adult) version, although some investigators declare themselves 'surprised' by how much children seem to know. As we shall argue below, this type of approach rules out any investigation of how children's views of the body are related to the social relations and cultures of childhood. Equally they fix and idealize adult knowledge, removing it from its historical, social and cultural context. Rather than being seen as a particular interpretation of nature, biological and medical knowledge is taken to be a simple image or reflection of it.

Antifoundationalists, on the other hand, are unwilling to make this distinction between the body and the representations that are made of it. In an extreme form antifoundationalists argue in an entirely idealist fashion: that there is no material body, there being only our perceptions of it, which are shaped by social circumstances. Somewhat less extreme is the view that even if the materiality of the body is conceded we only have access to it through discourses of various kinds. It is these discourses, or ways of representing the body, that structure and shape our experiences of it and the meanings we give to it. In this view, then, the task of social scientists is to analyse these representations and uncover the social processes through which they are made and have their effects.

Such an antifoundationalist view of anatomy, and childhood

bodies in particular, appears in the work of Armstrong (1983; 1987), though his construction of childhood bodies has rather different intellectual roots from those more traditionally to be found within the sociology and anthropology of childhood. These derive from the important role that he assigns to childhood, as a cultural construction, in the constitution of twentieth-century medicine. Following Foucault, he challenges the conventional idea that sociology and biology are mutually exclusive. Writing from within medical sociology, his purpose is to undermine the idea that human anatomy is a secure material context for understanding medicine as a social practice: 'Human anatomy has maintained its hegemony over sociology for too long. Its influence is so pervasive that its dominance has virtually been built into sociological thought. Surely it is now time to challenge the cognitive ordering held under the sovereignty of anatomy' (Armstrong 1987: 65).

Armstrong refutes the claim that there is a biology outside of social life to which we might refer when trying to understand the enterprise of biomedicine. Instead, he argues, the body should be seen as a socially constructed knowledge. He insists, therefore, that at any historical moment the body is to be understood not as an underlying reality but as a form of knowledge shaped by the social circumstances of its production, demonstrating this by tracing changes in biomedical views of the body, particularly the classification of its pathologies. Following Foucault (1974) Armstrong looks for sharp breaks in the history of medical thought when one paradigm for understanding the body has been replaced by an incommensurable alternative. In this way, knowledge is understood as a complex discursive formation which governs what can and cannot be thought or said about its object: this object which it creates in theory it then appears to discover in practice. Thus knowledge of the body is not to be understood as a more or less accurate representation of some underlying and constant material reality, but as a way of looking and representing, which is sustained by and is sustaining of power relations and social practices. Armstrong asks:[1] 'What is the nature of the body? . . . The body is what it is perceived to be; it could be otherwise if perception were different' (1987: 66).

As the product of its perception – a construction, invention, classification or representation – the body is endlessly reconstructed and reinvented, and one of Armstrong's (1983) main concerns is to trace the construction of children's bodies in the development of paediatrics as a distinct medical discipline. Initially it was a speciality concerned with the diseases of children but later claimed a concern with the health and development of children as a whole. The emergence of modern biomedicine in the eighteenth century entailed the creation of an anatomy of pathology which could isolate and place disease within specific sites of the body. At this point there was little attention paid to the age or stage of development of the patient. Only gradually were distinctions made between adult and childhood versions of a pathological condition, and these classifications did not form the basis of a distinct medical specialism until the early twentieth century, the result, Armstrong argues, of societal changes in the relationship between children and adults.

The establishment of paediatrics as a specialism turned on a shift from an idea of disease *in* children to the diseases *of* children. And as childhood came to be thought of as distinct from adulthood, so medicine came to think of children's diseases and children's bodies as different from adult ones. From this point of view, childhood bodies were not so much discovered as invented and in the postwar years paediatricians have increasingly claimed that their object of attention is 'normal' childhood, usually expressed as a concern with positive health rather than merely the treatment of disease.

In fact, it was paediatrics which pioneered the shift, now more widely found in medicine, from a concern with diseases in the body to the body in its social context through the formalization of panoptical techniques for the surveillance and monitoring of populations, such as social surveys. These, Armstrong suggests, led to the creation of different versions of the body in childhood and different types of child: 'Nervous children, delicate children, neuropathic children, maladjusted children, difficult children, oversensitive children and unstable children were all essentially inventions of a new way of seeing childhood' (1983: 15).

Similarly, in considering the appearance of the phenomenon 'infant mortality' – that is to say, bodily death of children – Armstrong argues against its understanding as a historical constant, as merely a biological phenomenon waiting to be discovered. Rather, infant mortality is an invention, the product of a certain way of thinking about, recording and analysing the deaths of children. He points out that although the data used to calculate infant mortality rates had existed for decades, it was not until 1877 that these were established. New statistical practices were introduced in response to governmental concern with improving the health practices of the population through intervention in the private domestic sphere:

Housing, nutrition, hygiene and poverty became the analytic lines through which the domestic was brought from the private into the public domain. The relationship between infant and mother . . . rapidly became entangled in the web of analyses of domestic life . . . the infant mortality rate itself became, in a reflexive moment, an important indicator of social well-being. (Armstrong 1986: 213–14)

In this way, in agreement with Donzelot (1980), Armstrong sees the child – and particularly the child's body – constructed as a medico-social problem, so providing a gateway for the regulation of the private sphere, especially the domestic and familial.

The Inviolable Body: Child Abuse

This relatively denaturalized or antifoundationalist childhood body whose emergence Armstrong charts has taken on a highly significant symolic form in late modernity in relation to child abuse, which is cited here as an extended example. There is, it would seem, a revival of the focus on bodily purity, with the child's body seen as the very temple of the sacred (see chapter 1). Children's bodies are to be preserved at all costs, any violation signifying a transgressive act of almost unimaginable dimensions. To strike at the child is to attack the repository of social sentiment and the very embodiment of 'goodness'. Indeed such an act epitomizes absolute evil. And yet child abuse is a constant feature of the historical process as well as being a preoccupation of the contemporary collective consciousness. Such abuse is not singular in its manifestations, which include physical (Kempe et al. 1962), sexual (Finkelhor 1979), psychological and emotional (Garbarino and Gilliam 1980) forms. Its causes are manifold and it has a significant impact on the individual child.

What we might suggest, then, in line with Armstrong's arguments, is that the phenomenon of child abuse has emerged as a malign and exponential growth towards the conclusion of the twentieth century not because of any significant alteration in the pattern of our behaviour towards children but because of the changing patterns of personal, political and moral control in social life more generally. These have, in turn, affected our vision of childhood (Jenks 1994). Whereas an antique vision of the child rendered abuse unseen or unintelligible, modernity has illuminated mistreatment and highlighted the necessity of care. However, this vision of the child brings abuse into prominence not only through scrutiny and surveillance (Dingwall et al. 1986) but also through the peculiar structural demands on the constitution of personal identity and social relationships wrought by accelerative social change.

What is clearly true is that a vastly increased number of cases of child abuse are reported now than was the case thirty, or even twenty years ago. This primarily indicates a conceptual and methodological discrepancy between 'incidence' and 'prevalence' (Mayes et al. 1992), that is, the difference between its occurrence at a point in time and its occurrence over a period. However, at its inception the increase was viewed by many commentators as a social trend, and initial explanations for this were sadly simplistic. Face-value explanations were almost universally short-term and synchronic and contained correspondences with the phenomenon itself – for example, they referred largely to the transfiguration of the modern nuclear family and threats to its inherent stability.

We have already seen (chapters 1 and 4) that Ariès and De Mause, and a whole corpus of what we can refer to as neo-Enlightenment historians, have generated accounts of the evolution of childhood status that share certain tenets. These are (1) that at one time childhood as a category of persons was not part of societies' collective perceptions; (2) that childhood and patterns of child care gradually came into being; (3) that such an evolution has harnessed our affections for children but has been directed by the advancement of ideas in relation to philosophies of human nature, theories of education, economies of human capital, and the politics of human rights; (4) that the emotional, physical and psychological needs of children are increasingly attended to; and (5) that overall the experience of childhood in contemporary society supersedes all previous historical manifestations.

What none of these accounts provides, however, is any explanation for the unprecedented occurrence of child abuse in modern Western society. Indeed, if the logic of their arguments were to achieve its telos then the very phenomenon of child abuse would have disappeared. We must therefore reverse their arguments. It cannot be that once there were no distinguishable children and now the world is organized in relation to children; that once abuse of people was rife, and now abuse of children is unthinkable. Rather we must argue that child abuse is not an original event: there has never been a historical period or a particular society in which children's bodies were not exploited, sexually molested and subjected to physical and psychological violence (Inglis 1978; Jobling 1978; Kempe and Kempe 1978).

Kempe, the American paediatrician with a well-established research record in this field, concurs with the view that child abuse is a perennial feature of human societies. When in the 1960s radiologists in certain American hospitals began to publish reports on bone fractures in young children that were either not accounted for or inadequately explained by their parents, it was Kempe who generated the concept of the 'battered baby' and began to make public the syndrome of child abuse. The 'battered baby' became transformed, in the less accusatory parlance of the British social services, into the 'non-accidental injury', but it was Kempe's formulation of a new category of social problem that prevailed. However, the originality of the problem took on a different and more subtle form when Kempe drew a distinction between changing social practices and changing social perceptions in relation to child abuse.

> A book on child abuse could not have been written one hundred years ago. If an investigator from the 1970's were to be transported back to the nineteenth century so he could survey the family scene with modern eyes, child abuse would be clearly visible to him. In the past, however, it was largely invisible to families and their communities. Before it could be acknowledged as a social ill, changes had to occur in the sensibilities and outlook of our culture. (Kempe and Kempe 1978: 17)

And in similar vein Foucault has stated in relation to incest:

> Incest was a popular practice, and I mean by this, widely practised among the populace, for a very long time. It was towards the end of the nineteenth century that various social pressures were directed against it. And it is clear that the great interdiction against incest is an invention of the intellectuals . . . If you look for studies by sociologists or anthropologists of the nineteenth century on incest you won't find any. Sure, there were some scattered medical reports and the like, but the practice of incest didn't really seem to pose a problem at the time. (1988: 302)

Modern children are indeed embodied, but we need to theorize the nature of that embodiment further through accounting for how children themselves experience their bodies.

The Experiential Body of Childhood

While the body as a discursive formation tells us a great deal about the role of professions such as medicine and their part in the creation of frameworks through which the body is understood, it has little to say about the body as an experienced entity. For this we have to turn to those who have placed the lived worlds of children more centrally within the sociology of childhood. These writers are concerned to enter into the social worlds of particular children through the use of ethnographic methods, including participant observation and in-depth interviewing (see chapter 9). The two examples we discuss below share this approach, although in rather different circumstances. Both show the body as 'drenched with symbolic significance' (B. S. Turner 1984) and therefore as an important element through which children come to create their identities. James (1993) deals with the more commonly experienced contexts of children's everyday lives, focusing on how children create and enact categories of significant difference, especially bodily difference at home and in school. The work of Bluebond-Langner, on the other hand, reconstructs the more enclosed worlds of a summer camp for children with cancer and a leukaemia ward peopled by terminally ill children and their carers (Bluebond-Langner 1978).

James (1993) notes that bodily differences (of height and weight) have been employed to create 'the child' as an othered category in Western cultures. Cultural stereotypes about what constitutes a normally developing body for a child assume great importance, she argues, both for parents and for children themselves. Deviations from these normative notions can create intense anxiety. Among children, experiences of the body, and especially of bodily differences, function as important signifiers for social identity. In her ethnography James noted five aspects of the body that seemed to have particular significance for the children she studied: height, shape, appearance, gender and performance. Each of these acted as a flexible and shifting resource for children's interactions and emergent identities and relationships.

But although cultural stereotypes about each of these five features played an important role, children did not simply absorb them passively. Rather they actively apprehended and used them to comprehend not only their own body but also its relationship to other bodies. Through this, meanings for the body were forged. One explanation for this offered by James is that children have to come to terms not only with their own constantly changing bodies and those of their peers, but also with the changing institutional contexts in which meanings are given to these changes. For example, James reports how in the later stages of nursery school children came to think of themselves as 'big'; their apprehension of the difference between themselves and children just entering the nursery plus the significance of the impending transition to primary school signalled this identity. But once they had made the transition and were at the beginning of their career in primary school, they were catapulted back into being 'small' once again. This relativity produced a fluidity in their understanding of the relationship between size and status, generating what James identifies as a typical 'edginess' among children about body meanings. The body in childhood is a crucial resource for making and breaking identity precisely because of its unstable materiality.

Stereotypical relationships between size and age provided a well-used resource for children to make distinctions among themselves. Small size became a metaphor for age but, more importantly, it could be used to index, claim and achieve some autonomy as a person. An eight-year-old girl was eloquent about this experience:

> What I like [is] to be big and what [why?] I want to be older is because everyone treats me like I'm a little kid, like a baby. They say 'Camilla, will you do that?' Like I'm a little baby. And my [older] sister gave me this little toy to play with and, guess what, my mummy picked me up and put me in the chair and she goes 'I'll feed you in a minute' and I said 'No, I can feed myself'. And my sister she never gets dragged around like me. Like she always drags me around and shouts at me, like 'Camilla, you silly little girl. Why have you been in my drawers? Why are you wearing my bra?' (James 1993: 114)

Children's use of bodily differences as signifiers of identity was pervasive. Being 'fat' as well as being 'skinny' were seen equally as divergences from the norm, and thus both provided a resource for identity formation. However, while the children drew on the cultural availability of stereotypes of size a great deal, it was also true that almost any bodily variation could be given significance. For example, a boy with protruding teeth had this feature pointed out repeatedly, though the significance accorded to this ranged, circumstantially, from 'goofiness' to having a friendly smile.

Being labelled in these ways was for many children a fleeting or at least a temporary experience, but for those with longer term bodily differences – for example those who need to wear spectacles – this process of labelling could be transformed into a more enduring disadvantage. Such children risked permanent identification as weak or weedy. Nevertheless, even in these cases there was no necessary relationship between bodily difference and stigmatized identity. Much depended on the strategies adopted by the children in question: where one child might experience an underscoring and confirmation over time of an outsider identity, another might find ways of transforming difference into an advantage. Wearing spectacles might be welcomed or rejected as a sign of cleverness.

The importance of exploring the social context within which children interpret bodily difference is also strikingly illustrated by the work of Bluebond-Langner. In her study of a summer camp for North American children with cancer she noted that unconditional acceptance by their peers was one of the most valued aspects of these children's camp experience (Bluebond-Langner et al. 1991). At home their hair loss and other negative effects of therapy resulted in these children isolating themselves because of the teasing and stigmatization endured in their relationships with healthy children in their school or neighbourhood. In the social context of the camp, these bodily effects, by contrast, were taken up as signs of a different but shared identity.

In an earlier study, Bluebond-Langner (1978) also explored the contextualization of children's bodily knowledge by showing how terminally ill children in a leukaemia ward in North America were, over time, able to accumulate knowledge about their impending death by reading their own bodies, those of their fellow sufferers and the bodily dispositions adopted by their parents, nurses and doctors. Their prognosis was kept secret from the children, never disclosed by any of the adults whose care they were in. Bluebond-Langner shows how, through their active and acute interpretive skills, the children made sense of the hospital context. The children noted and remarked the passage through the ward of children who became progressively more ill, and of those who disappeared without explanation but who were grieved over. She shows, for example, how the children got to know that whispered conversations by nurses in the laundry room signalled that something they were not allowed knowledge of was under discussion: the children took pains to overhear and piece together for themselves an account of what was being said. She analyses, most movingly, why, even when they understood their own fate, the children did not reveal this to their parents: reading the bodies and worried faces of their family members, they judged their adult carers to be too fragile to be emotionally burdened further.

Reductionisms and their Avoidance

Although B. S. Turner's (1984) distinction between foundationalist and antifoundationalist accounts, identified and illustrated above, helps to differentiate between assumptions that different writers make about childhood bodies, ultimately, in his view, the division is problematic. To overcome the difficulties he proposes a form of methodological eclecticism, such as might be achieved by placing different accounts of childhood bodies side by side, as we have done in this chapter. Here James and Bluebond-Langner concentrate on the experience and changing meaning of the body for children, while Armstrong's (1983) account seeks to explore from a structural and discursive perspective how changing assumptions about the difference between adults' and children's bodies become codified into highly authoritative forms of knowledge. In some senses, then, these two kinds of accounts, although resting on quite different assumptions about the body, can be understood as complementary in asking different but equally valid questions.

In reviewing Turner's position, however, Shilling argues that it fails in its ambition to synthesize because its method is additive rather than relational: it attempts to 'combine foundationalist and anti-foundationalist frameworks without altering any of their basic parameters' (1993: 103). Consequently, it does not examine the dynamic relationships between the body in nature and the body in society. Accepting the necessity of steering a course between biological and social reductionism, Shilling attempts a synthesis by another route; this begins from the position that the body is unfinished at birth and that, over the life course, the body changes through processes that are simultaneously biological and social.

First, he asserts, the mind–body relationship has to be seen in the wider context of the culture–nature relationship, an argument which is drawn from both anthropological and feminist analyses. Important among the former is the theory of symbol and metaphor, sometimes called 'experiential reason', developed by Lakoff and Johnson (1980). They argue that there is a close, but not one-to-one, relationship between mind and body, resulting from the mind's location in and dependence on bodily mechanisms for a perception of the natural world. We exist, for example, in a world where gravity creates the phenomenon of motion as 'up' or 'down'. Human thought incorporates, draws on and elaborates this phenomenon so that happiness is 'up' and sadness is signalled by metaphors of descent. Feminist writers, though to different degrees, have in a comparable manner pointed to the irreducible biological differences which shape experience differently for men and women. While some feminist analyses tend towards biological reductionism (often with an inversion of male claims to superiority), others look to an interaction between biological and social processes in which natural differences are transformed or distorted into social ones (Orbach 1988; Chernin 1983). In these accounts the natural body is not only shaped by social relations but also enters into their construction as both a resource and a constraint. Second, and equally important, is Shilling's suggestion that once we grant the body a biological/physical existence, we can begin to see how it is fashioned by society through material practices such as diet or disciplinary regimes and by symbolic processes which provide interpretations for the body. How this can be instructive for our understanding of childhood and of childhood's potential contribution to social theories about the body we shall now explore.

Childhood and Embodiment

Shilling (1993) himself pays relatively little attention to childhood, which appears in relation to only two substantive topics. The first is an illustration of the processes by which society and culture work on and change biological bodies, an important aspect of what Elias (1982) has called the civilizing process. By this he intends not the emergence of a superior form of society but rather the long-term historical trend by which individuals in societies come to practise certain forms of internalized restraint and control over social behaviour. Included in this are many forms of behaviour concerned with bodily functions such as eating, copulating and defecating.

These behaviours are theoretically open-ended, but in the history of Western societies the process as described by Elias crucially entails the creation of a widening psychological distance between children and adults: 'growing up' in Western societies is the

individual civilizing process to which each young person is auto-
matically subject from the earliest days of childhood. What marks
off a child from an adult is taken to be the successful practice and
performance of internalized, even unconscious, control over the
body and its functions. This means, therefore, that young children
who have not yet learned the specific (and historically variable)
techniques of bodily control are culturally uncivilized. Indeed, Elias
suggests that many behaviours currently associated with children –
for example eating food with the hands or defecating as and where
the urge comes – were for a long period also practised by adults (see
chapter 4). In contemporary society, however, while allowances are
made for children's behaviour so long as they are learning to, for
example, use the lavatory or eat food with a knife and fork, children
must eventually acquire these skills if they are ever to be seen as
proper adults.[2]

This gradual and learned process of embodiment to which Elias
alludes, by which certain forms of behaviour become automatic because they are ingrained in bodily practice, is central to Bourdieu's
(1986) account of social class. This argues that different class positions are created by the ways in which different individuals and
groups have access to, deploy and are able to transform the different
combinations of 'capitals' available to them: cultural, social and economic. Economic capital consists of money and goods which household members have access to – though not necessarily equally – and
which are the basic resource that underpins the others. Cultural
capital comprises personal attributes of two types: institutional cultural capital – mainly formal educational qualifications – and embodied cultural capital – speech, tastes, etiquette, skills, identity, and
other values. Social capital consists of the contacts, networks and
group memberships which give potential access to sociability, the
skills acquired in using it and the opportunities for its acquisition. For
our purposes here, one might usefully add to this list, as Shilling
(1993) does, the notion of 'physical capital': the body itself is or
becomes a more or less endowed entity. In some respects, such as
health inequalities, the body itself may thus be part of the process by
which class relations are reproduced, a point often expressed explicitly by parents through the notion of a 'good start in life'.

In relation to childhood and embodiment the most important
point we can take from Bourdieu is that class distinctions (of taste,
speech, habit, etc.) are primarily embodied ones – a notion he ex-
presses through the term 'habitus'. Formed unconsciously, the habitus in effect underpins the socialization of children. It includes, for

example, the transmission of ingrained, taken-for-granted values and assumptions not only as a set of articulated entities but also as embodied practices. It is during childhood, therefore, that crucial aspects of habitus embodiment take place. Following Bourdieu it might be argued, then, that children are born into, apprehend and experience class difference from their earliest days of life through their bodies.

From the point of view of the new sociological approaches to childhood, though, this picture can be criticized on a number of grounds. It is certainly the case that the reception given to Bourdieu by Anglophone social theory has, as Jenks points out, emphasized '[cultural] reproduction as copy or imitation rather than as regeneration or synthesis' (1993: 118). Whether this interpretation of Bourdieu's ' habitus' is accurate is debatable but what is important is that there is an exhilarating elision in Bourdieu's work between its objective and subjective correlates which is not theoretically resolved: while the concept of ' habitus' permits the potential for grasping the agency of children in both apprehending and transforming culture and social relations, there is at the same time a pull, and a strong one, towards seeing them positioned as only the outcomes of reproduction, as simply embodiments of its passive points of transmission. This is compounded, as was argued in chapter 5, by a more or less comprehensive failure even to examine what children do in their 'play' with others.

However, given that socialization as a concept has dominated accounts of childhood it is not really surprising that this gap is generally to be found in sociological and anthropological accounts of childhood and the body. Indeed an examination of classic texts in the field reveals the same. Mauss's celebrated, and pioneering, discussion in 1934 of how even such a fundamental act as walking is shaped by the specific expectations of a culture assumes that children 'learn' about appropriate body dispositions and styles through a simple and gradual process of accretion (Mauss 1973). Similarly there is no space in Bateson and Mead's (1942) analysis of the embodiment of culture in Bali for the notion that there may be differences between adults and children in what is considered appropriate bodily conduct at different points in the life course.

An important theoretical point for us here, then, is that childhood itself might be thought of as exhibiting difference at the level of children's bodily conduct, and not just as – as yet – imperfect versions of adult members of a culture but as childhood beings. As Prendergast points out:

The issue of embodiment as a cultural process surfaces most poignantly at key points in the life cycle: the trajectory of the body is given
symbolic and moral value: bodily forms are paradigmatic of social
transition . . . Each stage requires that we adjust to and attend to our
body, or that of others, in an appropriate and special way. (1992: 1)

Even though this insight perhaps underplays the importance of
childhood as a set of social relations in favour of seeing it more as a
stage in a learning process, Bluebond-Langner's work, discussed
above, suggests how analytically promising it is to bring together a
perspective which includes *both* an appreciation of the importance
of embodiment *and* the active role of children in apprehending and
constructing their social world through that embodiment.

It is this which emerges so strongly in the theory of embodied
development originated by Merleau-Ponty (1964). The genesis of
this approach is found in a two-way critique of what Merleau-Ponty
describes as the mechanical and idealist versions of child development, exemplified by Pavlov and Piaget. The former reduces
children's conduct to physiological processes, resulting in an
overdeterminist picture, as O'Neill points out: 'the acquisition of
human habits is not a strictly determined reflex but the acquisition
of a capability for inventing solutions to situations which are only
abstractly similar and never identical to the original "learning situation"' (O'Neill, 1973: 68). At the same time Merleau-Ponty is equally
critical of the disembodied learning and consciousness with which
Piaget invests children, arguing that experience is in the first place
visceral.

This is precisely the direction taken, though in rather different
ways, by the research on childhood conducted by Toren (1993).
Drawing on Merleau-Ponty's arguments and developing a position
broadly similar to Shilling (1993), she views children as growing
and developing within a historically and socially situated body.
Mind, she argues, develops in the specific social, cultural and historical circumstances that shape it, not just as consciousness but also
as body, even at the level of the nervous system. Providing an
important counterbalance to Shilling's reliance on passive socialization, she also stresses the creative activity of children themselves
as people who inhabit a world which stands in relation to the adult
one but is not identical with it. She suggests, then, that studying
how children constitute knowledge about the world is crucial to
anthropological (and presumably also sociological) understanding
of social relations.

Again as others have done (see James 1979), Toren notes that there is a good deal of ethnographic evidence that children at different ages hold concepts about the social world which are direct inversions of those held by adults. By focusing on the embodied character of social interaction she is able to suggest both how this comes about and what its meaning may be. Her ethnographic work on Fijian children shows that they attribute an individual's status to the space they occupy in ritual. Adults do the reverse and attribute the meaning of the space to the persons who occupy it. [3] Becoming adult, therefore, involves not simply accumulating cultural knowledge but denying what was known at an earlier stage in life.

But to explain how this can come about entails the notion that social relations are embodied, as well as articulated through language. Children arrive at their interpretations of the world because they 'read' social relations in their embodiment and enactment alongside a (sometimes contradictory) verbalization: 'That children constitute the meaning of one aspect of a concept before the other suggests not that it is necessarily more simple, but that adult behaviour has rendered it the more salient – even when denied' (Toren 1993: 473). The study of children's concepts thus comes to reveal some of the embodied but denied or forgotten substrata of social relations.

Christensen (1993) extends this point about the different structure of meaning and bodily expression by showing that children might express bodily experiences in ways quite different from their adult care-takers. In an ethnographic study of Danish primary school children and their actions and relationships during episodes of sickness and minor accidents, one focus she develops is on how children give help to others. She noticed that teachers and other adults thought children complained too much about the minor cuts, grazes and bruises acquired during the course of the school day. In response to demands for attention, the adults tried to teach the children to make less fuss, sometimes by telling them and sometimes by ignoring their complaints. Observation of the children showed that they did draw attention to bodily experiences in very dramatic ways, often with the request to others to 'Look!' For the children, however, this demand was not one for medical attention or first aid – as adults tended to interpret it. Rather, the children were drawing on a wider practice, engaged in during all kinds of games, play and other activities, of asking others simply to share their experience of the body. In her interactions with the children Christensen, as an adult, came to learn that the culturally appropriate response was not to reprimand the child, or even to give them help. It was simply, and without fuss, to share in the act of looking (see also chapter 4).

Producing the Gendered Body

If the body is therefore to be apprehended as both biological and social – but unfinished as Shilling (1993) suggests in both respects – we would expect childhood to be one of the most intensive periods in which work on the body is accomplished. Gender differences and how these are created are a prime exemplar. As we pointed out above, while some feminist writers have based their arguments on reductionist and essentialist accounts of the irreducible biological differences between men and women, others have tended to view differences between male and female bodies as the product of both biology and society. Connell (1987) codifies these arguments in an extremely effective way in his discussion of the processes by which biology and society interact to produce gender differences. The first he calls negation. This refers to the way in which social classifications and practices both play down the many similarities and over-laps between the bodies of men and women and also emphasize their differences. In the extreme, differences can be invented so as to sustain the division of the sexes. Connell suggests that this process begins in babyhood. Children are dressed stereotypically in differ-ently coloured clothes so that what is not directly obvious – the sex of the baby – is socially signalled, and there is much evidence that adults interpret the behaviour of small babies according to sexual stereotypes of active boys and passive girls (Henshall and McGuire 1986). We might push this process back even further, as medical technologies are now able to predict the sex of a baby before birth.

A second process through which gender is produced is said to involve social practices which shape and change the actual physical body. The division of labour, for example, distributes men and women into occupations which have different implications for the body: women are over-represented in jobs which require them to display sympathy and concern for the emotions and bodies of others; men are more concentrated in occupations requiring displays of power and competition (Hochschild 1983; Tancred-Sheriff 1989). The body and its capacities are shaped by these different practices. Despite the fluidity of the body as a means of expression in childhood, noted by James (1993), similar broad processes are observable in childhood.

Prout (1989) shows how boys and girls in primary school responded differently in relation to the illness of their peers: the girls emphasized care and concern (expressed through home visits and 'Get Well' cards) where for the boys illness was much more likely to be understood as a competitive weakness. This was viewed both metaphorically and physically, expressed through their intense involvement in body contact sports like football. In addition, the boys dominated the public spaces (such as playing fields) where physical games of bodily skill and stamina took place; the girls were relegated to the margins of the playground and took part in far less physically demanding games. Not only did the schoolteachers exclude girls from physical team games but social relations among the children themselves echoed these practices (see chapter 5).

Each of these processes are illustrated by Prendergast's work on how girls in English society experience menarche. Criticizing previous studies for paying little attention to the social context in which girls learn about and experience their bodies, her starting point is that 'embodiment is culturally given, and that many aspects of social organisation, behaviour and interaction will contribute towards defining and shaping aspects of bodily experience' (1992: 3). Using a variety of different methods, including questionnaires, interviews and participant observation in school, she assembled the accounts and experiences of girls in school. From this it seems that girls are aware of periods from a relatively early age, although most primary schools do not include any mention of them in the curriculum. Menstruation is, however, a classic absent presence, a silence that speaks of embarrassment, negativity and secrecy. Although most secondary schools covered the topic in the formal curriculum, Prendergast argues that the more important aspects of school experience for girls were those of the hidden curriculum (see chapter 3).

Two features stand out. First, periods were a resource frequently used by boys (and sometimes teachers) to undermine and demean the girls :

> Negativity was expressed in a variety of forms: keeping girls under surveillance, unpleasant comments and language, calling girls names, shaming behaviour such as tipping out bags in public and in some cases actual physical harassment . . . Some shaming incidents continued to be activated and used by boys against particular girls for a long time . . . A common theme was the ways in which boys could draw on the idea of, and visualise, girls' bodies as dirty, polluted and out of control. (Prendergast 1992: 70)

Second, school policies and practices had an important effect on the girls' identification with their bodies. This occurred explicitly through the attitudes expressed by school staff to the girls and, more insidiously, through the material conditions in which girls learnt to cope with their periods: dirty toilets with inadequate supplies of hot water and towels; toilets with no door locks for privacy or which remained locked during lesson time or to which girls did not have easy access; inadequate provision of tampons; the refusal to give girls analgesics and rules which forbade girls to carry their own supplies. It seems, then, that what shapes the experience of the body in this example is not only ideas or representations of menstruation but their practical realization in the very material circumstances of the school. Together these, Prendergast argues, require the girls to invent strategies of survival through bodily deportment and concealment.

These studies suggest that the body and society are inextricably bound together in the process of their production. It makes little sense to ask what proportion is contributed by biology and society. Similar criticism can be made of the division between nature and nurture: nature and nurture interact in ways which make it impossible to discover what proportion of each is present in people. They are not reducible to either – any more than a cake can be 'unbaked' to prove that it is really more flour than eggs.

Conclusion: the Body Translated

One of the insights of Prendergast's (1992; 1995) work is that it places the body in relation to not only symbolic but also material culture. What produces a category such as menarche is not simply the biological event, nor the phenomenology of bodily experience, nor its relationships within structures of symbolic meaning. Although all of these are important, the distribution of material resources which shape the structure of practice in relation to it must be taken into account. We end this chapter, therefore, by discussing one of the possibilities this insight raises for the study of childhood in particular and social theory more generally, one which is not well developed as yet in the sociological and anthropological literature.

An important corpus of ideas in which these areas are explored is found in the social study of technology. Its leading theorist, Latour (1993), has argued that social life, far from being a pure construction of meaning, is rather mutually constructed from what he refers to as 'heterogeneous materials'. These include bodies and technologies as well as human minds. Each of these entities is given the capacity to enrol and order the others in a process referred to as 'translation'. These orderings or patterns are sometimes temporarily stabilized but more often constitute shifting and hybrid combinations. One consequence of this approach is that the boundaries between the human body and other entities becomes much more blurred than is normally thought to be the case. The body is seen as having extensions through the combinations made with various technological devices. What comes sharply into focus for our purposes here is the huge variety of associations children continually make with machines – bicycles, computers, toys , videos, televisions and so on.

An example of this approach is found in the work of Place (1997). He suggests that the different approaches to the phenomenon of the body might be integrated by looking at an instance where the bodies of children are intensively combined with technologies of various kinds. The ethnographic location he chose was the modern hospital, specifically a paediatric intensive care unit. He points out that in this particular location the human body is perforated, cannulated, intubated and catheterized before being connected to sets of technological artefacts which enable detailed examination of the functioning of the heart, kidneys, brain, lungs and other organs. Such artefacts generate sets of symbols (traces, numbers and images) which are manipulated by the doctors and nurses. Changes in these symbols are understood to relate to changes of a similar magnitude occurring within the corporeal body:

> In the process of connection to these artifacts the body is, in the situated vocabulary of the intensive care unit, 'sorted out'. Literally it is 'sorted' (the disordered body is ordered), 'out' (the internal body is externalised). At the same time the boundary of the body is extended and circumscribed by both corporeal (human) and non-corporeal (technological) elements. The body is, in this sense, 'technomorphic', revisable by connection to technological artifacts. (Place 1997)

In this setting the nurses and doctors, as well as the parents and child patients, are all concerned to maintain the integrity of the body. But what precisely is the child's body in these circumstances? Is it enclosed by the skin or is it bounded by the technologies used to treat and monitor it?

On the basis of his participant observation Place makes a distinction between what he calls 'child data' (what is happening within the corporeal body) and 'data child' (the visible manifestation of that corporeality through its connection to the surrounding techno- logical artefacts). The consonance of these two forms cannot, he argues, be taken for granted: the conditions whereby this similitude holds is constructed minute by minute and the work of the paediat- ric unit is precisely to maintain an association between 'child data' and 'data child'.

Place's insights give a fresh perspective on B. S. Turner's (1984) central divide between foundational and antifoundational views to which we referred at the start of this chapter: the body and repre- sentations of it are not necessarily mutually exclusive. Rather the 'child data' and the 'data child' mutually explicate each other; in this setting one is unthinkable without the other: 'One does not determine the other, with the necessary implication of prior and post status. They are conjoined, mutually explicating only when juxtaposed. When the two forms do separate, one becomes a set of meaningless symbols, the other a disordered mass of flesh and blood' (Place 1997).

We have come a long way, then, from the discussion of childhood bodies which opened this chapter to arguing that childhood itself might be seen as the product of such translations: that is to say, as varied, usually unstable orderings of the heterogeneous elements through which 'the body' is composed. Different children in differ- ent circumstances may be associated with different material re- sources – producing not 'the child' but many competing visions of childhood. Their bodies may, or in some versions of childhood may not, be crucial. In either case it is necessary to examine the bounda- ries of children's bodies and how these are experienced, constructed and shifted by the interpretations and translations of adults, chil- dren, nature and technology. The issue becomes not whether there exists a 'real' body as distinct from social constructions of it – because this would be taken for granted – but how different claims to 'speak for' this body and enrol it in the service of intentional social action are made. As social analysts we would then truly be able to give a certain symmetry to the claims of Armstrong's paedia- tricians and James's playfully serious schoolchildren.

9 Researching Childhood

The surge of interest in the study of children and childhood documented in the previous chapters is testimony to recent concern within the social sciences to place children more centrally within its remit. A great deal of this work is still in its infancy, the product of a young and enthusiastic scholarship whose research accounts are scattered across a wide range of publications and journals As yet these do not present a coherent theoretical focus. Indeed, previous chapters have attended to this diversity, drawing on a variety of different approaches and placing some seminal texts in the field alongside other, perhaps rather less well-known work. However, what have yet to be addressed in this volume, and more generally in the new social studies of childhood, are the methodological issues arising out of the different ways in which scholars are now carrying out their research with children.

In addressing this topic we take up the argument that problems, theories and methods in social science are interrelated and cannot easily be separated out. Doing research is a messy affair, as dependent on negotiation, adjustment, personal choices and serendipity as on careful and meticulous preparation. To this end Bulmer usefully reminds us of the distinctions to be made between general methodology, research strategy or procedure and research techniques. Of these, it is perhaps only the first that has a constancy in our researching. By 'general methodology' Bulmer intends 'the general principles guiding sociological investigation, concerned in the broadest sense with questions of how the sociologist establishes social knowledge and how he can convince others that his knowledge is correct' (1977: 40).

In Bulmer's opinion most consideration should be given to

research strategy, the styling of sociological work, for it is at this moment of choice that 'the particular crystallisation of theory and method' in any research study becomes clear (1977: 13). This is when a research design, informed by a particular view of the way the world works, involving the use of specific tools, will be put to the test.

Heeding Bulmer's three distinctions – between methodology, strategy and techniques – this chapter explores the linkages between them to be found in the different sociological approaches to the study of childhood which were identified in part I of this book and explored through the following substantive discussions. Here we consider separately their methodological aspects. This is not simply to allow us to make further and finer distinctions between these approaches in terms of the ways in which particular representations of childhood and 'the child' are achieved, nor is it to evaluate them. Rather, a discussion of methodology has become imperative. Childhood studies cannot – and indeed should not – escape the methodological critique characteristic of debate in the social sciences.

For example, in the 1980s social anthropology – but with parallels across the social sciences (see, for example, Brown 1977; Hunter 1990; Plummer 1983) – witnessed a crisis of representation following the epistemological upheaval set in train by what has become known as the 'writing culture' debate (Clifford and Marcus 1986). Its insights, by now widely debated, critiqued and in some quarters rejected, had at their centre a controversial discussion which drew attention to the constructed nature of ethnographic accounts. In short, the suggestion was made that the humanistic nature of participant observation research, often considered the keystone of social anthropological praxis and qualitative sociology, means that the explanations of social life offered by researchers in the form of written texts are inevitably marked by their particular and peculiar authorship and fieldwork style. The 'writing culture' debate

> showed us that anthropological representations are fundamentally products of asymmetrical power relations. In addition, it was argued that attention had to be paid to the syntactic dimensions of anthropological representation making, that realism and claims to objectivity and the rhetorical style of the omniscient author should be abandoned and that holism was unrealisable and politically reprehensible . . . (James et al. 1997)

Thus by 1986 the certainties of anthropology's subject matter (traditionally the 'other'), of its methods (traditionally those of participant observation), of its texts (traditionally the monograph) and of its intention (traditionally that of understanding rather than practice) seemed less secure. In one fell swoop ethnographies of other cultures were threatened with a loss of their authority, and, indeed the utility of the very concept of culture seemed at risk. However, all was not yet lost. This challenge from postmodernism engendered a robust response, particularly in relation to method and practice. It was argued that if the accounts anthropology produces are just that, then rather more attention should be given to the process of account making and to its potential reception beyond the confines of the academy. A positive benefit of this critique has been that 'anthropology has begun to develop new forms and styles of represent-ation and ways to include the voices of those being represented in the process of representation making' (James et al. 1997).

The lessons for the sociological study of childhood to be drawn from this reflexive methodological stance are clear. If, as we have been arguing throughout this volume, childhood is socially constructed, then as childhood researchers we must acknowledge that the interpretations of children's lives which we offer are just as marked by the social context of their generation as any of those from a previous era (Stainton-Rogers and Stainton-Rogers 1992). Indeed, this view is already apparent in Bradley's 1980s account of research traditions in developmental psychology where he noted, wryly, that 'scientific discussions of infancy make more sense as illustrations of what the world means to particular scientists than as products of a selfless attempt to describe what the world means to babies and their minders' (1989: 3). Our aim in this chapter, however, is not to require declarations of guilt or valour, or to promote liberal agonizing on the part of researchers. Rather it is to underline some of the correlates of the constructed character of concepts of childhood by attending to the methodological processes by which social scientists have variously made their particular versions.

Approaches to Childhood Research

Though each embodies a particular orientation towards 'the child', it is clear that the sociological approaches to the study of childhood which we outlined at the outset of this volume are none the less variously framed by two particular questions. These ask about how childhood is constituted in society and how the child is to be understood. Each approach explores the extent to which childhood is to be comprehended as a universal condition or better instanced in its cultural particularity. At the same time, within each approach a choice is made as to whether to emphasize childhood as structure or children as agents. In posing these, each makes some commentary on children's abilities as social actors and their status as social subjects.

In this respect Jenks's categorization of the elements through which the idea of the child is conceptualized in European and North American societies provides a useful starting place for pursuing the methodological import of these varied approaches, underlining once more the socially situated character of our theorizing about childhood. The twin themes are as follows: 'First, a belief that the child instances difference and particularity, and secondly, following from the former, a desire to account for the integration of that difference into a more broadly conceived sense of order and rationality that comprises adult society' (1982a: 10). In this way, the social status of child is, Jenks argues, constituted through a necessary relationship of difference with that of 'adult' (but one which is nevertheless contingent in its content), a process which marks out the identity of each. In exploring the research strategies embedded in different sociological approaches to the study of childhood, we ask, then, in what ways they contribute to or dissociate themselves from furthering that relationship of difference. A second consideration follows. If theorizing and account making is contextual, then some regard must also be given to the conceptual and ideational legacy bequeathed to us by presociological models of the child and, in particular, to the seductive transitional theorizing embedded in the model of the socially developing child. Naturalized in our everyday ideological discourses, how far do the current research strategies employed in different frameworks for child study manage to shake off or accommodate the universalizing determinism implicit in the idea of the socially developing child?

'Years Lived Through': Age and the Socially Developing Child

Characteristic of most sociological research into childhood up to the 1970s, as we explored in chapter 1, the model of the socially developing child assumes children to have a different social status from adults, a position predicated on an assumed deficit of rationality and competence. Making strong claims to be scientific and universalistic, it offers an ideal type of child up to the researcher as an object of study, drawing on the theoretical schemas and research techniques of developmental psychology. In an unquestioned endorsement of Piagetian ideas of developmental stages, such research takes place largely in the form of age-based studies of childhood, 'years lived through' being seen as the one variable which can be held unproblematically constant. In such an approach age consequently remains untheorized, with attention focused instead on 'social' differences such as those of class or ethnicity.

Examples of this kind of work can be found in any number of comparative cohort studies where, sliced through at a particular age, the child population is surveyed for instances of difference. Assumed to be united by the commonality of biological growth and psychological development, children are understood to be diversified only by class, region, gender and ethnicity (Newson and Newson 1976). Longitudinal studies similarly rely on a certain constancy of child development so that differences between groups of children are read off as signs of social inequalities which gradually differentiate between them over time. In this way traditional accounts of socialization, which implicitly confirm the model of the socially developing child, ironically also render it dependent on the rhythms of its biology. Using large-scale quantitative methods, such as survey techniques, and only rarely supplementing these with more qualitative approaches, such as interviews with parents (even more rarely with children), this research strategy seeks to gain an understanding and evaluation of patterns and rates of naturally occurring childhood change. It makes no attempt to seek out ways in which to engage with the subjectivity of children or to position children as social actors within the research design. In assuming the constancy of age, this approach both denies the agency of children and ignores the socially constructed character of childhood.

It is, then, in radical opposition to such a perspective that the more recent sociological approaches to childhood research can be situated. However, it is also clear that for many contemporary researchers the persuasive power of the model of the 'socially developing child' none the less remains implicit in their research strategies. And in many ways this comes as no surprise. Given the structural constraints through which childhood is constituted in societies, particularly those of Europe and North America, there are indeed likely to be many similarities between the life experiences of six- or seven-year-old children. These experiences are equally likely to contrast markedly with those of ten-year-olds, precisely because the institutionalization of childhood in these societies is managed for children through discrete age stages (see chapter 4). Thus we might well expect to see patterns of difference in social behaviour between one age group and another; the danger lies in assuming that these social differences are the inevitable or even necessary outcome of children's age or biological development. That route, as we have already explored in considering working children and childhood diversity, tends to lead to the pathologizing of difference both within and across cultures.

And yet so seductive is this framing, so familiar are we with models of child development, that many research designs uncritically incorporate some aspects of an age-based methodology as if it were a 'natural' and irrevocable part of childhood. For example, although the ages of children are often given in a study, there is rarely much information offered about why a particular age group is chosen. Was it especially pertinent to the topic – as is quite clear in studies of school transition (Measor and Woods 1984; Prout 1989) – or was it a more arbitrary decision, thereby demonstrating the unconscious assimilation by researchers of the model of 'the developing child' into their account? How often do researchers choose an age group simply because they feel that the children will be 'old enough' to engage effectively with the researcher's project, rather than because at that particular age in that particular society children are sharing a particular social, rather than simply developmental, experience? Rarely do we detail the ages of adult research subjects unless, as in the study of elderly people, it is pertinent to the research topic .

Problematizing Age

The need for explicit acknowledgement of the often implicit naturalizing of age in research design becomes even more pressing in comparative projects. Traditionally, surveys which compared and contrasted the lives of children at different ages implied that differences between one age group and another were an unmediated function of developmental change, of progression through the life course, an indication of the benefits (or dangers) of simply becoming older. It was a view often perpetuated through the inappropriate transposition into sociology of research tools used for psychological work on child development. Sociometric techniques used to research children's friendships are a case in point. Employing techniques designed to test affection and regard – reciprocal naming, picture sequencing and naming hierarchies – researchers were led to agonize about the instability and fickleness of children's social relationships when compared to those of adults, for the network diagrams which were produced using these techniques revealed many inconsistencies and anomalies (Foot et al. 1980). 'Growing up' seemed the only viable solution for the apparently friendless child. But when used within a social constructionist perspective, in which 'the child' is positioned as a social subject, these same tools and techniques began to yield a more positive outcome. Researchers began to take account of the meanings which children themselves attribute to their friendships, rather than simply assuming that the children lacked friends (Bigelow and La Gaipa 1980). And what was perhaps more important, a process of critical reflection led to a consideration of the ways in which the methods and techniques employed might in themselves shape the outcomes of the research (Hallinan 1981). Through, for example, recognizing that children are positioned in particular sets of power relations in the classroom and that their participation in sociometric testing might be shaped by styles of classroom interaction, friendship researchers acknowledged the need for different research methods to overcome these limitations. For some this led to the abandonment of tests and experimental designs in favour of more ethnographic approaches (Denscombe et al. 1986).

Thus, in understanding differences in social behaviour between children of different ages, an additional, or alternative, reading offered by the new social studies of childhood suggests that these might be interpreted as a sign of children's growing confidence in the age-based cultural contexts they frequent – the school, the youth club, the dancing class – rather than simply as a function of biological development. Furthermore, understanding that in many parts of the world a child's age impinges very differently on local conceptualizations of children's physical and social skills (see chapters 6 and 7) has alerted researchers to think more reflexively about age as a 'social' rather than a 'natural' variable among children. A recent report on children in the developing world demonstrates this shift in perspective clearly through its deliberate depiction of children as fully participating members of the community:

We know of a group of community workers who know every inch of the village in which they work, who are accepted by everyone, who want to help their community, who will work hard (for short periods of time) and cheerfully (all the time). Last month the health worker asked them to collect information about which children had been vaccinated in the village. Next Tuesday some of them will help remind the villagers that the baby clinic is coming and they will be at hand to play with the older children when mothers take their babies to see the nurse. Next month they plan to help the school teacher in a village clean-up campaign. These health workers are the boys and girls of the village. (Hawes and Scotchmer, cited in Save the Children Fund 1995: 36)

Such a rethinking could, we suggest, be usefully extended in the research design of studies of childhood in cultures where age is regarded as an inevitable, determining feature of children's development. Indeed, from a social constructionist perspective, it might be thought to be more important to do so, for it is precisely in these contexts that a child's experience of childhood will be primarily as an aged being.

A good illustration of this is evidenced by the fact that, in industrialized societies at least, schools are the places where children are most often studied. They house a ready-made and easily accessible population with whom a range of techniques can be deftly employed: ethnographic work, questionnaires, surveys and interviews. But aside from studies which specifically set out to explore children's experiences of school – studies of the learning process or life at school (see, for example, Hammersley and Woods 1984; Pollard 1985; Whyte 1983; B. Davies 1982; Walkerdine 1985; Delamont 1980; Askew and Ross 1988) – how often are reflections offered on the ways in which the school as a research site works to naturalize the model of the socially developing child within our studies? As an age-based institution which is hierarchically organized into age classes and shot through with particular power relations, might it not shape the form and style of the research process? To what extent, for example, are we led to design our research with the age stratific-ation of the school in mind and what implications might this have for our research? Would findings about sexuality, gender, ethnicity, friendship, bullying, play and work, for example, look different if they had been gathered outside the context of the school or other child-specific, age-based institutions such as youth clubs or day-care centres.

What little evidence we do have suggests that this might, indeed, be the case. James (1993), for example, notes that the often remarked gender divisions in the friendships and play of young children (Lever 1976) may be a function of the school system itself and that, at home or in the street, children may socialize much more in mixed-sex groupings. In one of the few studies to explore children's lives at home and at school, Mayall (1994a) indicates that data gained from children at school may be refined or changed in discussion at home where different power relations pertain. Thus competent children may not simply be older children; they may be those who are skilled negotiators of these differences of space and place (James and Prout 1995).

A further observation for research design, arising from the insights developed through a social constructionist approach to childhood study, highlights another way in which the discourse of the socially developing child remains an insidious 'natural' feature of our understanding of childhood. The focus here is on language and the questioning of young children's linguistic competency, as noted long ago by the radical psychologist R. D. Laing. In the introduction to his book *Conversations with Children*, first published in 1978, he records how his verbatim reporting of children's conversations was greeted with incredulity. Did he invent the dialogue he included? Did he shape its flow, amend its style? In effect, his interlocutors asked, is it possible that children can say such things? Can they be as naive and at the same time as seemingly competent as their conversations suggested and what should we adults make of their talk with us and between themselves? Some seventeen years later this questioning has resurfaced as social scientists begin to take on a more child-centred perspective in their work and as lawyers in the United States and Western Europe grapple with the testimonies of child witnesses. Precisely because the social space of childhood has been determined for so long through the model of the developing child, questions are now being asked about what children can say and what status children's words can have.

In this respect it is significant that sociological research with children has largely looked in two directions – backwards towards infancy and forwards to adolescence. Childhood's middle years – from four to ten years old – are comparatively little studied. One explanation for this may be that by researching those who have few words and those who have many, the 'problem' of linguistic competence is seemingly reduced. Mothers and other adult care-takers can interpret the infant's babbling for us, and the words of older children, those deemed developed, have lost their ambiguity. But notwithstanding research which demonstrates that ambiguity and misinterpretation are key features of all social interaction (Rapport 1993), anxiety surfaces about how to interpret the speech of younger children. What should we do with the ungrammatical pronouncements of a five-year-old? What significance do the words of a child who muddles genders have? Is it a deliberate ploy or merely a linguistic error? That an implicit model of 'the socially developing child' feeds such uncertainty may be one reason why research design has tended to favour certain ages of childhood.

Childhood in Social Structure

Despite being the subject of extensive sociological critique the legacy of the model of the 'socially developing child' therefore continues to shadow much of our research work with children. In reflecting on a methodology for childhood study, we should pause to consider the challenge to traditional research design offered by taking account of the socially constructed character of 'age'. At the very least, if we wish to retain age as a useful marker, we should recognize its theoretical location within the model of the socially developing child and consider its import. More innovatively, we might consider directly the implications which age has as a social rather than natural variable for the study of childhood. Research by Qvortrup (1990) and Frones (1995) does just that – and in so doing creates a new theoretical direction. In mapping out the ways in which age works to create a specific social structural space for children in Western industrialized societies, both researchers exploit the benefits to be gained from large-scale quantitative research methods in which 'age' is used as a category marker. But they do so without accepting an implicit naturalization of childhood.

In his analysis of publicly available statistics, for example, Qvortrup (1990) demonstrates how children are rendered invisible in public accounts through the absence of child-specific statistics. Aggregation within those for 'the family' or for 'children under 16' leads, he argues, to a process of political marginalization. This may, on the one hand, deny children rights of citizenship and, on the other, lead to a misrepresentation of children's experiential position as members of different age groups within the social structure. This obfuscation of children's experience underestimates, for example, the effect of parental unemployment on children's lives and overestimates the number of children living without siblings. Similarly, Hernandez argues that using parents as the unit of account in calculating the number of children living in poverty in the US can be misleading:

> the distribution of children's economic status can be quite different from that of parents and other adults. Thus, whether the unit of analysis is children or an adult-based measure can make a critical difference in measuring and interpreting the actual status of children vis-à-vis the families in which they are living. (1994: 16)

This work (and other trenchant critiques such as Saporiti 1994) suggests that it is possible to utilize the techniques of large-scale survey and statistical sociology in the service of more recent concepts of children and childhood. It requires, however, a shift in the underlying vision of children, a determination to include them as social actors and the imagination to develop new techniques. As the appreciation of such possibilities spreads, there is a growing number of instances in which researchers have been able to include children in the production of data. The Australian Living Standards Study took a relatively straightforward approach. Information was collected from household members about fourteen spheres of life and questionnaire modules were included which related specifically to children and were to be filled in by them (Brownlee and McDonald 1993). Not only did the approach suggest that the benefits of income may not be equally distributed within families but also that standard of living is not determined only by cash. In any case children may have a specific experience to report. The British Household Panel Study, an annual face-to-face survey of a representative sample of 5,000 households, did not originally gather information directly from household members who were children. In 1994, however, it began to develop more specific methodologies for children's participation. Because children may find it difficult to find the privacy to answer questions in their homes, a technique was developed of a pre-recorded interview supplied on a cassette together with a personal 'Walkman' tape player. Children used this equipment, apparently with success, to answer questions in a self-completion booklet.

Frones's work uses a combination of statistical sources and small-scale local studies to describe changes in the social space of childhood in Norwegian society where a gender revolution seems to be occurring: girls are making rapid advances vis-à-vis boys in terms of educational achievement. This analysis of age-cohort studies in terms of a generational dynamic taking place over time suggests that this newly gendered space will shortly become seen as 'traditional' and even 'natural' by the children, if not by their teachers:

> The choice of further education is, for example, experienced by young people as the choice of the majority if it is chosen by the majority of their fellow students, even if this was the choice of a minority among age groups just a few years older. Modern upbringing takes place in a series of institutional contexts that on the one hand are controlled by the wider society and on the other hand contain a population with an ability to develop new interpretations and lifestyles, new social praxises, very rapidly, through the turnover of generations in educational institutions. (Frones 1995)

Frones's work shows the potential of combining survey work with smaller-scale local studies. Indeed, in his work children's agency comes very directly into view precisely by asking how large-scale effects such as the shifts in gendered patterns of academic and occupational achievement come about through the construction of age-specific subcultures created by children but made possible by organizational changes in the schooling system.

Researchers and Researched among the Tribal Children

As noted in chapter 1, that which we call 'the tribal child' acknowledges children's different social status in celebration of the relative autonomy of the cultural world of children. In part a response to the overwhelming dominance of the model of 'the developing child' in which children's incompetence is assumed, research within this tradition begins from an understanding of the child as socially able. Characteristic of some of the work carried out during the 1970s, and finding parallels with contemporaneous work on youth subcultures (Hebdige 1979), features of 'the tribal child' continue to inform present research strategies and methods.

Ethnographic approaches, now central in childhood research, were in fact first adopted by those working with the model of 'the tribal child', for the battle to establish the integrity of a child's perspective on the social world, in the face of dominant developmental approaches, was indeed akin to an anthropologist's task. These researchers were endeavouring to describe another people's world-view – a separate children's culture with belief systems and social practices foreign to an adult's eye. Parallel projects require parallel methodologies (Hastrup 1987). But just as many anthropological monographs mistakenly work hard at 'othering' other cultures in an effort to highlight their differences (Fabian 1983), as we have seen in chapter 5, so too has ethnographic work among children often 'othered' the world of the child. It has done so by making central those children's activities which reflect differences from, rather than similarities with, the adult world. This has led to the creation of a wide gulf between the social worlds of adults and children which has been far from inconsequential.

During the late 1970s this approach argued strongly for recognition of an autonomous community of children, relatively independent from the world of adults, in which children established their own rules and agendas. Such a child-centred approach required child-centred cultural contexts, so that the family and household became displaced as research sites by the school or the club. Traditionally the place for socialization research, the family was conceived as an unsuitable site within which to develop this radically changed perspective on child research.

Thus for a while it seemed that only for those working with children in non-industrialized societies did the family remain a research site (P. Reynolds 1989; 1996).[1] Such children clearly had a childhood which was already so different from a Western childhood through their involvement in family labour and other economic activities that there was no necessity to 'other' them in the conceptual work of exploring a child's perspective. More prosaically, in cultures where the discursive space of childhood is less marked and child-centred institutions such as schools are not routinely available, the family or household had inevitably to remain as the key site for researching children.

This rupturing of children's and adults' social worlds yielded other changes in research design. Just as anthropologists find perhaps the greatest differences between cultures to lie in expressive systems of belief such as religion, ritual and symbolism, so ethnographers of childhood saw in children's language and games eloquent arenas for revealing children's difference. Moreover, that the requirement to play is in part what has historically defined the child and differentiated it from the adult who must work (see chapters 5 and 6) simply underscored the emphasis placed by ethnographers on children's play. The net result is a large and still expanding body of ethnographic work on children's games and verbal lore in which children's competency and skill with the different cultural rules of a separate world of childhood is visibly endorsed. What are less readily available, however, are accounts of the more mundane everydayness of being in a family or the day-to-day experiences of becoming adult. In the rush to establish firm boundaries to the child's world, links with the world of adults were perhaps inevitably underplayed (Munday 1979). The fact that children do grow up, that they eventually leave the child's world, was something which, though it was not forgotten, it was tempting to suppress.

Though problematic, this implicit forgetting did have some benefits. Unlike the traditional model of 'the socially developing child' which downplayed children's abilities in relation to those of adults, the tribalizing of children allowed children's status as research subjects to be framed by a cultural relativism. Children were no longer simply to be judged as non-adult and found wanting. Children were just different, a perspective which cast a new light, for example, on the question of children's linguistic competency: what children meant was what they said and the ethnographer's job became one of translation and then interpretation. Nor was it any longer a problem that these meanings might not be congruent with those of the adult world. Any ambiguity was welcomed as an illustration of the child's perspective on the world, a competently different point of view (James 1979). Particularistic in the extreme, this approach celebrates the diversity which children represent.

This new and concentrated focus on children's language is admirably demonstrated by B. Davies. She shows how, much to their teacher's astonishment, the children she interviewed were able to demonstrate a far greater degree of 'linguistic competence in terms of vocabulary, style and analytic muscle' in conversation with her than they showed daily in classroom activities (1982: 163). This she ascribes to her non-directive participatory role among the children, which stemmed from her desire to see children as 'people with a perspective of their own and strategies of their own for dealing with the social world that they perceive; as people who have, in fact, a culture of their own' (1982: 1).

But although making substantial contributions to childhood research, the model of 'the tribal child' has not produced a strong reflexive methodological critique about the radical partitioning of the worlds of adults and children. Thus, although ethnographers keenly describe the process of doing research with children, their accounts do not, for example, adequately address the possibility that cultural models of childhood are necessarily part of children's own conceptions of who they are, and that, as consequence, they may shape children's relationships with adult researchers. Mandell (1991), for instance, describes her status vis-à-vis her child subjects as one of being 'least adult' and details how she accomplished this. Rejecting the research role of detached observer, Mandell opts for complete involvement and refuses the position of an authoritative adult in the children's world. She climbs into the sandpit and joins them on the swings, arguing that such participatory activities distance her adult self for the children. The key question here is not whether being 'least adult ' is possible (clearly it may be) or whether it works (it may well do) but how far it is desirable. Might not more, or at least different, things be learned about children and their social world by adopting the more middle ground of semi-participant or friend?

Let us elaborate. If, as Fine (1987: 222) argues, it is not possible for adults to 'pass unnoticed' in the company of children – age, size and authority always intervene, something which Mandell also reluctantly notes – then might it not be worth reflecting on the significance of those differences? In what circumstances do they assume importance and when are they irrelevant? In ethnographic work with children, on which occasions are researchers forced to backtrack to their adult selves and what might this reveal about the social construction of childhood and children's own understanding of their status as children which is shaped by particular discourses of 'the child'? Such benefits would add to that noted already by Fine and Sandstrom, that 'there is methodological value in maintaining the differences between sociologists and children – a feature of interaction that permits the researcher to behave in certain "non kid" ways – such as asking ignorant questions' (1988: 17). If, as Geertz (1983) argues, anthropologists do not have to turn native in order to argue from the natives' point of view, then it is clear that childhood researchers need not pretend to be children.

These criticisms are not intended to signal the retreat from ethnography. Far from it. Rather, it is to suggest that if we admit the inevitability of the differences between children and ourselves as researchers, acknowledging that, however friendly we are or however small, we can only ever have a semi-participatory role in children's lives, then we might develop tools and techniques specifically for work with children on those occasions when our adultness prohibits our full participation (see below).[2] Noting which differences make a difference between us, and when they do (Bateson 1973), may be as, if not more informative than attempting to tribalize ourselves in our efforts to work consistently with a model of 'the tribal child'.

Researching Children as a Minority Group

The heuristic value of adopting a reflexive stance towards research roles with children can be seen in the last approach, which we called in chapter 1 'the minority group child'. Researchers working with this methodological framework do not see themselves as unobtrusive participants in a separate child's world. Instead, children are envisaged as competent participants in a shared, but adult-centred, world and it is through this mutual understanding that the research relationship develops. Less emphasis is given to the children's social lives with other children, attention being focused instead on children's perspectives on and comprehension of an adult world in which they are required to participate. That two strands of research predominate in the work of those using this model of the child – serious illness and work – is not surprising. In industrialized societies both these are conceptually aspects of adults', rather than children's, lives. Death and labour have no natural place in the ideology of a safe, happy and protected childhood (Holt 1975; Ennew 1986). To research these areas, then, is to study children engaging with adult affairs but, and this is significant, largely excluded from them in terms of political, economic and social institutions.

Bluebond-Langner's method of fieldwork (see chapter 8) with terminally ill children was a direct consequence of her encountering children who were professional patients. By nine years old they had been hospitalized 'as many as fifty times [and] had learned a great deal about how the hospital operated, how to manipulate various people and the meanings of various kinds of staff behaviour and expressions' (1978: 238). Her book describes these children dealing with an adult world from whose decisions they were continually excluded while none the less being subject to its regulation and treatment regimes. In this context Bluebond-Langner's role as researcher varied, both in time and between children. Not fitting the available conventional adult categories of nurse, doctor or parent, she became a kind of friend with whom they could talk and, at times, someone over whom the children could exert control. For her, these were not children inhabiting another world in which she, as an adult, learned to participate. They were people facing difficult choices, with particular needs and desires, and thus her questioning was directed by the children and subject to their permission. Participating only when asked, she withdrew on request. In her account, then, there is little sense of the researcher attempting to pass as a child; her relationship with the children was as between equals.

In research on children's consent to surgery, which explores the question of children's rights and decision-making, Alderson is explicit that a model of 'the adult child' frames her research strategy. She observes that any difference between researching children and adults

> lies mainly in the interviewer if she protectively forces children into an adult–child relationship, instead of treating them as mature, competent people. Some children are shy or hesitant, like some adults, but we also met confident, fluent eight-year olds. Adults tend to make more connections, and to reply in more detail at greater length than very young children. This difference is a matter of degree rather than of kind, and is perhaps less due to immaturity than to children's inexperience. When they are experienced they give mature replies. (1993: 71)

Like those who would tribalize the child, great emphasis is placed on giving voice to children's own perspectives, but here it is not a vision of a world apart, another culture heard from. Rather the reverse: in these accounts children are observing and analysing the actions of their adult care-takers. Where possible, verbatim reportage of children's own opinions about their treatment and about the actions of doctors, nurses and parents is provided, for children are seen as competent commentators on their illness experiences. To these, Bluebond-Langner and Alderson add their own analytic interpretations, explaining and extending the children's accounts.

Bearison, however, warns against the latter practice. He contends that children's words alone should constitute the analysis. We need look no further:

> simply listen to the children speaking in their own voices about issues and events that are important to them. There is a great deal to be learned and appropriated from their narratives. They teach us the value of listening to children on their own terms without judging them so that their internal voices will become louder in our time. (1991: 26)

While his bold presentation of children's narratives is reminiscent of recent experimental ethnographic writing in social anthropology, such an extreme rendering of 'the minority group' does little to effect a sociological understanding of children's lives. Bearison offers us few clues as to how we might approach the narratives he presents, so that the children we hear lose, rather than gain, any individuality or personhood. Unlike in Alderson's or Bluebond-Langner's work, we do not know which of the seventy-five children he interviewed is speaking to us. Are they the words of a three- or a nine-year-old child, an Afro-American child, a Hispanic boy or a Caucasian girl? We simply do not know. And yet, if these were adult narratives, it is precisely such details that, as sociologists and anthropologists, we would insist on. By omitting these in his desire to clearly articulate children's own views on having cancer, Bearison's approach ironically replicates the universalizing tendencies of the model of 'the developing child' to which it (and he) is so fundamentally opposed.

This elision of childhood diversity in the struggle to reclaim children's competency and status is a central tension in the minority group approach. Even in its most sophisticated renderings, age and gender – key differentials of childhood – may be played down as sociological markers of differences between children in the struggle to demonstrate children's practical competence when confronting the starkness of ill-health and disease or the adult world of work. Drawing on her fieldwork in a Norwegian fishing community, Solberg (1994), for example, argues strongly that age should be ignored if we wish to see children's perspective on work. In the fishing community children bait fishing lines alongside adults and each baiter is expected to complete the task, irrespective of their status. Child labour, often exoticized and problematized in the literature (see chapter 6) is in this account presented as a normal dimension of these children's lives. Children are capable members of the baiting team.

And yet it is clear that in industrialized societies, and increasingly in those of the South, conceptions of age, and to a lesser extent gender, do set certain boundaries to concepts of childhood which work both to prescribe and limit children's activities through delineating specific arenas of action for 'the child'. Where these lines are drawn tells us about the differences between the social status of child and adult; how they are negotiated tells us about children's abilities as social actors. In our research design we should explore the duality of this structuring of children's lives.

Ethics and Techniques for Studying Children

In considering the social status of children, ethical considerations are never far from the surface of the discussion and have a clear bearing on child research. It is not our intention here to offer a resolution to particular problems but to indicate some of the dilemmas which may be faced in any research with children. Notwithstanding the professional codes of conduct to which any researcher should adhere, it would seem that researching children does raise a number of particular issues. Alderson (1995) and others involved in children's rights have led the way in arguing for greater consideration to be given to the ethics of child research. As Morrow and Richards (1996) point out in their review of the available literature, this effectively centres on the two central issues of informed consent and protection.

Morrow and Richards note that gaining informed consent for children to participate in research often amounts in practice to gaining consent from adult gate-keepers such as parents and teachers. Social and legal rules position children as minors with few decision-making rights so that consent inevitably gets delegated to those who are deemed to have responsibility for children. Gaining assent from children, on other hand, does not ensure certainty either. Children are in a multitude of ways subject to sets of power relations, at home and at school, which may lead to a practical compliance through the fear of sanction (see also Hill et al. 1996: 132).

That children are deemed as needing protection in the research relationship is also a function of conceptualizations of childhood 'as a period of powerlessness and responsibility' (Morrow and Richards 1996). For Lansdown (1994) this vulnerability takes two forms: first, a dependency on adults incurred through their physical weakness and limited social experience; and second, a structural vulnerability through which their position as social, political and economic actors is marginalized. Both these vulnerabilities may put children 'at risk' in the research relationship through their placing of 'too much' trust in the adult researcher. Notwithstanding these dilemmas, the greater ethical issue facing child researchers is shaped by wider social constructions of 'the child', as Morrow and Richard make clear:

> Children's perceived vulnerability means that a further fundamental difference is that the obligations, duties and responsibilities that researchers have towards their subjects are qualitatively different when working with children and relate to adult responsiblities towards

children in general. Thus, if a child discloses that he or she is at risk of harm, then the assumption is that the researcher has a duty to pass this information on to a professional who can protect the child/other children at risk. . . . Researchers need to recognise their moral obligations as adults to protect children at risk even when this may mean losing access to, or the trust of, the children concerned if they do intervene. (1996: 98)

Strong though the case for this is, as in debates on children's rights an over-emphasis on protection invites the charge that what resides beneath the rhetoric of welfare is the attempt to exclude children from participation (Archard 1993; Alderson and Goodey 1996). In research this would mean, for example, a return to the practice of producing data about children but not with them. Such pressures are sometimes spoken about by government-funded researchers in the US where the notion of children speaking independently of their parents might be seized on as an attack on 'family values'.

It is becoming clear from our survey of the implications for research design arising out of the different approaches to child study that while children as research subjects may be envisioned as sharing the status of adults, they are none the less thought to possess somewhat different competencies and abilities. It is up to researchers to engage with these more effectively. Although we would not necessarily want to insist that the study of children requires researchers to develop innovative research strategies and techniques, it does behove researchers to reflect on the methods we use to study children. While ethnographic research and qualitative interviewing are now perhaps the most favoured research strategies for studying children's lives, children's limited social experience, combined with their unequal structural position in society, may mean that we need to refine these methods and techniques. Observation, participation and interviewing all entail implicit assumptions about children's competency, as we have seen: tools of the trade they might be but they are far from value-free.

Moreover, acknowledging that children have different abilities but are none the less competent and confident in them allows us to consider the methodological import of Hebdige's (1979) observation that those who lack power in society may find other forms and means of self-expression beyond the purely verbal. For children the body is clearly an important resource of non-verbal communication, something already recognized in our previous discussions (see chapter 8). But children use other mediums of communication – drawings and stories for example – which have been less well documented as a resource (cf. Steedman 1982). If we dispense with arguments about the necessary relationship between age and accomplishment, sociological approaches to children's art or written work opens up considerable methodological possibilities. Through their schooling, in industrialized societies at least, children are accustomed to paint and draw and are actively encouraged to express themselves on paper. Having been taught these skills, they use them daily and, unlike most adults, are accomplished practitioners. It behoves us to make use of these different abilities rather than asking children to participate unpractised in interviews or submit them unasked to our observational and surveilling gaze. Talking with children about the meanings they themselves attribute to their paintings or asking them to write a story allow children to engage more productively with our research questions using the talents which they possess (Wilkinson 1988: 81–90; Ennew 1994: 67–9).

One example, drawn from some recent research, illustrates this point well (James 1993). In a class of four- and five-year-old children a group of boys and girls were painting pictures of their families. Robbie drew a picture of his mother, his sister and himself. He was challenged by Tom with the question 'Where's your dad?' and, before Robbie could reply, Tom said 'I expect he's dead.' As if this were a matter of fact rather than speculation, Tom resumed his own painting, while Robbie compared his picture with those of the other children. A while later he screwed up his painting and embarked on another. This time there were four figures. By way of explanation to Tom, Robbie said 'This is when we lived in London, Daddy was there.' The questioning routines of an interview, unfamiliar to children, would surely have yielded far less information about notions of belonging and social difference than did this brief interchange over a painting.

A second reason to pay closer attention to method and technique is the recognition that much of children's social experience is, again in industrialized societies at least, highly structured by the adult world, to the extent that 'free play' in school can only take place at times and in places previously designated for that freedom. This means that children's social relationships with adults (however friendly and well meaning) often take place as mediated relationships centred on tasks, where adults assume the directive role as teacher, youth club leader, swimming instructor, gym teacher and so on. To be friends with children – the role adopted by many researchers – is from the children's point of view a potentially uncertain and disruptive action. It leaves many questions unanswered. Who is this woman? What does she want and why does she want it from us? What book is she writing and why can't our names be in it?

Children may be rightly suspicious or cautious. In her account of doing research with children, James (1993) describes how not all the children wished to join in the research and how for others her interests were definitely not theirs. It was fun to chat about food and football but not about friendship. However, when engaged in a mutual project – such as keeping a chart or diary, writing a story, making a tape-recording – the children were working in a style which was not only familiar to them but one over which they had more control. Thus the power relationship evoked between adult researcher and child informant in a standard one-to-one interview becomes diffused when 'group interviews' are held instead. As Hood, Kelley and Mayall (1996) note, the social mismatch between adult interviewer and child subject may be lessened in group interviews where children have support from their peers. Though the narrative structure of the interview may become less structured, the shifting of control to children themselves permits them to become enthusiastic informants rather than reluctant subjects.

From these examples it is clear, then, that engaging children in what might be called 'task-centred activities' which exploit children's particular talents and interests might provide a better way of allowing children to express their ideas and opinions than the use of more 'talk-centred' methods such as interviews or questionnaires. Some progress has already been made in this direction through the use of activities adapted from participatory rural appraisal techniques used in community projects in the developing world. Baker et al. (1996) for example describes the use of 'spider diagrams' for exploring the health status and beliefs of street children in Nepal and their use of drama and video as ways of involving children on a more equal footing in the research project. Hanssen's (1996) innovative development of the 'network interview method'[3] involved children in Sri Lanka drawing answers to questions about the giving and receiving of care. Kefyalew (1996) used focus groups and role play with great success among children in Ethiopia. Indeed, Kefyalew notes that although his assistants ranked such participatory approaches rather unfavourably before beginning the research, they became convinced of their value through using them.

However, as Paul Connolly points out, the adoption of innovative, child-centred methods does not in itself necessarily allow children's voices to be heard. In his discussion of studies of racism and children, he argues that what is important is that researchers should reflect in the first instance on their own stance towards children: 'it is not simply a question of choosing the right methods in seeking out the authentic voices of young children but is rather a matter of engaging with the underlying and preexisting values and assumptions that researchers have about childhood and the influence they may exert within the research process' (Connolly, forthcoming). As he demonstrates, if a researcher remains wedded to a model of child development which sees a growing competence with age, then their ways of approaching children and the later interpretation of the data will necessarily reflect this position. The substitution of picture-ranking attitudinal tests for more ethnographic methods will have little, if any, effect.

Conclusion

It is timely, not to say urgent, that a discussion about methods of researching childhood takes place. In the first place there is a need to pay heed to methodology lest the upsurge of research activity about children and childhood fails to reap a proper and considered benefit. Furthermore, given the particular character of childhood as a phenomenon, the reconstruction of children as social actors and the consequent view of children as the new subjects, rather than objects, of research, we should pause to ask whether our standard research techniques, which as social scientists we so readily employ, are indeed the most appropriate. Although, in our view, studying children need not of itself necessitate the adoption of new or exotic techniques, time to reflect may allow us to be both more adventurous and more critical of the standard methodological array. We have, therefore, highlighted features of actual research strategies, tracing how the style and design of any particular exploration has in the past and may in the future be more innovatively reflected in the specific techniques and tools commissioned for its artistry. At the same time, this chapter has delineated some of the ways in which methodology bears witness to underlying ontological assumptions about the social world and children's place in it. It is to these fundamental theoretical questions that we return in the final section of this book.

Part III
Theorizing Childhood

10 Theorizing Childhood

The overarching concern of this book has been to provide an analytic framework that will act both to consolidate the now burgeoning array of childhood studies and to indicate trails and pointers for the development of future work in this area. However, as social scientists we are only too acutely aware of the double-edged consequences of such an endeavour. In one sense such a marking-out of territory is always useful. It offers a structuring, a security and a consolidation for a research community which is gratifying to its members. It can provide a unity of purpose, an expanded fund of knowledge through 'critical mass', a unification of topic with which to meet the demands for research of user groups and, finally, an external identity, professionalization and status through the solidarity of a subdiscipline. All of these effects are, of course, the social and, indeed, ethnomethodological outcomes and practices contained within the Kuhnian notion of a paradigm: 'a scientific paradigm stands for the entire constellation of beliefs, values, techniques and so on shared by the members of a given community' (Kuhn 1970: 175).

However, paradigms are not simply social rules of conduct that bind communities together through spontaneous loving bonds. Paradigms also contain deep-rooted assumptions and principles, both epistemological and ontological, as Kuhn was himself quick to point out: 'What are the fundamental entities of which the universe is composed? How do these interact with each other and in what sense? What questions may be legitimately asked about such entities and what techniques employed in seeking solutions?' (Kuhn 1970: 4–5). Paradigms provide a knowledge about what actually and properly constitutes a phenomenon and also about the best and most appropriate way to find out more about that phenomenon. In this sense, then, such principles offer control, if not also constraint, and their activation is, most fundamentally, political. Here is a second, perhaps less welcome, consequence of our endeavour.

However, although as authors of this book we are not shy concerning our knowledge of the territory of childhood studies, or indeed our combined parts in pioneering that territory through setting out some of its perimeters (Jenks 1982b: James and Prout 1990b), our concerted purpose here is *not* one of legislation and closure. On the contrary, as the earlier chapters have sought to demonstrate, part of our intention has been precisely to seek out and reveal the mechanisms by which such constraints come to be placed on our understandings of childhood and, in turn, institutionalized into the form of everyday knowledge. We have explored, for example, the principles of certainty by which people within Western culture 'know' that children are natural, universal creatures who, eventually, simply 'grow up'! At the same time, we have drawn attention to the vast body of literature written with a concern for the history and cultural specificity of childhood which indicates that the sociocultural context in which the 'natural' child lives and has lived varies considerably. The phenomenological outcome of this well-documented diachronic instability has been a recognition that concepts of childhood are not constant. Thus, as a social status, childhood has to be recognized and understood through routine and emergent collective perceptions that are grounded in changing politics, philosophy, economics, social policy or whatever. Such knowledge is a central feature of this book: it insists that we must envision the child within a broad cultural context.

However, at the same time, the territory of childhood is populated with persuasive ideas that have, through time, burdened us with a particular vision of the child. This has, we suggest, ultimately overwhelmed our capacity to theorize childhood in the rapidly transforming conditions of late modernity, an unfortunate consequence for two reasons: one, that we might operate with an inappropriate set of expectations and demands on today's children; and two, that we risk remaining unreflexive in our research concerning our own relationship with childhood. As C. Wright Mills warned us over fifty years ago, a failure of critical reflexivity in our approach to the social world can lead to a normalization of our topic and a routinization of our methodology and levels of understanding.

Writing with a concern for the complacency of early deviance theorists he stated that 'an analysis of textbooks in the field of social disorganization reveals a common style of thought which is open to social imputation. By grasping the social orientation of this general perspective we can understand why thinkers in this field should select and handle problems in the manner in which they have' (Mills 1943: 47).

Although we are not suggesting here that the contemporary study of childhood is in need of such a severe indictment, we would none the less point to the need for a constant vigilance over the kinds of attention we pay to our growing body of knowledge. A second insistent theme of this book has been, then, that our problems need to be forged analytically rather than simply received as difficulties or dilemmas stemming from contemporary practice. As we stated at the outset, children have become supremely an issue of our time. Nations are investing in educational and moral futures and public concerns abound with issues of protection, rights and citizenship in relation to the young. It is all too easy to become embroiled in the urgent hyperbole of paedophilia, child abuse, child pornography, childhood criminality or even the perpetual party political battle ground of educational standards: they are all 'the' issues of today and appear to require an immediate answer, or at least an opinion.

Though heeding such demands for research, our more central endeavour must always be to understand analytically this urgent focus on childhood: for example, to explore what it is that elevates these issues to absolute centrality and renders them so pressing, and to analyse why childhood itself has become such a newly contested terrain. Only by concentrating on these more theoretical concerns do we retain the possibility of speaking about childhood as a social status in its own right, with its own agendas. Indeed, we suggest, only with such an analytic and theoretically focused perspective is it possible to attend properly and responsibly to those external, policy-driven demands for research. Without such a focus, childhood is condemned to remain, as in the past, simply an epiphenomenon of adult society and concern.

Such, then, is *our* concern in this concluding chapter: to draw together the analytic threads of this volume and indicate directions in which the new social studies of childhood might not only be more productively theorized but might, in itself, make a more than modest contribution to social theory.

Childhood and Social Theory

The initiative in theorizing childhood has derived largely from advances within sociology and anthropology, disciplines which we as authors represent, and which provide potential for further interdisciplinary study.[1] Indeed, as we have sought to demonstrate throughout, this firm grounding of 'childhood' within what are essentially sociological concerns derives from the intimate relationship between 'the child' and the idea of social order. Although adults themselves have to be constrained into social order, in true Durkheimian fashion children offer living exemplars of the very margins of that order, of its volatility and, in fact, its fragility. On a momentary basis, children exercise anarchistic tendencies and asociality up to the limits of adult tolerance and often beyond, hence their temporal and spatial confinement in 'childhood' (see chapters 3 and 4). They are unstable, systematically disruptive and uncontained, so that, as individual manifestations of 'childhood', children are cognitively managed, though barely, under a variety of different rubrics: children's 'creativity', 'self-expression', 'primitiveness', 'simplicity' or just 'ignorance' all feature as traditional, often developmental, 'explanations' of how children are. For adults to replicate such conduct beyond celebration or intoxication would be to invite the categorization of eccentricity at best (Hockey and James 1993), or, at worst, insanity:

> madness does not represent the absolute form of contradiction, but instead a minority status, an aspect of itself that does not have the right to autonomy, and can live only grafted onto the world of reason. Madness is childhood. Everything in the Retreat is organised so that the insane are transformed into minors. They are regarded as 'children who have an overabundance of strength and make use of it'. (Foucault 1967: 123)

Children, then, represent a potential challenge to social order by virtue of their constant promise of liminality, which as Van Gennep in *The Rites of Passage* of 1908 and latterly V. Turner (1974) have shown, maps out the space of the ordered and the normal. In this case, this is the taken-for-granted, adult world. Thus, in the same way that criminological studies serve to delineate normative behaviour in judicial codes, childhood studies might be seen to police the boundaries between the morally acceptable and the morally unacceptable, though this may not be their usual intent. The metanarrative remains, none the less, the problem of order:

> We can now, perhaps, begin to see that the persistent and deeper analytic theme, stemming from the emblematic role of childhood as an idea, is a more fundamental orientation towards the preservation of both social and sociological worlds. When we talk of the child we are also talking of recollections of time past, images of current forms of relationship and aspirations towards future states of affairs . . . It is precisely because of this conceptual complexity that any analysis of childhood must rigorously attempt to open up the boundaries that have been placed around the experience, whether such boundaries are commonsensical, sociological, educational, psychological, medical or biological in type. In this way it becomes increasingly possible to actually topicalize 'the child' for social theory. (Jenks 1996b: 11)

It is in this sense, then, that we argue that childhood is fundamentally wedded to a central concern of social theory.

Future analytic work in the new social studies of childhood is poised to continue the productive exploration of this contribution through a further conjoining of disciplines. Sociologists, anthropologists, psychologists, social geographers, historians, philosophers and theorists from sociolegal studies all have a great deal to add to the total mosaic of our knowledge about children and childhood, with each of these disciplinary interests usefully attending to different theoretical aspects. In this way, confirmation will be achieved of the view expressed through this volume that without addressing childhood there can be no adequate account of the social. To this end the following sections sketch in some of the key theoretical dimensions which might begin to be investigated in a concerted, interdisciplinary study of childhood.

As a starting point we would point to four core, yet linked, sociological dichotomies (see Jenks, forthcoming) which can usefully orient our thinking:

> Structure and agency
> Identity and difference
> Continuity and change
> Local and global

In what follows, we will seek to explain further and integrate these dichotomies with the four dominant discourses of childhood that we predicted at the outset and which we have employed to organize our analysis through this volume:

> The social structural child
> The socially constructed child
> The minority group child
> The tribal child

And in considering the interplay between these conceptual arenas here, we offer an understanding of, first, the ways in which thinking about childhood necessarily reflects the nature of the social, and secondly, childhood's own contribution to furthering our understanding of that social world. By way of conclusion, then, we would argue that the core sociological dichotomies with which contemporary social science engages provide a promising and constructive platform for the different orientations towards research with children which comprise the new social studies of childhood. Finally, and by turns, it also becomes apparent that childhood studies can have a great deal to say about the nature of those dichotomies.

Sociological Dichotomies

In outlining these four sociological dichotomies we shall be neither prescriptive nor exhaustive. Instead, our intention is to pick out the key ways in which they speak to or about childhood through a recursive glance at the substance of our text. We begin with that most fundamental dichotomy: structure and agency.

Structure and agency

It is incontestable that the concept of social structure is foundational to the discipline of sociology. Structure is *the* primary heuristic device, developed to explain the social as a realm of being different from and in excess of the actions of individuals or even the sum of those actions. If, as sociology asserts as its basic ontology, society exists as an objective reality, then it becomes essential to demonstrate that there is a tangible mode of organization which regulates both individual conduct and the patterns of interaction that are sustained between individuals. Society is nothing more, and nothing less, than these patterns of interaction or what we might call social relationships. And social structure is the transformation of these relationships into the form of an idea; that is, 'structure' is the way that sociology conceptualizes these social relationships and their various manifestations.

It is sociologically problematic to imagine society to be merely the aggregation of behaviours or the collection of acting individuals alone. This is because society, in its manifold forms, is made up of the different ways that actions and individuals are gathered together into groups or communities of people. Are we to suppose that the groupings that comprise society are made up of individuals who, as dynamic individuals, actively constitute and make real their relationships together and in so doing generate society as a process? Does 'society' issue from their actions? Or, on the other hand, are we to suppose that the patternings of organization around social relationships take on a life of their own which perpetuates those relationships and produces a 'society', despite the actions of individuals?

In the latter explanation – which we can term the structural account – what is being claimed is that the individual is relatively passive in respect of making the social; structure appears as a set of objective and external conditions which determines the conduct of societal members as they enter into different relationships or groups. This contrasts with the first position – the agency account – where we are looking instead at free will generating the social as process.

But we need to be clear. Although undoubtedly there is a dichotomy at work, these explanations also form a continuum: both positions conceptualize 'the social' as being made up of relationships between compliant members which are organized, that is structured, in recognizable ways. 'The social' therefore has an objectivity, a real existence. From within the first position society is regarded as if its structures were manufactured through the actions of people in concert; these individuals are the creative agents of their own subjectively meaningful courses of action and thus develop their interrelationships directly through this agency. From within the second position the society and its structures are treated as synonymous: the social is a sedimented network of interrelationships that itself acts to determine the conduct of individuals. This determinism functions through the conditions imposed on the choices made available and constraints that are placed on human behaviour. So we have a dichotomy that is also continuous in its lived experience.

Within social theory these two positions live suspended in a relatively antagonistic tension. They are not seen to be compatible and they are the source of many oppositions in accounting for social phenomena. On the other hand, real social relationships and their causality dwell perpetually in the hinterland between these extremes, and a radical adherence to either position at the expense of the other leads to the generation of impossible difficulties: social action continuously and reflexively creates and is produced by both agency and structure at one and the same time (Giddens 1984).

All this is, as we have seen, pertinent for a social theorizing of childhood. Indeed, childhood has long been a magnificent testing ground for this dichotomy between agency and structure for, as chapter 1 explored, most questions raised about children's competencies, rights, responsibilities and needs have been located in the space between these poles. The varieties of this reasoning are infinite. But what lurks behind this spectrum of theoretical accounts is some sense that it is adult society which constitutes the structure and the child the agent, and that the former determines or socializes the latter. Whether the child's becoming is witnessed as the emergence of Chomsky's deep structural competence (1965), the Parsonian 'appropriate internalisation of normatively oriented need dispositions' (1951) through Cicourel's notion of ' the acquisition of a sense of social structure' (1970) or through Speier's 'acquisition of interactional competencies' (1970), the dichotomy remains. Indeed, in much traditional theorizing about children it is presented as elementary to the adult–child relationship and thus to its intellig-ibility.

Identity and difference

Our second dichotomy is that of identity and difference, itself a sophistication of an earlier sociological binary between self and other. The new formulation implies a process of establishing identity-with and difference-from as a continuous issue of self and status definition and redefinition. Fluid and with an emphasis on a changing dialectic, it contrasts with the more traditional distinction between the self and other. This depended on a strong sense of interiority and identity and postulated a locatedness and constancy for categorical systems that enabled the fixity of the other. Such a view did not fit well with the emerging post-structuralist being of the second half of the twentieth century and, in anthropology for example, set in train a political critique.

But despite its various contemporary iterations, questions of identity and difference have been threaded continuously through traditional accounts of childhood, figuring most prominently in those centred on childhood and becoming. From Piaget's 'decentring' of the child, through Freud's journey from id to super-ego, to G. H. Mead's space between the I and the Me, ideas of identity and difference engage with discourses of the child. In all of these we find multiple reworkings of the understanding that if the individual instances a kind of project or trajectory of self-intent, this only gains any sensibility over and against the needs and meanings of the assumed sense of the collectivity. Thus children's, as anyone's, journey into identity is about forging a relationship with the problem of order such that any definition of self and not-self can be sustained. Children learn who they are through interaction with (usually) the adult other. The spatiality of this journey has therefore been both cognitive and interactional, and intimately enmeshed with the persistent question of reflexivity.

Continuity and change

What of the dichotomy that is maintained between continuity and change? Children have been regarded as a precise index of this dimension. They exude a newness, a fresh and forward-looking perspective in their becoming, while at the same time providing us with a strong and lasting, even nostalgic, sense of ourselves and our aspirations projected forward into tomorrow (James and Prout 1990a). Through children, and in relation to childhood, account has been taken of both the recognition of change and the experience of consistency in everyday social relations. As noted, the space of childhood might always have existed, but it has had a changing profile and intent (Qvortrup 1994).

To capture the shifting qualities of this dichotomy, an appropriate analytic tool has been that of 'cultural reproduction'. As chapter 4 began to explore, the idea of cultural reproduction makes reference to the emergent, temporal quality of the experience of everyday life, albeit through a variety of theoretical positions. It is a concept which serves to articulate the dynamic process that renders sensible the utter contingency of, on the one hand, the stasis and determinacy of social structures and, on the other, the innovation and agency inherent in the practice of social action. Cultural reproduction allows us to contemplate the necessity and

complementarity of both continuity and change in social experience and enables us to regard children as ontologies, as life courses
and as instances of generations, as Bourdieu's (1986) work on the
modern system of education has shown. This he saw as integral to
the 'reproducing' of the culture of the dominant classes through
their children, a mechanism of mass socialization which helped to
ensure their continued dominance and also to perpetuate their
covert exercise of power (Jenks 1993). As this volume has variously explored, though children bear the marks or categorizations
of their social reproduction, they are also positioned as the very
agents of cultural reproduction.

Local and global

The last of our dichotomies and of perhaps more recent interest in
social science is that between the local and the global. This is in part
about the past and the future, but also about a wholesale social
movement from the diverse to the generalizable. As a pan-social
tendency, what we are witnessing here is no accidental historical
confluence of epistemologies or topicalities but a more general, and
perhaps even conscious, consequence of the effects of globalization.
As the constraints of geography increasingly recede and the world
moves steadily towards the status of 'a single place', then the questions that we previously asked about identity and difference have
become more directed. They look now towards issues of personhood
and the general state of human ontology in the context of a more
common ecology, economy and technoscientific culture. This is not,
however, to ignore or gloss over the gross material divergence that
is still rife across human experience, taken on a comparative basis
(see chapters 6 and 8). Instead, it is to point to the tendency for an
international and transcontinental politics, economics and style of
information exchange and manipulation to dominate the experience
of being human.

Of course, social action remains situated locally, as does its interpretation. However, the causal structural forces which affect its
history and development are often driven from sources which are
not confined within particular, recognizable boundaries. Whether
we are considering lifestyles in Europe and North America or subsistence in the South, children's fashion in New York or street
children in Guatemala, boy soldiers in Bosnia or the Green Cross
Code, we must still attend to the fact that the society which is

shaping and constraining the everyday experience of children extends beyond the limits of the nation-state (see chapter 7).

Indeed, nowhere has been left untouched by the march of modernity, and although the concrete manifestations of modernity are concentrated, its impact and iconography are diffuse. With its tendencies towards globalization, understood as the universalization of experience, modernity has had dramatic effects on our comprehension of space and time. As we have seen in previous chapters, the child emerges as a mediating figure but also a symbol, particularly in relation to issues of social identity and those of risk and welfare. Children have become a source of our concerns about the nature of identity in a rapidly changing world, and also a consequence of the accumulating dangers that are its essential products, as we have variously explored in our discussions of child work, health and the body. Furthermore, if we turn to children, we also encounter symptoms of the structural problems that we have either constructed or conspired to reproduce both socially and culturally, from the localism of 'stranger danger' to the globalism of Internet pornography. What is critical about this dichotomy, when revisited as a continuum, is that it places the universalism of 'childhood' in vivid relief with its particularity.

In isolating these core dichotomies within sociological theorizing, what we have shown is that the substantive topics of 'children' and 'childhood' do not, and of course cannot, escape their remit. And, indeed, they should not. To this end, we shall now demonstrate their integration with the discourses of childhood that have organized our thinking in this book and, in this way, reveal the contribution which the new social studies of childhood can potentially make to social theory.

We do so by suggesting that there are a clustering of concerns within social theory, which map on to the four major philosophical dimensions of voluntarism and determinism, and universalism and particularism (see figure 2), and that these composite dimensions provide a broad base from which to begin to ask a more integrated set of questions about the relationships between agency and structure, identity and difference, continuity and change and local and global. And it is through locating the four distinctive voices of the new social studies of childhood within this matrix of sociological concern that we are able to indicate the kinds of questions about the social world which can be asked and the kind of answers that are likely to be given by contemporary childhood research.

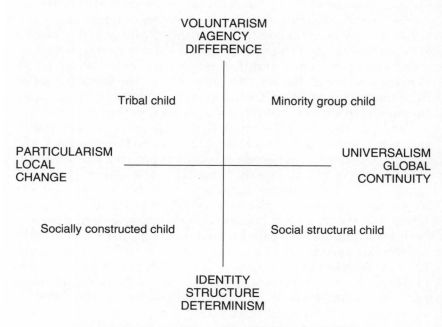

VOLUNTARISM
AGENCY
DIFFERENCE

Tribal child   Minority group child

PARTICULARISM   UNIVERSALISM
LOCAL   GLOBAL
CHANGE   CONTINUITY

Socially constructed child   Social structural child

IDENTITY
STRUCTURE
DETERMINISM

Figure 2 Theoretical field for the social study of childhood

Childhood's Dichotomies

The substantive body of our text has seen the affirmation of four new and different ways of seeing 'the child'. To recap, these are, nominally, the social structural child; the socially constructed child; the tribal child; and the child as a minority group. Though each topic has been differentially addressed through these approaches – for example, issues about child labour and diverse childhoods are usually characterized by more structural approaches, while child-centred studies predominate in discussions of children's play – the apparent differences between these approaches mask a series of family resemblances. These, we argue, unify them in their opposition to or rejection of the central analytical features associated with the more traditional model of the developing child, rehearsed in our introductory chapter. Thus the differences turn out to be less important than the resemblances!

In any case, our purpose is not to generate a separatist typology. To repeat: we are concerned to provide an analytic framework that will consolidate the new social studies of childhood and provide pointers for its development. To this end we shall emphasize the overlaps and areas of agreement between the four discourses rather than attempt to demarcate their differences and begin an arid process of rigid and permanent separation.

The primary distinction between the traditional conception of the socially developing child (which in chapter 1 we cite as an example of *transitional* theorizing) and our fourfold classification of 'new' approaches to the child (those we called in chapter 1 *sociological* conceptions of the child) is the one to be made between notions of 'becoming' and 'being'. The model of the socially developing child, characteristic of socialization theory, is always engaged with the process of change and alteration, the compulsion for this ontological nomadism being the end goal of adult society. This is always assumed and always prestated. The developing child is thus essentially epiphenomenal, its very 'becoming' rendering it incomplete:

> Understood from within a variety of disciplines and perspectives, and also across a range of different sets of interests, childhood receives treatment as a stage, a structured process of becoming, but rarely as a course of action or a coherent social practice. The type of 'growth' metaphors that are readily adopted in discussions about childhood all pertain to the character of what is yet to be and yet which is also presupposed. Thus childhood is spoken about as: a 'becoming'. (Jenks 1996: 9)

In contrast, our four 'new' discourses of childhood understand the child as 'being'. The child is conceived of as a person, a status, a course of action, a set of needs, rights or differences – in sum, as a social actor. And as we have seen throughout this volume, this new phenomenon, the 'being' child, can be understood in its own right. It does not have to be approached from an assumed shortfall of competence, reason or significance. The 'being' child is not, however, static, for it too is in time. Like all social actors, it populates history. Thus there is no necessity to abandon ideas of past and future just because we have shifted from a conceptual framework that is predicated on becoming: 'The child is active in its own right, not simply imitatively, but as . . . an agent in its own construction and as naturally an agent as any adult, in the sense of agency that concerns the initiation of action by choice' (Wartofsky 1981: 199).

To summarize: the epistemological break that we have claimed for new sociological approaches to the study of childhood is the move to study real children or the experiences of being a child. The socially developing model, by contrast, rarely addressed children at all: children were either the embodiments of growth or the indices through which transitions and changes might be assessed and measured. Traditional developmental psychology, for example was outstanding in its dedication to fitting the child to a 'stage' or 'level' of attainment, and socialization theory, in its mimicry, searched childhood expressions for evidence of adult interactional skills as steps towards the achievement of adulthood. Such approaches remain ignorant of the everyday, synchronic experience of the child actually living in the social world 'as a child'.

To be more specific as to the insights offered in the new social studies of childhood, we shall therefore revisit our four new discourses of childhood. Highlighting their analytical characteristics, we shall show not only how they provide different views of childhood but that these new envisionings are fundamentally sociological, rather than developmental, in character. As Christensen (forthcoming) observes, 'childhood' in itself is not an analytic category; it is an empirical phenomenon which is 'in need of' analysis. In this volume this has been achieved through addressing children and childhood, both implicitly and explicitly, in terms of the core sociological dichotomies which characterize sociological analyses.

The social structural child

Here, instead of operating with the view that children are marginal to society and awaiting integration as adults, theorists view childhood as a constant and recognizable component of all social structures, across space and time:

> The idea of childhood as an integral form is worthwhile to compare with the conventional wisdom that children are to become integrated into society. We have . . . chosen a different perspective than childhood as a transient phase of one single individual's life: rather we suggest that it is a *permanent form*, which never disappears, even if its members change continuously, and even if it is itself historically at variance. This latter point is an important one since its historical variability accounts for its dynamic qualities, and it remains necessary to understand the mutual influence of generations at any given time. The interrelationships of childhood with other structural forms

– age groups, social classes, etc. – change continuously depending on social system and social formation. Thus we have to follow the structural change of childhood as well as of any other socio-economic groupings: they are mutually influencing each other and they are in principle exposed to the same external forces. (Qvortrup 1994: 23)

Children are a structural category, they are part of the very constitution of social life and should therefore be understood as an integral form within every and any social system. Children have always been and will continue to be in and of the society, whatever its present manifestation. There is a strong sense of the universality of childhood and of the status identity of 'child'. Childhood is not and could never be conceived of as a historical invention. As such, in this approach, the child becomes a unit of analysis *sui generis* and thus comparable with other units that comprise the social system.

Within this discourse, then, though analysts are interested in the experience of childhood, this is often in terms of its interrelationships with other categories in the society. How is childhood experienced in relation to adolescence or adulthood? Such work lends itself readily to the variety of other forms of institutional approaches to the social world and gains considerably from the information derived through the use of demographic techniques and quantitative data. Once the category of childhood has been conceptually established and thus rendered less problematic, or at least not an interpretive issue, then measuring and assessing the relative features of comparative contexts can begin. Thus Qvortrup (1994) was able to initiate a wide-scale five-year international programme of research into the comparative living conditions of children in industrial societies administered through the European Centre for Social Welfare Policy and Research in Vienna and involving twelve different countries (see chapter 8 and 9).

However, although the 'social structural' approach allows empirically for different appearances of the childhood phenomenon, it remains, at heart, committed to a global more than a localized conception of the child. Indeed, it is from this level of empirical plenitude that it derives its persuasive strength and political impact. Internationally there are lots of children; they are a global phenomenon. And, as we have seen, we can begin to make comparative statements about nation-states according to the provision made for this substantial segment of their citizenry. Similarly, if childhood constitutes a coherent, recognizable status of personhood, then children can claim a strong sense of identity with each other; they are recognizable internally and can experience the solidarity that derives from a recognition of a shared location in the social structure.

This discourse allows clear parallels to be drawn, for example, between childhood and social class, prefigured in the early Marxist feminist perspective of seeing women as a social class. In such a view children's structural difference is subject to structural differentiation. Similarly, children have to be understood in relation to socioeconomic factors, in relation to the public and the private, to their relative exercise of power and to the social facilitation of their unique intent, either as a group or as individuals:

> I think there is a case for saying that adult–child relations are relations of production in which the labour of one class (children) is exploited by another (adults). It is a big claim to make, but amounts to saying that the quality of life enjoyed by adults is enhanced by their control over the process of growing up that constitutes the activities of childhood, and that the quality of life for children as they grow up is therefore reduced. This is the nature of the exploitation of one class by another. (Oldman 1994: 163)

In summary, then, discourses centred around 'the social structural child' claim childhood as a generalizable category, an enduring (though changing) feature of the social structure of any society and one which is universal, global and in possession of a recognizable identity.

The minority group child

Moving to our second discourse, that of the 'minority group child', in many senses what we see is an embodiment of the empirical and politicized version of the 'social structural child'. Within this mode of discourse, childhood is also understood as a universal category in relation to its rights, qualities of personhood and status identity. An early manifesto for the 'minority group child' was proposed by Holt, who stated:

> Only in recent years did I begin to wonder whether there might be other or better ways for young people to live. By now I have come to feel that the fact of being a 'child', of being wholly subservient and dependent, of being seen by older people as a mixture of expensive nuisance, slave, and super-pet, does most young people more harm

than good. I propose instead that the rights, privileges, duties, responsibilities of adult citizens be made *available* to any young person, of whatever age, who wants to make use of them. (1975: 15)

This mode recognizes that children are structurally differentiated within societies and that, as such, they experience the exercise of power differently, and in particular in its institutionalized and legitimated forms. It is also taken as basic that such children have their needs and rights variously ascribed and constricted according to the dominant paternalistic ideologies, albeit activated for 'good' and 'caring' reasons:

> concepts of rights were originally based on values of rationality, independence and freedom. Since these characteristics are identified with adulthood rather than with childhood, they contribute to common assumptions that children should be denied civil rights; instead the child's need for protection is usually emphasized. (Alderson 1993: 45)

Similarly, from a sociolegal perspective, Roche has argued that:

> a commitment to children's rights requires a respect on the part of the majority (adult) traditions to the different lives led by our children and their different, and at times awkward, voices in the private as well as the public world. There will be inconsistent stories. Such new conversations will be difficult because, despite the cosiness of the word, they do not take place between equals and because in this postmodern world our traditional reference points of right and wrong have been eroded. (1996: 37)

And considering the growing discrepancy between our gradually more enlightened views on the minority group status of children and their policy provision, Masson has stated that: 'There remains a wide gulf between the view that young people mature and can become independent before their majority and the practical reality of dependence constructed by a shift of state resources away from this age group' (1995: 229).

As a status that inhabits all societies, 'minority group' childhood is also conceived of as a universal experience. Globally, all children are to different degrees exploited, and their human rights are underexpressed and inappropriately exercised. Empirically this occurs across a spectrum of degrees of liberation, marked by differences of gender and ethnicity, for example. But a group pronounced as 'minority' cannot publicize such internal stratifications without thereby weakening the solidarity of its newly demarcated groupness, as became clear in the early days of feminism: black working-class women probably had more in common structurally with black working-class men than they did with white middle-class women.

This parallel is not unintentional: whereas 'the social structural child' claims metaphorical (and more substantive) links with the analysis of social class, 'the minority group child' can be seen in relief alongside the women's movement. It, too, is subject to processes of discrimination that are hierarchically distributed through gender and through age. Thus, as befits a group that is claiming a difference from the mainstream of society and a marginal status, the discourse associated with the 'minority group child' also has a political constancy, although this is not to downplay its active role in advocating change. But a group that needs to become for-itself rather than merely in-itself has to be understood, analytically, through continuity rather than in terms of an adaptability to change. In this way theorists working from the perspective of 'the minority group child' present childhood as timeless.

In sum, 'the minority group child' approach is universalistic, differentiated and global, and fails to find liberation through the historical process. It sees children as conscious and active beings with a consciousness awaiting mobilization.

The socially constructed child

Our third discourse of childhood is that of the 'socially constructed' child. This child belongs to social structures but without any sense of fixity. But what is outstanding in this formulation of childhood is the commitment to a radical relativism. This statement is not, however, to to be taken as a criticism or dismissal. Rather, this relativism is a considered analytical device to enhance the particular and partial, or perspectival, nature of an understanding of childhood, a refinement of the phenomenological strategy of 'bracketing'. It involves the coupled epistemological practices of returning to the phenomenon itself and then showing how it is constituted or variously established in everyday life. Thus, within the 'socially constructed' child mode of discourse, there is no essential child but always one that is built up through constitutive practices, in either a strong or a weak sense.

A strong sense of the social construction of childhood would be a brand of historicism that sees the child as a product of its time and material conditions, a kind of Marxist child who is determined by its relation to the means of production; the means of parenting; or even the means of educational provision. Stainton-Rogers, for example, captures this sense in his discussion of relative 'social realities':

> There are no hard-and-fast principles for defining when disagreements about how things are seen become significant enough to talk about them as different social realities. However, it is usually assumed that the more distant people are from one another (in terms of historical time, geographical location, culture or class) the more likely they are to have different world views. It is also generally accepted that ideologies imply different social realities, so that Marxists and capitalists 'see the world differently' . . . Contrasted social realities can co-exist within a complex society and even do battle 'inside our own heads'. When social constructionists look at childhood, it is to these different social realities that they turn. (1989: 24)

A weak sense of the social construction of childhood, on the other hand, would be found in the kind of discourse theory which states that the child is brought into being through the dominant modes of speech that exist concerning age, dependency, development (Burman 1994) or the family. For example:

> This concept of discourse goes beyond De Saussure's parole/langue distinction by positing 'discourse' as sets of concepts and the language through which they are thought as inseparable from and fused with social practices and institutions. Ideas, concepts, knowledge, modes of speaking, etc. codify social practices and in turn constitute them. Within these discourses subject positions (such as 'the child') are created. Seen from this point of view, then, different discourses of childhood constitute childhood (and children) in different ways – not only as sets of academic knowledge but also in social practices and institutions. (James and Prout 1990b: 25)

Such work (Jenks 1982b; James and Prout 1990b) falls within the 'social constructionist' framework and was part of a calculated attempt to free the child from the constraints of naturalism by placing childhood squarely in the realm of the culturally located and thus humanly constituted. Through this device alone the child became available for discussion and childhood open to contestation. Multiple discourses and finite structural forces could now be seen to contribute to our collective appreciation of the condition of childhood. Thus, through visibility, these discourses became open to deconstruction and the structural constraint was present for analysis. Finally, within the 'social construction of childhood' mode of discourse, time becomes a critical dimension and permits the very understanding of childhood to be seen as historically contingent.

Thus within this approach our understanding of childhoods is always properly disjunctive; it is always structured, in either a strong or weak fashion but is none the less temporal and susceptible to change. Inevitably, therefore, the 'socially constructed' child is a local rather than a global phenomenon and tends to be extremely particularistic.

The tribal child

Finally we arrive at our fourth discourse of childhood, the one we have referred to as the 'tribal child'. Just as the 'minority group' child stood in a particular relationship to the 'social structural' child, so too the 'tribal child' can, in many senses, be read as the empirical and potentially politicized version of the 'socially constructed' child. We might suppose that, although a metaphoric rather than a strictly descriptive category, this manner of speech about childhood finds its origins in the literature of anthropology from Lucien Lévy-Bruhl, Franz Boas, through Margaret Mead and up until the present day:

> While all cultures have given meaning to physical differences of sex and age, it can be argued that the social worlds in which these physical signs become significant are so profoundly different that we are already doing analytical violence to complex constellations of meanings and practices when we single out notions of male and female or childhood and adulthood and attempt to compare them cross-culturally. These terms already presuppose a world of *Western* cultural assumptions – for example, that sexual or age differences are self-evidently dichotomous and that they define the parameters for exclusive identities. (Stephens 1995: 5–6)

But it also emerges in a dramatic and more populist form in the ethnographic work of the Opies, as chapter 5 explored:

> the folklorist and anthropologist can, without travelling a mile from his door, examine a thriving unself-conscious culture (the word 'culture' is used here deliberately) which is as unnoticed by the sophisticated world, and quite as little affected by it, as the culture of some

dwindling aboriginal tribe living out its helpless existence in the
hinterland of a native reserve . . . As Douglas Newton has pointed
out: 'The world-wide fraternity of children is the greatest of savage
tribes, and the only one which shows no sign of dying out.' (Opie and
Opie 1977: 25)

However, the discourse of the 'tribal' child speaks neither of an
integrated and functional segment of a social system, nor of an
oppressed group within a social structure. Though the 'tribal'
child is inevitably, and to varying degrees, contingent on existing
formations or social realities, it is understood both politically and
analytically in terms of its separateness. But this separateness and
potential insulation is itself achieved; it is not naturally, or even
geronto-cratically, given. Rather, the separateness of the 'tribal'
child is an issue of self-sustaining autonomy and therefore a critical expression of agency over structure. In this sense the Opies'
earlier formulation of a 'culture' of childhood might, after all,
prove to be an important one. 'Tribal' children inhabit a social
category that is, in essence, their own. Their culture is to be regarded as the self-maintaining system of signs, symbols and rituals that prescribes the whole way of life of children within a
particular sociohistorical setting.

Clearly such an understanding derives much from sociological
and anthropological views of culture, rather than those of critical
aesthetics, but the political challenge it presents and the urgency of
its demands for articulation share far more with the concept of a
'subculture' that has mutated through Althusser and Gramsci into
the vocabulary of contemporary Cultural Studies. Thus the independence from the adult world that is presupposed in the
conceptualization of the 'tribal' child offers a potential for resistance to the normalizing effects of age hierarchies, educational
policies, socialization theories and child-rearing practices. Taking
Hall's view of culture/subculture as being 'that level at which
social groups develop distinct patterns of life and give expressive
form to their social and material . . . experience' (Hall et al. 1976:
27) we can also see that the 'tribal' child requires, if not shouts out
for, understanding in its own right. It is not part of a supportive
social pyramid constructed in the worship of the rational adult
world.

Although Cultural Studies eventually absorbed criticism for its
overarching attachment to the adolescent experience, it is not hard
to see how a conceptualization such as subculture is highly appeal-

ing in relation to an understanding of both youth and childhood. As Hebdige put it:

> We can now return to the meaning of youth subcultures, for the emergence of such groups has signalled in a spectacular fashion the breakdown of consensus in the post-war period . . . the challenge to hegemony which subcultures represent is not issued directly by them. Rather it is expressed obliquely in style. The objections are lodged, the contradictions displayed . . . at the profoundly superficial level of appearances: that is, at the level of signs . . . Style in subculture is, then, pregnant with significance. Its transformations go 'against nature', interrupting the process of 'normalization'. As such, they are gestures, movements towards a speech which offends the 'silent majority', which challenges the principle of unity and cohesion, which contradicts the myth of consensus. (1979: 17–18)

The very particularism and thus analytical isolation of the 'tribal' child lends itself to the methods of anthropology and, indeed, we find an almost constant application of the use of ethnography in this kind of work. So, for example, Kelly-Byrne (1989), acting as a babysitter for a considerable period, adopted the research role of participant observer in the play of her charge. This work generated an actively engaged study of a child's play activity from the perspective of the child and thus revealed something of the encoded workings and symbolic exchange of the 'tribe'. And we also find that Buckingham's (1994) analysis of children's culture in relation to the mass media shows that it allows them an autonomy of cultural reception. This frees them from the more obvious and popular views that they are simply and passively prey to the determinacy of adult corruption through film, video and TV (see also Morley 1995).

The persistent emphasis on the particular character of the 'tribal' child and its inevitable refusal to be formulated on a global basis lead to other interesting and demystifying elements within this discourse. 'Tribal' children do not have to fall under the sway of either romantic or Enlightenment fables. Such children may be nasty; brutish; bullies; wholly self-interested or self-absorbed; selfish; pitiless; racist and sexist. These 'tribal' subcultures, not aspiring to stated adult morality, do not have to be 'nice'. Indeed, we learn daily that real children are sexual, and sometimes killers. The 'tribal' child is voluntaristic and particularistic; it exercises a strong sense of self-determinacy and is finitely located in specific times and spaces.

Conclusion

In conclusion, then, we can see how the new social studies of childhood engage variously with the core dichotomies which, as argued earlier, have shaped, and will certainly continue to shape the questions asked and interpretations offered by social scientists. Though the intensity and comprehensiveness of this engagement may vary between researcher and accounts, it is the potential for this address which is important. Approaches which stress children's agency raise different questions about localities and processes of social change than those which favour more structured approaches. The tribal child discourse explores children's agency in different, localized settings, whereas a more social constructionist perspective looks at the conditions for the possibility of those child identities in particular locales. Similarly, ideas about childhood difference and children's identies gain analytic strength when placed alongside questions of structure, agency and globalization. The minority group perspective makes us ask about how children's 'differentness' is actively taken up in a global context; the social structural approach can explore how children's structural position works to shape a universal, but varying, status identity of 'child'.

However, looked at overall, as in figure 2, this diagrammatic representation is not simply tidy and convenient but, we anticipate, useful also. In raising some new questions, or rephrasing old questions in a new light, it also recognizes that in existing theoretical and empirical work there is a possibility for movement across and between these approaches. Thus the 'socially constructed' child and the 'tribal' child often stand in a close relation, collude or even experience elision in the approaches adopted in childhood studies. And an identical fluidity and potential for creativity exists between the 'social structural' child and the 'minority group' child. Movements in the other direction are, however, relatively rare. Thus the 'social structural' child and the 'socially constructed' child are locked in different, and even antagonistic, formulations, as are the 'minority group' child and the 'tribal' child. [2]

Recognizing in this way the overlaps and possible areas of synthesis between approaches is, therefore, to reiterate the intention of this volume: not to close off debate but, on the contrary, to open it up for wider discussion, especially in terms of social theory. It has also been our intention to present a broad account of the different ways in which childhood studies can, through careful theorizing, engage more effectively and incisively with those policy or welfare debates which for so long have shaped the direction of research. The four approaches which we have identified and illustrated through the body of the text represent, then, a platform for future research initiatives and modes of inquiry that might usefully stem from the new social studies of childhood, to combine in the endeavour that is *theorizing childhood*.

Notes

Chapter 1 The Presociological Child

1 We acknowledge none the less that it is inconceivable to achieve a form of speech about the social that is disembodied or context-free.
2 Though the growing divergencies with the idealist Rousseau are in danger of rendering the two philosophers utterly incompatible, despite their different starting points there is a congruence over the learning process.

Chapter 2 The Sociological Child

1 A major commonality between the models can be seen here in terms of the obvious essentialism that their shared positivism brings to bear.
2 In fact, such original phenomenology appeared rather too 'wild' for the standards of British reason but was rendered acceptable through the mediation of Berger and Luckmann (1966) and Schutz (1971).

Chapter 3 Childhood in Social Space

1 We make no apology for focusing on urban childhood here for, with a few exceptions (see Ward 1990; Valentine, forthcoming), relatively little research work has as yet been carried out among 'rural' children in European/North American contexts. But for a discussion of rural childhood elsewhere, see chapter 7.
2 The term 'South' is now commonly accepted terminology for the developing countries. It is taken to exclude countries like Australia and Japan.

Chapter 4 The Temporality of Childhood

1 As La Fontaine (1986) argues, the term 'child' can function as both a kin and status category.
2 The controversy surrounding what has become known as the Gillick case, concerning the provision of contraceptive advice for young people, de-stabilized the notion of age as an index of competence. For a full account see Kennedy (1988).

Chapter 5 Play as Childhood Culture?

1 Corsaro (1992) discusses processes of production and social reproduction in children's peer culture, and pays particular attention to language use.

Chapter 6 Working Children

1 Chattel slavery is marked by the comprehensive rights of ownership of the slave by the slave master; debt bondage arises from the pledging of labour services by a debtor to a creditor by way of guarantee and where these do not go towards the liquidation of the debt or the where the length and nature of these services is not specified; serfdom arises from tenure to land being conditional on the tenant living and labouring on that land, rendering services to the owner but not being able to move away or otherwise change status.

Chapter 7 One Childhood or Many?

1 Again this is a complex question because of the range and diversity of the social contexts in which children might participate. For example, Mayall (1993) suggests that English children experience looking after their health in very different ways at home and at school: the former is negotiative and it is assumed that children have the right to a voice, while the second deals with children as an administrative batch subject to bureaucratic rules. The divide between home and school may be much more varied and complex than this perhaps overdrawn picture implies.
2 It might be argued, for example, that someone is trapped in poverty if they do not have the means to travel for a job interview. This, however, opens up a debate about what is considered acceptable or normal at a particular time. In the UK the most used measure is the level at which an adult (defined for these purposes as over twenty-four?!) becomes eligible for Supplementary Benefit, the most basic level of state social security payments. Political and academic argument over this has led some to argue that even those whose incomes are at 140 per cent of Supplementary Benefit should be counted as poor. In 1988 the UK government decided to stop publishing any statistics on

family income in relation to SB levels; the result has been that a number of independent researchers and research institutes have developed a variety of their own measures.

3 However, it is not clear that all these effects are caused by poverty. Factors such as racial disadvantage and parental divorce are also important. Similarly, in the US it is suggested that long-term effects are compounded of a number of interacting factors which centre on poverty and the life conditions through which it is lived and experienced.

Chapter 8 The Body and Childhood

1 In this view the very category 'biology' is an invention of nineteenth- and twentieth-century thought, not a great, permanent and universal underpinning of human societies. Thus it becomes possible to ask how and why the particular forms and contents of biology came to be made the way they were.

2 Those adults who do not achieve these skills or who in old age lose them risk infantilization, see Hockey and James 1993.

3 Similar examples can be used to show that Euro-American children see racial categories as evaluative when adults deny that this is the case.

Chapter 9 Researching Childhood

1 The recent 'discovery' of childhood by family sociologists has begun to change this picture (Brannen and O'Brien 1996).

2 For an excellent account of ethnographic wok with children see Corsaro (1996).

3 This method involves children taking an active part in the interview process, picking questions out for the interviewer to ask and then 'posting' answers into special boxes predesignated as representing people involved in caring relationships with them.

Chapter 10 Theorizing Childhood

1 This is not to underplay the contribution already made by psychology (see, for example Burman 1994; 1996; Woodhead 1996), social geography (see Sibley 1995; Valentine 1996; forthcoming), history (see Cunningham 1991; Steedman 1995); sociolegal studies (see Freeman 1979) and philosophy (see Archard 1993). Indeed the phrasing 'the new social studies of childhood' endeavours to get round such exclusivity and exclusions.

2 This observation leads us, perhaps, to another level of metatheory – that we may be witnessing an opposition between materialist and idealist positions. Thus the 'social structural' child and the 'minority group' child, being materially based, are less radically opposed to the earlier transitional paradigm of the 'developing' child than are the 'socially constructed' and 'tribal' child. This we have already alluded to in chapter 8.

References

Abdalla, A. (1988) 'Child Labour in Egypt: Leather Tanning in Cairo'. In A. Bequele and J. Boyden (eds), *Combating Child Labour*, Geneva: International Labour Office.

Adam, B. (1990) *Time and Social Theory*, Cambridge: Polity Press.

Alanen, L. (1992) *Modern Childhood: Exploring the 'Child Question' in Sociology*, Research Report 50, University of Jyvaskyla, Finland.

Alderson, P. (1993) *Children's Consent to Surgery*, Buckingham: Open University Press.

Alderson, P. (1995) *Listening to Children: Children, Ethics and Social Research*, London: Barnardo's.

Alderson, P. and Goodey, C. (1996) 'Ethics of Research with Disabled Children', *Children and Society* 10(2): 106–17.

Aldridge, J. and Becker, S. (1993) *Children Who Care: Inside the World of Young Carers*, Loughborough: Department of Social Sciences, Loughborough University.

Allan, G. and Crow, G. (eds) (1989) *Home and Family: Creating the Domestic Space*, London: Macmillan.

Allatt, P. (1993) 'Becoming Privileged: The Role of Family Processes'. In I. Bates and G. Risborough (eds), *Youth and Inequality*, Milton Keynes: Open University Press.

Ambert, A. (1986) 'The Place of Children in North American Sociology'. In P. Alder and P. Alder (eds), *Sociological Studies of Child Development*, Greenwich, Conn.: JAI Press.

Ambert, A. (1995) 'Toward a Theory of Peer Abuse', *Sociological Studies of Children* 7: 177–207.

Amit-Talai, V. (1995) 'The Waltz of Sociability: Intimacy, Dislocation and Friendship in a Quebec High School'. In V. Amit-Talai and H. Wulff (eds), *Youth Cultures: A Cross-Cultural Perspective*, London: Routledge.

Archard, R. (1993) *Children: Rights and Childhood*, London: Routledge.

Archer, L. J. (1988) *Slavery and Other Forms of Unfree Labour*, London: Routledge.

Ariès, P. (1962) *Centuries of Childhood*, London: Cape.

Armstrong, D. (1983) *Political Anatomy of the Body: Medical Knowledge in Britain in the Twentieth Century*, Cambridge: Cambridge University Press.

Armstrong, D. (1986) 'The Invention of Infant Mortality', *Sociology of Health and*

Illness 8: 211–32.

Armstrong, D. (1987) 'Bodies of Knowledge: Foucault and the Problem of Human Anatomy'. In G. Scambler (ed.), *Sociological Theory and Medical Sociology*, London: Tavistock.

Askew, S. and Ross, C. (1988) *Boys Don't Cry*, Milton Keynes: Open University Press.

Atkins, E. et al. (1981) 'The British Birth Cohort: An Account of the Origins, Progress and Results of the National Survey of Health and Development'. In S. A. Mednick and A. E. Baert (eds), *Prospective Longitudinal Research: An Empirical Basis for the Primary Prevention of Psychological Disorders*, Oxford: Oxford University Press.

Baker, R. with Panther-Brick, C. and Todd, A. (1996) 'Methods Used in Research with Street Children in Nepal', *Childhood* 3(2): 171–94

Bateson, G. (1973) *Steps to an Ecology of Mind*, London: Paladin.

Bateson, G. and Mead, M. (1942) *The Balinese Character*, New York: Academy of Sciences.

Bauman, Z. (1987) *Legislators and Interpreters: On Modernity, Postmodernity and Intellectuals*, Cambridge: Polity.

Baxter, P. T. W. and Almagor, V. (eds) (1978) *Age , Generation and Time*, London: Hurst.

Bearison, D. J. (1991) *'They Never Want to Tell You': Children Talk about Cancer*, Cambridge: Harvard University Press.

Beck, U. (1992) *Risk Society*, London: Sage.

Bennett, C. (1994) 'Underclass of '94', *Guardian*, 16 Mar.

Bequele, A. and Boyden, J. (eds) (1988) *Combating Child Labour*, Geneva: International Labour Office.

Berger, P. and Luckmann, T. (1966)*The Social Construction of Reality*, Harmondsworth: Penguin.

Bergman, W. (1992) 'The Problem of Time in Sociology', *Time and Society* 1(1): 81–134.

Bernardi, B. (1985) *Age Class System: Social Institutions and Polities based on Age*, Cambridge: Cambridge University Press.

Bernstein, B. (1967) 'Open Schools – Open Society', *New Society*, 14 Sept., pp. 351–3.

Bernstein, B. (1971) 'On the Classification and Framing of Educational Knowledge'. In M. Young (ed.), *Knowledge and Control*, London: Collier Macmillan.

Bigelow, B. J. and La Gaipa, J.-J. (1980) 'The Development of Friendship Values and Choice' . In H. C. Foot, A. J. Chapman and J. R. Smith (eds), *Friendship and Social Relations in Childhood*, London: John Wiley.

Blackburn, C. (1991) *Poverty and Health: Working with Families*, Milton Keynes: Open University Press.

Bluebond-Langner, M. (1978) *The Private Worlds of Dying Children*, Princeton: Princeton University Press.

Bluebond-Langner, M., Perkel, D. and Goertzel, T. (1991) 'Paediatric Cancer Patients' Peer Relationships: The Impact of an Oncology Camp Experience', *Journal of Psychosocial Oncology* 9(2): 67–80.

Bourdieu, P. (1986) *Distinction*, London: Routledge and Kegan Paul.

Boyden, J. (1990) 'Childhood and the Policy Makers: A Comparative Perspective on the Globalisation of Childhood'. In A. James and A. Prout (eds), *Constructing and Reconstructing Childhood*, Basingstoke: Falmer Press.

224 *References*

Boyden, J. (1991) *Children of the Cities*, London: Zed Books.

Boyden, J. (1994) *The Relationship between Education and Child Work*, Child Rights Series no. 9, Florence: Innocenti Occasional Papers.

Boyden, J. and Myers, W. (1994) *Exploring Alternative Approaches to Combating Child Labour: Case Studies from Developing Countries*, Child Rights Series no. 8, Florence: Innocenti Occasional Papers.

Bradley, B. (1986) *Visions of Infancy*, Cambridge: Polity Press.

Bradshaw, J. (1990) *Child Poverty and Deprivation in the United Kingdom*, Economic Policy Series no. 8, Florence: Innocenti Occasional Papers.

Bradshaw, J., Ditch, J., Holmes, H. and Whiteford, P. (1993) *Support for Children: A Comparison of Arrangements in Fifteen Countries*, London: HMSO.

Brake, M. (1987) *Comparative Youth Culture*, London: Routledge.

Brannen, J. (1995) 'Young People and their Contribution to Household Work', *Sociology* 29(2): 317–38.

Brannen, J. and O'Brien, M. (1995) 'Childhood and the Sociological Gaze: Paradigms and Paradoxes', *Sociology* 29(4): 729–37.

Brannen, J. and O'Brien, M. (eds) (1996) *Children in Families: Research and Policy*, London: Falmer.

Briggs, J. (1986) 'Expecting the Unexpected: Canadian Inuit Training for an Experimental Life-style', paper delivered to the 4th International Conference on Hunting and Gathering Societies, London School of Economics.

Bromley, R. (1988) *Lost Narratives: Popular Fictions, Politics and Recent History*, London: Routledge.

Brown, R. H. (1977) *A Poetic for Sociology: Towards a Logic of Discovery for the Human Sciences*, Cambridge: Cambridge University Press.

Brownlee, H. and McDonald, P. (1993) 'In Search of Poverty and Affluence: An Investigation of Families Living in Two Melbourne Municipalities', Working Paper 10, Australian Institute of Family Study, Melbourne.

Buckingham, D. (1994) 'Television and the Definition of Childhood'. In B. Mayall (ed.), *Children's Childhoods*, London: Falmer.

Buck-Morss, S. (1986) 'The Flaneur, the Sandwichman and the Whore: The Politics of Loitering', *New German Critique* 13(9): 99–142.

Bulmer, M. (ed.) (1977) *Sociological Research Methods*, London: Macmillan.

Burman, E. (1994) *Deconstructing Developmental Psychology*, London: Routledge.

Burman, E. (1996) 'Local, Global or Globalised: Child Development and International Child Rights Legislation', *Childhood* 3(1): 45–66.

Caldwell, J. C. (1982) *The Theory of Fertility Decline*, London: Academic Press.

Carlton, J. (1991) 'The Social Services Perspective', *Children and Society* 5(1): 21–7.

Castells, M. (1977) *The Urban Question*, London: Edward Arnold.

Castells, M. (1978) *City and Power*, London: Macmillan.

Chernin, K. (1983) *Womansize: The Tyranny of Slenderness*, London: The Women's Press.

Chomsky, N. (1965) *Aspects of the Theory of Syntax*, Cambridge, Mass.: MIT Press.

Christensen, P. (1993) 'The Social Construction of Help among Danish Children', *Sociology of Health and Illness* 15(4): 488–502.

Christensen, P. (1997) 'The Cultural Performance of Sickness amongst Danish Schoolchildren', draft Ph.D thesis, Hull University.

Christensen, P. (forthcoming) 'Vulnerable Bodies: Cultural Meanings of Child, Body and Illness'. In A. Prout (ed.), *Childhood and the Body*, London: Macmillan.

Cicourel, A. (1970) 'The Acquisition of Social Structure'. In J. Douglas (ed.), *Understanding Everyday Life*, London: Routledge and Kegan Paul.

Clarke, K. (1985) 'Public and Private Children: Infant Education in the 1820s and 1830s'. In C. Steedman, C. Urwin and V. Walkerdine (eds), *Language, Gender and Childhood*, London: Routledge.

Clifford, J. and Marcus, G. E. (1986) *Writing Culture*, Berkeley: University of California Press.

Cockburn, T. (1995) 'The Devil in the City: Working Class Children in Manchester 1860–1914', paper delivered at the BSA Conference, University of Leicester, 11 Apr.

Connell, R. (1987) *Gender and Power*, Cambridge: Polity Press.

Connolly, M. and Ennew, J. (1996) 'Introduction: Children Out of Place', *Childhood* 3(2): 131–47.

Connolly, P. (1995) 'Boys Will Be Boys? Racism, Sexuality and the Construction of Masculine Identities among Infant Boys'. In J. Holland, M. Blair and S. Sheldon (eds), *Debates and Issues in Feminist Research and Pedagogy*, Clevedon: Multilingual Matters in assoc. Open University Press.

Connolly, P. (forthcoming) 'In Search of Authenticity: Researching Young Children's Perspectives'. In A. Filer, A. Pollard and D. Thiessen (eds), *Pupil Perspectives*, London: Falmer Press.

Cooper, R. and Law, J. (1995) 'Organisation: Proximal and Distal Views'. In S. Bacharach and P. Galiardi (eds), *Research in the Sociology of Organisations*, Greenwich, Conn.: JAI Press.

Cooter, R. (ed.) (1992) *In the Name of the Child: Health and Welfare 1880–1940*, London: Routledge.

Corrigan, P. (1979) *Schooling the Smash Street Kids*, London: Macmillan.

Corsaro, W. A. (1979) ' We're Friends Right? Children's Use of Access Rituals in a Nursery School', *Language in Society* 8: 315–36.

Corsaro, W. A. (1985) *Friendship and Peer Culture in the Early Years*, Norwood, N.J.: Ablex.

Corsaro, W. A. (1992) 'Interpretive Reproduction in Children's Peer Cultures', *Social Psychology Quarterly* 58: 160–77.

Corsaro, W. A. (1996) 'Transitions in Early Childhood: The Promise of Comparative Longitudinal Ethnography'. In R. Jessor, A. Colby and R. A. Shweder (eds), *Ethnography and Human Development*, Chicago: University of Chicago Press.

Coveney, P. (1957) *Poor Monkey*, London: Rockcliff.

Cunningham, H. (1991) *The Children of the Poor: Representations of Childhood since the Seventeenth Century*, Oxford: Blackwell.

Danziger, K. (ed.) (1971) *Readings in Child Socialization*, Oxford: Pergamon.

Davies, B. (1982) *Life in the Classroom and Playground*, London: Routledge and Kegan Paul.

Davies, E. (1972) 'Work Out of Schools', *Education*, 10 Nov.

Dawe, A. (1970) 'The Two Sociologies', *British Journal of Sociology* 21(2): 207–18.

Delamont, S. (1980) *Sex Roles and the School*, London: Methuen.

De Mause, L. (ed.) (1976) *The History of Childhood*, London: Souvenir.

Denscombe, M., Szulc, H., Patrick, C. and Wood, A. (1986) 'Ethnicity and Friendship: The Contrast between Sociometric Research and Fieldwork Observation in Primary School Classrooms', *British Educational Research Journal* 12(3): 221–35.

Denzin, N. (1977) *Childhood Socialization*, San Francisco: Jossey-Bass.

Dingwall, R., Eekelaar, J. and Murray, T. (1986) *The Protection of Children: State Intervention and Family Life*, Oxford: Blackwell.

Donzelot, J. (1980) *The Policing of Families*, London: Hutchinson.

Duncan, G. J. (1994) 'The Economic Environment of Childhood'. In A. C. Huston (ed.), *Children in Poverty*, Cambridge: Cambridge University Press.

Eisenstadt, S. N. (1956) *From Generation to Generation*, New York: Free Press.

Elias, N. (1982) *The Civilizing Process*, Oxford: Blackwell.

Elkin, F. and Handel, G. (1972) *The Child and Society: The Process of Socialization*, New York: Random House.

Ennew, J. (1986) *The Sexual Exploitation of Children*, Cambridge: Polity Press.

Ennew, J. (1994) *Street and Working Children: A Guide to Planning*, London: Save the Children Fund.

Ennew, J. and Milne, B. (eds) (1989) *The Next Generation: Lives of Third World Children*, London: Zed Books

Evans-Pritchard, E. E. (1940) *The Nuer*, Oxford: Oxford University Press.

Fabian, J. (1983) *Time and the Other: How Anthropology Makes its Object*, New York: Columbia University Press.

Field, N. (1995) 'The Child as Labourer and Consumer: The Disappearance of Childhood in Contemporary Japan'. In S. Stephens (ed.), *Children and the Politics of Culture*, Princeton: Princeton University Press.

Fine, G. A. (1987) *With the Boys*, Chicago: Chicago University Press.

Fine, G. A. and Sandstrom, K. L. (1988) *Knowing Children: Participant Observation with Minors*, Qualitative Methods Series, Newbury Park: Sage.

Finkelhor, D. (1979) *Sexually Victimized Children*, New York: Free Press.

Fogelman, K. (ed.) (1983) *Growing Up in Great Britain*, London: Macmillan.

Foley, W. (1974) *A Child in the Forest*, London: British Broadcasting Corporation.

Foot, H. C., Chapman, A. D. and Smith, J. R. (1980) *Friendship and Social Relations in Children*, London: John Wiley.

Foucault, M. (1967) *Madness and Civilization*, London: Tavistock.

Foucault, M. (1974) *The Archaeology of Knowledge*, London: Tavistock.

Foucault, M. (1977) *Discipline and Punish*, London: Penguin.

Foucault, M. (1988) *Politics, Philosophy, Culture*, ed. L. Kritzman, New York: Routledge.

Freeman, M. (1979) *Violence in the Home: A Socio-legal Study*, Farnborough: Gower.

Frones, I. (1994) 'Dimensions of Childhood'. In J. Qvortrup et al. (eds), *Childhood Matters: Social Theory, Practice and Politics*, Aldershot: Avebury.

Frones, I. (1995) 'Gender Revolution: Cohorts, Children and Social Change', paper delivered to the Childhood and Society Seminar, Institute of Education, London.

Furstenberg, F. F. Jr, Brooks-Gunn, J. and Morgan, S. P. (1987) *Adolescent Mothers in Later Life*, Cambridge: Cambridge University Press.

Fyfe, A. (1989) *Child Labour*, Cambridge: Polity Press.

Gamble, R. (1979) *Chelsea Childhood*, London: British Broadcasting Corporation.

Garbarino, J. and Gilliam, G. (1980) *Understanding Abusive Families*, Cambridge, Mass.: Lexington Books.

Geertz, C. (1975) *The Interpretation of Culture*, London: Hutchinson.

Geertz, C. (1983) *Local Knowledge: Further Essays in Interpretive Anthropology*, New York: Basic Books.

Gell, A. (1992) *The Anthropology of Time*, Oxford: Berg.

Gellert, E. (1962) 'Children's Conceptions of the Content and Function of the Human Body', *Genetic Psychology Monograph* 65: 293–405.

Giddens, A. (1984) *The Constitution of Society: Outline of a Theory of Structuration*, Cambridge: Polity Press.

Giddens, A. (1991) *Modernity and Self-Identity*, Cambridge: Polity Press.

Gilbert, N. (ed.) (1993) *Researching Social Life*, London: Sage.

Glauser, B. (1990) 'Street Children: Deconstructing a Construct'. In A. James and A.Prout (eds), *Constructing and Reconstructing Childhood: Contemporary Issues in the Sociological Study of Childhood*, London: Falmer.

Golding, W. (1958) *Lord of the Flies: A Novel*, London: Faber.

Goodnow, J. (1988) 'Children's Household Work: Its Nature and Functions', *Psychological Bulletin* 103(1): 5–26.

Goslin, D. (ed.) (1969) *Handbook of Socialization Theory and Research*, Chicago: Rand McNally.

Gottlieb, J. and Leyser, Y. (1981) 'Friendship between Mentally Retarded and Non Retarded Children'. In S. R. Asher and J. M. Gottman (eds), *The Development of Children's Friendships*, Cambridge: Cambridge University Press.

Grint, K. (1991) *The Sociology of Work: An Introduction*, Cambridge: Polity Press.

Grugeon, E. (1988) 'Children's Oral Culture: A Transitional Experience'. In M. Maclure, T. Phillips and A. Wilkinson (eds), *Oracy Matters*, Milton Keynes: Open University Press.

Hall, C. (1985) 'Private Persons versus Public Someones: Class, Gender and Politics in England, 1780–1850'. In C. Steedman, C. Urwin and V. Walderine (eds), *Language, Gender and Childhood*, London: Routledge.

Hall, S., Clarke, J., Jefferson, P. and Roberts, B. (1976) *Resistance through Rituals*, London: Hutchinson.

Hallden, G. (1991) 'The Child as a Project and the Child as Being: Parents' Ideas as Frames of Reference', *Childhood and Society* 5(94): 334–56.

Hallden, G. (1992a) 'Establishing Order: Small Girls Write about Family Life', Working Paper 2, Department of Education, Stockholm University.

Hallden, G. (1992b) 'Man Alone or Parallel Lives: Small Boys Write about Family Life', Working Paper 3, Department of Education, Stockholm University.

Hallden, G. (1994) 'The Family – a Refuge from Demands or an Arena for the Exercise of Power and Control – Children's Fictions on their Future Families'. In B. Mayall (ed.), *Children's Childhoods*, London: Falmer.

Hallinan, M. (1981) 'Recent Advances in Sociometry'. In S. R. Asher and J. M. Gottman (eds), *The Development of Children's Friendships*, Cambridge: Cambridge University Press.

Hammersley, M. and Woods, P. (eds) (1984) *Life in School*, Milton Keynes: Open University Press.

Hanssen, E. (1996) 'Finding Care on the Street: Processes in the Careers of Sri Lankan Street Boys', *Childhood* 3(2): 247–60.

Hardman, C. (1973) 'Can There Be an Anthropology of Children?' *Journal of the Anthropology Society of Oxford* 4(1): 85–99.

Hardman, C. (1974) 'Fact and Fantasy in the Playground', *New Society*, 26 Sept.

Hassard, J. (ed.) (1990) *The Sociology of Time*, London: Macmillan.

Hastrup, K. (1987) 'Fieldwork amongst Friends: Ethnographic Exchange within the Northern Civilisation'. In A. Jackson (ed.), *Anthropology at Home*, London: Tavistock.

Hebdige, D. (1979) *Subculture: The Meaning of Style*, London: Methuen.

Hebdige, D. (1990) 'Introduction' to 'Subjects in Space', special edition, *New Formations* 11.

Hendrick, H. (1990) 'Constructions and Reconstructions of British Childhood: An Interpretive Survey, 1800 to the Present'. In A. James and A. Prout (eds), *Constructing and Reconstructing Childhood*, London: Falmer Press.

Henshall, C. and McGuire, J. (1986) 'Gender Development'. In M. Richards and P. Light (eds), *Children of Social Worlds*, Cambridge: Polity Press.

Hernandez. D. J. (1994) 'Children's Changing Access to Resources: A Historical Perspective', *Social Policy Report (Society for Research in Child Development)* 8(1): 16–17.

Hill, M., Laybourn, A. and Borland, M. (1996) 'Engaging with Primary-Aged Children about their Emotions and Well-Being', *Children and Society* 10(2): 129–44.

Hillman, M., Adams, J. and Whitelegg, J. (1990) *One False Move: A Study of Children's Independent Mobility*, London: Policy Studies Institute.

Hindess, B. (1973) *The Use of Official Statistics in Sociology: A Critique of Positivism and Ethnomethodology*, London: Macmillan.

Hobbs, S., Lavalette, M. and McKechnie, J. (1992) 'The Emerging Problem of Child Labour', *Critical Social Policy* 12(1): 93–105.

Hochschild, A. (1983) *The Managed Heart: Commercialisation of Human Feeling*, Berkeley: University of California Press.

Hockey, J. and James, A. (1993) *Growing Up and Growing Old*, London: Sage.

Holt, J. (1975) *Escape from Childhood*, Harmondsworth: Penguin.

Hood, S., Kelley, P. and Mayall, B. (1996) 'Children as Research Subjects: A Risky Enterprise', *Children and Society* 10(2): 117–29.

Howell, S. (1987) 'From Child to Human: Chewong Concepts of Self'. In G. Jahoda and I. M. Lewis (eds), *Acquiring Culture*, London: Croom Helm.

Hunter, A. (ed.) (1990) *The Rhetoric of Social Research Understood and Believed*, New Brunswick, N.J.: Rutgers University Press.

Huston, A. C. (ed.) (1994) *Children in Poverty*, Cambridge: Cambridge University Press.

Hutson, S. (1995) 'Children without Families? Young Homeless People and Young People from Care Talking'. In J. Brannen and M. O'Brien (eds), *Childhood and Parenthood: Proceedings of ISA Committee for Family Research Conference on Children and Families, 1994*, London: Institute of Education.

Inglis, I. (1978) *Sins of the Fathers*, London: Peter Owen.

Ivy, M. (1995) 'Have You Seen Me? Recovering the Inner Child in Late Twentieth-Century America'. In S. Stephens (ed.), *Children and the Politics of Culture*, Princeton: Princeton University Press.

James, A. (1979) 'Confections, Concoctions and Conceptions', *Journal of the Anthropology Society of Oxford* 10(2): 83–95.

James, A. (1983) 'The Structure and Experience of Childhood and Adolescence: An Anthropological Approach to Socialization', Ph.D thesis, Durham University.

James, A. (1986) 'Learning to Belong: The Boundaries of Adolescence'. In A. P. Cohen (ed.), *Symbolising Boundaries*, Manchester: Manchester University Press.

James, A. (1993) *Childhood Identities: Self and Social Relationships in the Experience of the Child*, Edinburgh: Edinburgh University Press.

James, A. (1995a) 'On Being a Child: The Self, the Group and the Category'. In A. P. Cohen and N. Rapport (eds), *Questions of Consciousness*, London: Routledge.

James, A. (1995b) 'Talking of Children and Youth: Language, Socialization and Culture'. In V. Amit-Talai and H. Wulff (eds), *Youth Cultures: A Cross-Cultural Perspective*, Routledge: London.

James, A., Hockey, J. and Dawson, A. (eds) (1997) *After Writing Culture*, London: Routledge.

James, A. and Jenks, C. (1996) 'Public Perceptions of Childhood Criminality', *British Journal of Sociology* 47(2): 315–31.

James, A. and Prout, A. (1990a) 'Re-presenting Childhood: Time and Transition in the Study of Childhood'. In A. James and A. Prout (eds), *Constructing and Reconstructing Childhood*, Basingstoke: Falmer Press

James, A. and Prout, A. (eds) (1990b) *Constructing and Reconstructing Childhood*, Basingstoke: Falmer Press.

James, A. and Prout, A. (1995) 'Hierarchy, Boundary and Agency: Toward a Theoretical Perspective on Childhood'. In A. Ambert (ed.), *Sociological Studies of Childhood* 7: 77–101

James, A. and Prout, A. (1996) 'Strategies and Structures: Towards a New Perspective on Children's Experiences of Family Life'. In J. Brannen and M. O'Brien (eds), *Children and Families: Research and Policy*, London: Falmer Press.

Jenkins, R. (1983) *Lads, Citizens and Ordinary Kids*, London: Routledge and Kegan Paul.

Jenks, C. (1982a) 'Constituting the Child'. In C. Jenks (ed.), *The Sociology of Childhood: Essential Readings*, London: Batsford.

Jenks, C. (ed.) (1982b) *The Sociology of Childhood – Essential Readings*, London: Batsford.

Jenks, C. (1989) 'Social Theorizing and the Child: Constraints and Possibilities'. In S. Doxiadis (ed.), *Early Influences Shaping the Individual*, NATO Advanced Studies Workshop, London: Plenum.

Jenks, C. (ed.) (1993) *Cultural Reproduction*, London: Routledge.

Jenks, C. (1994) 'Child Abuse in the Post-modern Context: An Issue of Social Identity', *Childhood* 2(4): 111–21.

Jenks, C. (1995a) 'Decoding Childhood'. In P. Atkinson, B. Davies and S. Delamont (eds), *Discourse and Reproduction: Essay in Honour of Basil Bernstein*, Cresskill N.J.: Hampton.

Jenks, C. (1995b) 'Watching your Step: The History and Practice of the Flaneur'. In C. Jenks (ed.), *Visual Culture*, London: Routledge.

Jenks, C. (1996a) *Childhood*, London: Routledge.

Jenks, C. (1996b) 'The Postmodern Child'. In J. Brannen and M. O'Brien (eds), *Children and Families: Research and Policy*, London: Falmer Press.

Jenks, C. (ed.) (forthcoming) *Core Sociological Dichotomies*, London: Sage.

Jobling, M. (1978) 'Child Abuse: The Historical and Social Context'. In V. Carver (ed.), *Child Abuse: A Study Text*, Milton Keynes: Open University Press.

Johnson, V., Hill, J. and Ivan-Smith, E. (1995) *Listening to Smaller Voices: Children in an Environment of Change*, London: Action Aid.

Justice, J. (1986) *Policies, Plans and People: Culture, Health and Development in Nepal*, Berkeley: University of California Press.

Kanbargi, R. (1988) 'Child Labour in India: The Carpet Industry of Varanasi'. In A. Bequele and J. Boyden (eds), *Combating Child Labour*, Geneva: International Labour Office.

Karp, J. (1996) 'Caste-Iron Certitude: Rehabilitation Scheme Takes Aim at Feudalism', *Far Eastern Economic Review* 159(10): 57–8.

Kefyalew, F. (1996) 'The Reality of Child Participation in Research: Experience from a Capacity Building Programme', *Childhood* 3(2): 203–14.

Kelly-Byrne, D. (1989) *A Child's Play Life: An Ethnographic Study*, New York: Teachers College Press.

Kempe, C. et al. (1962) 'The Battered Child Syndrome', *Journal of the American Medical Association* 181: 17–24.

Kempe, R. and Kempe, C. (1978) *Child Abuse*, London: Fontana.

Kennedy, I. (1988) *Treat Me Right*, Oxford: Clarendon Press.

Kennedy, S., Whiteford, P. and Bradshaw, J. (1996) 'The Economic Circumstances of Children In Ten Countries'. In J. Brannen and M. O'Brien (eds), *Children in Families*, London: Falmer.

Kovarik, J. (1994) 'The Space and Time of Children at the Interface of Psychology and Sociology'. In J. Qvortrup et al. (eds), *Childhood Matters: Social Theory, Practice and Politics*, Aldershot: Avebury.

Kuhn, T. (1970) *The Structure of Scientific Revolutions*, Chicago: University of Chicago Press.

La Fontaine, J. (1986) 'An Anthropological Perspective on Children in Social Worlds'. In M. Richards and P. Light (eds), *Children of Social Worlds*, Cambridge: Polity Press.

Lakoff, G. and Johnson, M. (1980) *Metaphors We Live By*, Chicago: University of Chicago Press.

Laing, R. D. (1978) *Conversations with Children*, London: Penguin.

Lansdown, G. (1994) 'Researching Children's Rights to Integrity'. In B. Mayall (ed.), *Children's Childhood: Observed and Experienced*, London: Falmer Press.

Latour, B. (1993) *We Have Never Been Modern*, Hemel Hempstead: Harvester / Wheatsheaf.

Lavalette, M. (1994) *Child Employment in the Capitalist Labour Market*, Aldershot: Avebury.

Lee, N. (1995) 'Judgement, Responsibility and Generalised Constructivism', paper delivered to the Conference on The Labour of Division, Centre for Social Theory and Technology, Keele University, Nov.

Lever, J. (1976) 'Sex Differences in the Games Children Play', *Social Problems* 23: 478–87.

Le Vine, R. et al. (1994) *Child Care and Culture: Lessons from Africa*, Cambridge: Cambridge University Press.

Lewis, J. (1986) 'Anxieties about the Family and the Relationship between Parents, Children and the State in Twentieth Century England'. In M. Richards and P. Light (eds), *Children of Social Worlds*, Cambridge: Polity Press.

Lowe, G., Foxcroft, D. and Sibley, D. (1993) *Adolescent Drinking and Family Life*, Reading: Hardwood Academic.

Mackay, R. (1973) 'Conceptions of Children and Models of Socialisation'. In H. P. Dreitzel (ed.), *Childhood and Socialisation*, London: Macmillan.

MacLennan, E. et al. (1985) *Working Children*, London: Low Pay Unit.

McNamee, S. (forthcoming) 'Youth, Gender and Video Games: Power and Control in the Home'. In G. Valentine and T. Skelton (eds), *Geographies of Youth Culture*, London: Routledge.

McRobbie, A. and Garber, J. (1976) 'Girls and Subcultures'. In J. Clarke, S. Hall, T. Jefferson and B. Roberts (eds), *Resistance Through Rituals*, London: Hutchinson.

Mandell, N. (1991) 'The Least-Adult Role in Studying Children'. In F. Waksler (ed.), *Studying the Social Worlds of Children*, London: Falmer Press.

Massey, D. (1984) *Spatial Divisions of Labour*, London: Macmillan.

Masson, J. (1995) 'The Children's Act 1989 and Young People: Dependence and Rights to Independence'. In J. Brannen and M. O'Brien (eds), *Childhood and Parenthood*, London: Institute of Education.

Matthews, M. H. (1992) *Making Sense of Place: Children's Understanding of Large-Scale Environments*, Hemel Hempstead: Harvester Wheatsheaf.

Mauss, M. (1973) 'Techniques of the Body' (1934), *Economy and Society* 2: 70–88.

Mayall, B. (1993) 'Keeping Healthy at Home and School: It's my Body So It's my Job', *Sociology of Health and Illness* 15(4): 464–87.

Mayall, B. (1994a) *Negotiating Health: School Children at Home and at School*, London: Cassell.

Mayall, B. (ed.) (1994b) *Children's Childhoods: Observed and Experienced*, London: Falmer.

Mayall, B. (1995) 'Children as a Minority Group: Issues and Prospects', paper presented to the Seminar on Childhood and Society, Institute of Education, London.

Mayall, B. (1996) *Children, Health and the Social Order*, Buckingham: Open University Press.

Mayer, P. (ed.) (1970) *Socialisation: The Approach from Social Anthropology*, London: Tavistock.

Mayes, G., Currie, E., Macleod, K., Gilles, J. and Warden, D. (1992) *Child Sexual Abuse*, Edinburgh: Scottish Academic Press.

Mayhew, H. (1985) *London Labour and the London Poor* (1861), Harmondsworth: Penguin.

Mead, M. (1978) *Culture and Commitment*, Garden City, N.Y.: Anchor.

Mead, M. and Wolfenstein, M. (1954) *Childhood in Contemporary Cultures*, Chicago: Chicago University Press.

Measor, L. and Woods, P. (1984) *Changing Schools: Pupil Perspectives on Transfer to a Comprehensive School*, Milton Keynes: Open University Press.

Merleau-Ponty, M. (1964) *The Primacy of Perception*, Chicago: Northwestern University Press.

Miles, M. and Harvey, D. (1991) 'Paediatricians and the Children Act', *Children and Society* 5(1): 34–9.

Mills, C. Wright (1943) 'The Professional Ideology of Social Pathologists', *American Journal of Sociology* 49(2): 904–13.

Morley, D. (1995) 'Television: Not So Much a Visual Medium, More a Visual Object'. In C. Jenks (ed.), *Visual Culture*, London: Routledge.

Morris, L. (1990) *The Workings of the Household*, Cambridge: Polity Press.

Morrison, A. and McIntyre, D. (1971) *Schools and Socialization*, Harmondsworth: Penguin.

Morrow, V. (1994) 'Responsible Children? Aspects of Children's Work and Employment outside School in Contemporary UK'. In B. Mayall (ed.), *Children's Childhoods: Observed and Experienced*, London: Falmer.

Morrow, V. (1995) 'Invisible Children? Toward a Reconceptualisation of Childhood Dependency and Responsibility'. In A. Ambert (ed.), *Sociological Studies of Childhood* 7: 207–31.

Morrow, V. and Richards, M. (1996) 'The Ethics of Social Research with Children: An Overview', *Children and Society* 10(2): 90–105.

Morss, J. (1990) *The Biologising of Childhood: Developmental Psychology and the Darwinian Myth*, London: Lawrence Erlbaum.

Munday, E. (1979) 'When is a Child a "Child"? Alternative Systems and Classification', *Journal of the Anthropology Society of Oxford* 10(3): 161–72.

Musgrave, P. W. (1987) *Socialising Contexts: The Subject in Society*, London: Allen and Unwin.

Myers, R. (1992) *The Twelve Who Survive: Strengthening Programmes of Early Child Care and Development in the Third World*, London: Routledge/UNESCO.

Nasman, E. (1994) 'Individualisation and Institutionalisation of Childhood in Today's Europe'. In J. Qvortrup, M. Bardy, G. Sgritta and H. Wintersberger (eds), *Childhood Matters*, Aldershot: Avebury.

Newson, J. and Newson, E (1976) *Seven Years Old in the Home Environment*, London: Allen and Unwin.

Nichols, T. (1992) 'Different Forms of Labour'. In *Work, Employment and Society* 6 (1): 135–46.

Nieuwenhuys, O. (1994) *Children's Life Worlds: Gender, Welfare and Labour in the Developing World*, London: Routledge.

Oakley, A. (1994) 'Women and Children First and Last: Parallels and Differences between Women's and Children's Studies'. In B. Mayall (ed.), *Children's Childhoods: Observed and Experienced*, London: Falmer.

O'Brien, M. (1991) 'Allocation of Resources in Households: A Child's Perspective', paper presented to the European Commission Conference on Children, Family and Society, Luxemburg.

Okely, J. and Calloway, H. (eds) (1992) *Anthropology and Autobiography*, London: Routledge.

Oldman, D. (1994) 'Childhood as a Mode of Production'. In B. Mayall (ed.), *Children's Childhoods: Observed and Experienced*, London: Falmer.

O'Neill, J. (1973) 'Embodiment and Child Development: A Phenomenological Approach'. In H. P. Dreitzel (ed.), *Recent Sociology 5*, New York: Collier.

O'Neill, J. (1994) *The Missing Child in Liberal Theory*, Toronto: University of Toronto Press.

O'Neill, J. (1995) 'On the Liberal Culture of Child Risk: A Covenant Critique of Contractarian Theory'. In A. Ambert (ed.), *Sociological Studies of Children, Volume 7*: Greenwich, Conn.: JAI Press.

Opie, I. and Opie, P. (1969) *Children's Games in Street and Playground*, Oxford: Oxford University Press.

Opie, I. and Opie, P. (1977) *The Lore and Language of Schoolchildren* (1959), Oxford: Oxford University Press.

Orbach, S. (1988) *Fat is a Feminist Issue*, London: Arrow Books.

Osborne, A. F., Butler, N. R. and Moulis, A. C. (1984) *The Social Life of Britain's Five Year Olds*, London: Routledge and Kegan Paul.

Pahl, R. E. (1984) *Divisions of Labour*, Oxford: Blackwell.

Parsons, T. (1951) *The Social System*, London: Routledge and Kegan Paul.

Parton, N. (1985) *The Politics of Child Abuse*, London: Macmillan.

Pattison, R. (1978) *The Child Figure in English Literature*, Athens: University of Georgia Press.

Piaget, J. (1972) *Psychology and Epistemology* (1927), trans. P. Wells, Harmondsworth: Penguin.

Pickvance, C. (1985) 'The Rise and Fall of Political Movements and the Role of Comparative Analysis', *Environment and Planning. D. Society and Space* 3: 31–53.

Place, B. (forthcoming) 'The Constructing of Bodies of Critically Ill Children: An Ethnography of Intensive Care'. In A. Prout (ed.), *Childhood and the Body*, London: Macmillan.

Plummer, K. (1983) *Documents of Life*, London: Allen and Unwin.

Pollard, A. (1985) *The Social World of the Primary School*, London: Holt, Rhinehart and Winston.

Pollard, A. and Filer, A. (1996) *The Social World of Children's Learning*, London: Cassell.

Pollock, L. (1983) *Forgotten Children: Parent–Child Relations 1500–1900*, Cambridge: Cambridge University Press.

Pond, C. and Searle, A. (1991) *The Hidden Army: Children at Work in the 1980s*, London: Low Pay Unit.

Postman, N. (1982) *The Disappearance of Childhood*, New York: Delacotte Press.

Prendergast, S. (1992) *'This is the Time to Grow Up': Girls' Experiences of Menstruation in School'*, Cambridge: Health Promotion Trust.

Prendergast, S. (1995)'The Spaces of Childhood: Psyche, Soma and the Social Existence. Menstruation and Embodiment at Adolescence'. In J. Brannen and M. O'Brien (eds), *Childhood and Parenthood*, London: Institute of Education.

Prout, A. (1987) 'An Analytical Ethnography of Sickness Absence in an English Primary School' Ph.D thesis, Keele University.

Prout, A. (1989) 'Sickness as a Dominant Symbol in Life Course Transitions: An Illustrated Theoretical Framework', *Sociology of Health and Illness*11(4): 336–59.

Prout, A. (1992) 'Work, Time and Sickness in the Lives of Schoolchildren'. In R. Frankenberg (ed.), *Time, Health and Medicine*, London: Sage.

Prout, A. (1996) 'Objective vs Subjective Indicators or Both? Whose Perspective Counts? Or the Distal, the Proximal and Circuits of Knowledge', paper delivered to the Workshop on Monitoring and Measuring the State of the Children – Beyond Survival, Jerusalem.

Putallaz, M. and Gotman, J. M. (1981) 'Social Skills and Group Acceptance'. In S. R. Asher and J. M. Gottman (eds), *The Development of Children's Friendships*, Cambridge: Cambridge University Press.

Qvortrup, J. (1990) 'A Voice for Children in Statistical and Social Accounting: A Plea for Children's Right to be Heard'. In A. James and A. Prout (eds), *Constructing and Reconstructing Childhood*, Basingstoke: Falmer Press.

Qvortrup, J. (ed.) (1993) *Childhood as a Social Phenomenon: Lessons from an International Project*, Eurosocial Report 47, Vienna: European Centre.

Qvortrup, J. (1994) 'Childhood Matters: An Introduction'. In J. Qvortrup et al. (eds), *Childhood Matters*, Aldershot: Avebury.

Qvortrup, J. (1995a) 'Childhood and Modern Society: A Paradoxical Relationship'. In J. Brannen and M. O'Brien (eds), *Childhood and Parenthood: Proceedings of ISA Committee for Family Research Conference on Children and Families, 1994*, London: Institute of Education.

Qvortrup, J. (1995b) 'From Useful to Useful: The Historical Continuity of Children's Constructive Participation'. In A. Ambert (ed.), *Sociological Studies of Children, Volume 7*, Greenwich, Conn.: JAI Press.

Qvortrup, J., Bardy, M., Sgritta, G. and Wintersberger, H. (eds) (1994) *Childhood Matters: Social Theory, Practice and Politics*, Aldershot: Avebury.

Rapport, N. (1993) *Diverse World Views in an English Village*, Edinburgh: Edinburgh University Press.

Reynolds, P. (1989) *Children in Cross-Roads: Cognition and Society in South Africa*, Claremont: David Phillip.

Reynolds, P. (1996) *Traditional Healers and Childhood in Zimbabwe*, Ohio: Ohio University Press.

Reynolds, V. (1974) 'Can There Be an Anthropology of Children? A Reply', *Journal of the Anthropological Society of Oxford* 5(1): 32–8.

Richards, M. and Light, P. (eds) (1986) *Children of Social Worlds*, Cambridge: Polity Press.

Riches, P. (1991)'The New Children Act: An Overview', *Children and Society* 5(1): 3–10.

Ritchie, O. and Kollar, M. (1964) *The Sociology of Childhood*, New York: Appleton Century Crofts.

Rival, L. (1993) 'State Schools against Forest Life: The Impact of Formal Education on the Huaorani of Amazonian Ecuador', mimeo.

Robertson, P. (1976) 'Home as a Nest: Middle Class Childhood in Nineteenth Century Europe'. In L. de Mause (ed.), *The History of Childhood*, London: Souvenir.

Roche, J. (1996) 'The Politics of Children's Rights'. In J. Brannen and M. O'Brien (eds), *Children and Families*, London: Falmer.

Rogers, G. and Standing, G. (eds) (1981) *Child Work, Poverty and Underdevelopment*, Geneva: International Labour Office.

Rose, N. (1989) *Governing the Soul*, London: Routledge.

Rutherford, F. (1971) *All the Way to Pennywell*, Durham: Institute of Education.

Said, E. (1986) *The Author, the Text and the Critic*, London: Faber.

Salazar, C. (1988) 'Child Labour in Colombia: Bogota's Quarries and Brickyards'. In A. Bequele and J. Boyden (eds) (1988) *Combating Child Labour*, Geneva: International Labour Office.

Samuel, R. (1994) *Theatres of Memory: Past and Present in Contemporary Culture*, London: Verso.

Saporiti, A. (1994) 'A Methodology for Making Children Count'. In J. Qvortrup et al. (eds), *Childhood Matters*, Aldershot: Avebury.

Save the Children Fund (1995) *Towards a Children's Agenda*, London: Save the Children Fund.

Sawyer, R. (1988) *Children Enslaved*, London: Routledge.

Schildkrout, E. (1978) 'Roles of Children in Urban Kano'. In J. La Fontaine (ed.), *Age and Sex as Principles of Social Differentiation*, London: Academic.

Schildkrout, E. (1980) 'Children's Work Reconsidered', *International Social Science Journal* 32(3): 479–89.

Schutz, A. (1971) *Collected Papers*, vol. 1, The Hague: Martinus Nijhoff.

Schwartz, T. (1976) 'Relations among Generations in Time-Limited Cultures'. In T. Schwartz (ed.), *Socialisation as Cultural Communication*, London: University of California Press.

Schwartzman, H. B. (1978) *Transformations: The Anthropology of Children's Play*, New York: Plenum.

Sennett, R. (1993) *The Fall of Public Man*, London: Faber.

Sgritta, G. B. and Saporiti, A. (1989) 'Myth and Reality in the Discovery and Representation of Childhood'. In P. Close (ed.), *Family Division and Inequalities in Modern Society*, London: Macmillan.

Sharp, R. and Green, A. (1975) *Educational and Social Control: A Study of Progressive Primary Education*, London: Routledge and Kegan Paul.

Sheridan, A. (1980) *Foucault: The Will to Truth,* London: Tavistock.

Shilling, C. (1993) *The Body and Social Theory,* London: Sage.

Shipman, M. (1972) *Childhood: A Sociological Perspective,* Slough: National Foundation for Educational Research.

Sibley, D. (1995) 'Families and Domestic Routines: Constructing the Boundaries of Childhood'. In S. Pile and N. Thrift (eds), *Mapping the Subject: Geographies of Cultural Transformation,* London: Routledge.

Sklair, L. (1991) *The Sociology of the Global System,* Hemel Hempstead: Harvester Wheatsheaf.

Slukin, A. (1981) *Growing Up in the Playground,* London: Routledge and Kegan Paul.

Smith, N. and Katz, C. (1993) 'Grounding Metaphor: Towards a Spatialized Politics'. In M. Keith and S. Pile (eds), *Place and the Politics of Identity,* London: Routledge.

Solberg, A. (1990) 'Negotiating Childhood: Changing Constructions of Age for Norwegian Children'. In A. James and A. Prout (eds), *Constructing and Reconstructing Childhood,* Basingstoke: Falmer Press.

Solberg, A. (1994) *Negotiating Childhood: Empirical Investigations and Textual Representations of Children's Work and Everyday Lives,* Stockholm: Nordic Institute for Studies in Urban and Regional Planning.

Song, M. (1996) '"Helping Out": Children's Labour Participation in Chinese Take-Away Businesses in Britain'. In J. Brannen, J. and M. O'Brien (eds), *Children and Families: Research and Policy,* London: Falmer Press.

Speier, M. (1970) 'The Everyday World of the Child'. In J. Douglas (ed.), *Understanding Everyday Life,* London: Routledge and Kegan Paul.

Stadum, B. (1995) 'The Dilemma in Saving Children from Child Labor: Reform and Casework at Odds with Families' Needs', *Child Welfare* 74: 33–55.

Stafford, C. (1995) *The Roads of Chinese Childhood: Learning and Identification in Angang,* Cambridge: Cambridge University Press.

Stainton-Rogers, R. (1989) 'The Social Construction of Childhood'. In W. Stainton-Rogers, D. Harvey and E. Ash (eds), *Child Abuse and Neglect,* London: Open University Press.

Stainton-Rogers, R. and Stainton-Rogers, W. (1992) *Stories of Childhood: Shifting Agendas of Child Concern,* London: Harvester Wheatsheaf.

Stainton-Rogers, W., Harvey, D. and Ash, E. (eds) (1989) *Child Abuse and Neglect,* London: Open University Press.

Steedman, C. (1982) *The Tidy House.* London: Virago.

Steedman, C. (1995) *Strange Dislocations: Childhood and the Idea of Human Interiority 1780–1930,* London: Virago.

Stephens, S. (ed.) (1995) *Children and the Politics of Culture,* Princeton: Princeton University Press.

Stone, L. (1979) *The Family, Sex and Marriage in England 1500–1800,* Harmondsworth: Penguin.

Sutton-Smith, B. (1977) 'Play as Adaptive Potentiation'. In P. Stevens (ed.), *Studies in the Anthropology of Play,* New York: Leisure Press.

Tancred-Sheriff, P. (1989) 'Gender, Sexuality and the Labour Process'. In J. Hearn, D. Sheppard, P. Tancred-Sheriff and G. Burrell (eds), *The Sexuality of Organisation,* London: Sage.

Tattum, D. P. and Lane, D. A. (eds) (1989) *Bullying in Schools,* Stoke-on-Trent: Tentham Books.

Taylor, S. (1989) 'How Prevalent Is It?' In W. Stainton-Rogers, D. Harvey and E. Ash (eds), *Child Abuse*, Milton Keynes: Open University Press.

Tesson, G. and Youniss, J. (1995) 'Micro-sociology and Psychological Development: A Sociological Interpretation of Piaget's Theory'. In A. Ambert (ed.), *Sociological Studies of Children, Volume 7*, Greenwich, Conn.: JAI Press.

Thompson, D. (1989) 'The Welfare State and Generational Conflict: Winners and Losers'. In P. E. Johnson et al. (eds), *Workers vs Pensioners: Intergenerational Justice in an Ageing World*, Manchester: Manchester University Press.

Thorne, B. (1993) *Gender Play: Girls and Boys in School*, New Brunswick, N.J.: Rutgers University Press.

Toren, C. (1993) 'Making History: The Significance of Childhood Cognition for a Comparative Anthropology of Mind', *Man* 28(3): 461–78.

Trevor, W. (1976) *The Children of Dynmouth*, London: Bodley Head.

Turner, B. S. (1984) *The Body and Society: Explorations in Social Theory*, Oxford: Blackwell.

Turner, B. S. (1989) 'Ageing, Status and Sociological Theory', *British Journal of Sociology* 40(4): 588–607.

Turner, B. S. (1992) *Regulating Bodies: Essays in Medical Sociology*, London: Routledge.

Turner, V. (1974) *Dramas, Fields and Metaphors: Symbolic Action in Human Society*, Ithaca, N.Y.: Cornell University Press.

UNICEF (1989) *The State of the World's Children, 1989*, Oxford: UNICEF/Oxford University Press.

Urry, J. (1995) *Consuming Places*, London: Routledge.

Valentine, G. (1996) 'Children Should be Seen and Not Heard? The Role of Children in Public Space', *Urban Georgaphy* 17(3): 205–20.

Valentine, G. (forthcoming) 'A Safe Place to Grow Up? Parenting Perceptions of Children's Safety and the Rural Idyll', *Journal of Rural Studies*.

Van Gennep, A. (1960) *The Rites of Passage* (1908), London: Routledge and Kegan Paul.

van Oosterhout, H. (1988) 'Child Labour in the Philippines: The Muro-Ami Deep-Sea Fishing Operation'. In A. Bequele, and J. Boyden (eds), *Combating Child Labour*, Geneva: International Labour Office.

Wadsworth, M. E. J. (1981) 'Social Class and Generation Differences in Pre-school Education', *British Journal of Sociology* 32: 560–82.

Wadsworth, M. E. J. (1986) 'Evidence from Three Birth Cohort Studies for Long Term and Cross-Generational Effects on the Development of Children'. In M. Richards and P. Light (eds), *Children of Social Worlds*, Cambridge: Polity Press.

Walkerdine, V. (1985) 'On the Regulation of Speaking and Silence'. In C. Steedman, C. Urwin and V. Walkerdine (eds), *Language, Gender and Childhood*, London: Routledge.

Wallerstein, I. (1974) *The Modern World System*, New York: Academic Press.

Ward, C. (1977) *The Child in the City*, Harmondsworth: Penguin.

Ward, C. (1990) *The Child in the Country*, London: Bedford Square Press.

Wartofsky, M. (1981) 'The Child's Construction of the World and the World's Construction of the Child: From Historical Epistemology to Historical Psychology'. In F.Kessel and A.Seigal (eds), *The Child and Other Cultural Inventions*, New York: Praeger.

White, B. (1995) 'Globalization and the Child Labour Problem', mimeo, Institute of Social Studies, The Hague.

White, G. (1977) *Socialization*, London: Longman.

Whiting, B. B. and Whiting, J. W. M. (1975) *Children of Six Cultures: A Psychosocial Analysis*, Cambridge: Harvard University Press.

Whiting, J. W. M. (1958) 'The Function of Male Initiation Ceremonies in Puberty'. In E. E. Maccoby, T. M. Newcomb and E. L. Hartley (eds), *Readings in Social Psychology*, New York: Holt.

Whittaker, A. (1985) 'Bonded Labour – India's Slavery', *The Reporter* 13(2) (Anti-Slavery Society, London).

Whyte, J. (1983) *Beyond the Wendy House*, London: Longman.

Wilkinson, S. R. (1988) *The Child's World of Illness*, Cambridge: Cambridge University Press.

Willis, P. (1977) *Learning to Labour*, Farnborough: Saxon House.

Wilson, A. (1980) 'The Infancy of the History of Childhood: An Appraisal of Phillipe Ariès', *History and Theory* 19(2): 132–54.

Wintersberger, H. (forthcoming) 'Children: Costs and Benefits', paper to International Workshop on Monitoring and Measuring the State of the Children, Jerusalem. To be published in A. Ben-Arieh and H. Wintersberger (eds), *Monitoring and Measuring the State of Children – Beyond Survival*, Eurosocial Report 26, Vienna: European Centre for Social Welfare Policy and Research.

Wolff, J. (1985) 'The Invisible Flaneuse: Women and the Literature of Modernity', *Theory, Culture and Society* 2(3): 37–46.

Woodhead, M. (1996) *In Search of the Rainbow: Pathways to Quality in Large-Scale Programmes for Young Disadvantaged Children*, Early Childhood Development: Practice and Reflections 10, The Hague: Bernard van Leer Foundation.

Wright, P. (1987) 'The Social Construction of Babyhood: The Definition of Infant Care as a Medical Problem'. In A. Bryman et al. (eds), *Rethinking the Life Cycle*, London: Macmillan.

Wrong, D. (1961) 'The Oversocialized Conception of Man in Modern Sociology', *American Sociological Review* 26: 183–93.

Wulff, H. (1995) 'Introducing Youth Culture in its Own Right: The State of the Art and New Possibilities'. In V. Amit-Talai and H. Wulff (eds), *Youth Cultures: A Cross-Cultural Perspective*, London: Routledge.

Young, M. (ed.) (1971) *Knowledge and Control: New Directions for the Sociology of Education*, London: Collier Macmillan.

Zelitzer, V. A. (1985) *Pricing the Priceless Child: The Changing Social Value of Children*, New York: Basic Books.

Index

Index by Fiona F. Barr